THE MIEGUNYAH PRESS

*This is number seventy-two in the
second numbered series of the
Miegunyah Volumes
made possible by the
Miegunyah Fund
established by bequests
under the wills of
Sir Russell and Lady Grimwade.*

*'Miegunyah' was the home of
Mab and Russell Grimwade
from 1911 to 1955.*

REMEMBERED GARDENS

PHOTOGRAPHS BY HOLLY KERR FORSYTH

Holly Kerr Forsyth

REMEMBERED GARDENS

EIGHT WOMEN & THEIR VISIONS OF AN AUSTRALIAN LANDSCAPE

THE
MIEGUNYAH
PRESS

THE MIEGUNYAH PRESS
An imprint of Melbourne University Publishing Ltd
187 Grattan Street, Carlton, Victoria 3053, Australia
mup-info@unimelb.edu.au
www.mup.com.au

First published 2006
Text © Holly Kerr Forsyth 2006
Design and typography © Melbourne University Publishing Ltd 2006
Images © Holly Kerr Forsyth unless otherwise indicated

page ix: *Rosa* 'Buff Beauty' and 'Pierre de Ronsard' adorn the fence and archway at Rossie and Gayford Thompson's property Baladonga, in the Coolah district of western New South Wales.

page xii: The reflection garden in Judy and Gordon Cope-Williams' winery garden, at Romsey in the foothills of the Macedon Ranges

pages 16–17: detail from painting of Elizabeth Macarthur (Dixson Galleries, State Library of New South Wales, DG221, reproduced with permission); Banksia rose

pages 38–9: detail from miniature of Georgiana Molloy (from private collection, Mrs J. Bunbury, Marybrook, Busselton); *Agapanthus* 'Peter Pan'

pages 68–9: detail from photograph of Mrs Charles Meredith [Louisa Anne Meredith] (Allport Library and Museum of Fine Arts, State Library of Tasmania, reproduced with permission); *Spiraea* spp. (may)

pages 102–3: detail from photograph of Una Falkiner (unknown); *Clematis paniculata*

pages 124–5: detail from photograph of Winifred West (reproduced in Priscilla Kennedy, *Portrait of Winifred West*, Fine Arts Press, Sydney, 1976); *Dahlia* 'Bishop of Llandoff'

pages 148–9: detail from photograph of Beatrice Bligh (courtesy of Michael Bligh); jasmine and clematis

pages 180–1: detail from photograph of Edna Walling (courtesy of Barbara Barnes); *B. serrata* (old man banksia)

pages 214–15: Judith Wright: Lines from 'South of My Days', reproduced with the permission of the publishers from the volume *A Human Pattern: Selected Poems* (ETT Imprints, Sydney, 1999); detail from photograph of Kath Carr (courtesy of Alan Baldick); *Isopogon anemonifolius* (drumsticks)

Edited by Clare Coney
Designed by Mary Callahan
Typeset in Minion by J & M Typesetting and Mary Callahan
Printed in Singapore by Imago

National Library of Australia Cataloguing-in-Publication entry

Forsyth, Holly Kerr, 1953– .
Remembered gardens : eight women and their visions of an
Australian landscape.

Bibliography.
Includes index.
ISBN 0 522 85243 2.

1. Gardens—Australia—History. 2. Gardening—Australia—
History. 3. Women gardeners—Australia. I. Title.

635.0994

Notes

It is useful to clarify here the use of first names and surnames throughout this book. The women discussed are referred to by their first name. If they were professional women, however, like the garden designer Edna Walling, or a writer, or artist, surnames are used. When referring to the childhood of a designer, or to the period before she was married, first names are used; surnames are used once she accepted her first commission.

All quotations retain original spellings and punctuation. ? indicates a word that was obscured or difficult to decipher.

The debts I have accumulated in the several years since this project germinated are too numerous to list, and indeed, it would be impossible to name everyone involved. This book was born from the research for my doctoral thesis, completed in 2004 at the University of New South Wales and titled 'From the British Pastoral to the Australian Arcadia: Women, Transferred Vision and the Reconstruction of Landscape'.

Not a word could have been written without the guidance and support of my supervisor, Associate Professor Ian Bickerton. He demanded reflection upon areas I had not previously considered as relevant to the meaning of gardens. For an academic, whose desire to write and research always weighs on heart and mind, the time given in directing a demanding student is especially generous. I am delighted that this book will provide for The Ian J. Bickerton History Prize, to be presented annually to a student at the University of New South Wales, in an area of Australian History. I was indeed privileged to also receive generous advice and detailed observations, over several drafts, from my co-supervisor, Professor John Gascoigne.

The antiquarian bookseller Tim McCormick can perhaps be credited with my interest in women in historic gardens, over and above a passion for gardening in general. One birthday Tim gave me a rare first edition of Beatrice Bligh's *Down to Earth,* the story of her garden making at Pejar Park, her home on the Wollondilly River, north-west of Goulburn on the Southern Tablelands of New South Wales. Reading her words I realised that garden making was not just about gardening: here was a record of history, and not just garden history, but also a tale of separate spheres, of gender relations, of space and boundaries, of aspirations, economics and demographics. It was a social history. From then I started to search out stories of women who arrived as frontier settlers to Australia, and who turned to the garden to provide them with so much apart from simply sustenance or flowers. They became, to me, 'my girls'. Other booksellers were generous in listening to my theories, and giving me theirs, as we discussed the out-of-print books that they were sourcing for me.

The research for this book was facilitated by the dedicated staff of so many libraries, the repositories of vital archives and so much fascinating information, but places that can also confront a reader with a frustrating code, to be broken only with the help of librarians. Staff of libraries all over the world deserve my thanks, from Gaye Juhl and her colleagues at the library at the University of New South Wales, to Elizabeth Ellis and Paul Brunton at the Mitchell Wing of the State Library of New South Wales, to those at the National Library in Canberra, the La Trobe in Melbourne, the Battye in Perth, to the staff at the Cumbria Records Office, Carlisle, on the Scottish border—where I found gold in the form of a diary in which Georgiana Molloy recorded her dreams for her garden in Western Australia in the context of Repton and his Red Books. At Meriden School in Sydney, archivist Diana Tilley-Winyard was generous with her suggestions for avenues of research when I encountered a 'dead end'—and not only concerning my research on past student Kath Carr.

Sue Home sought out gardens and owners whom she knew might fill in some of the silences for me; she travelled with me on several research trips and not only made coffee in the sleety cold of a Scottish spring but confirmed my transcriptions of cross-hatched letters and of diaries. Many people generously spent time with me, recalling their knowledge of these country gardens and their creators. Ivan Saltmarsh, and Ivan and Deidre Pearson helped me find the gardens of Louisa Anne Meredith. There was Dizzy Carlyon, who grew up on one of the Falkiner properties, who gave me so much background on life on large pastoral estates and who put me in touch with so many who remembered Una. Suzanne Falkiner, Una's great-niece, and David Bruce Steel, Una's grandson, also were generous with their time and gave me access to private family papers. Beatrice Bligh's children, Lucinda Nicholson and Michael and Hugh Bligh, generously reminisced about their mother and gave me access to her private archive. Barbara Barnes, Edna Walling's niece and the executor of her estate, shared her time and memories, as well as a wealth of fascinating Walling material; Peter Watts generously gave me access to his Walling archive. Susie Sutherland sent me a letter she had received from Walling, recommending Kath Carr as the only landscaper who would design Susie's garden as she, Walling, would want. Such a gift is treasure to any researcher and provides concrete proof to verify the anecdotal evidence that is crucial, but sometimes unreliable. Rhonda and Bill Daly, like all Carr's clients, were generous in sharing their knowledge of her work, and in their hospitality. Alan Baldick provided vital background to his sister, Kath Carr.

At Melbourne University Publishing, my thanks to Louise Adler for her support of this book. Tracy O'Shaughnessy brought her clear vision to the tone and style of the book, and Catherine Cradwick was meticulous as she shepherded the book toward completion. My thanks to Mary Callahan for her inspired design that has captured the spirit of these women and the landscape on which they gardened, and for her care.

So many people also provided me with a bed, a wonderful meal and a glass of wine as I travelled more than 100 000 kilometres, visiting some 700 gardens and archives around the country, finding context and depth for the stories of Australia's women. Other friends provided a shoulder when, at times, the task seemed too great.

Extended periods of quiet time were necessary to write this book. At the Thredbo Alpine Club Peter and Lona Berlowitz cooked wonderful meals for me when, in the 'quiet season', I would work amidst the solitude of the Snowy Mountains' beautiful high country. And to Lillian Soto, who stepped into the breach at home, time and time again, to keep things in order, while I indulged in my peripatetic lifestyle, I owe an enormous debt of gratitude.

It is my husband, Ross, and children, Olivia, Camilla, Angus and Tom, however, for whom I reserve my greatest praise and thanks for their patient support over so many years.

Contents

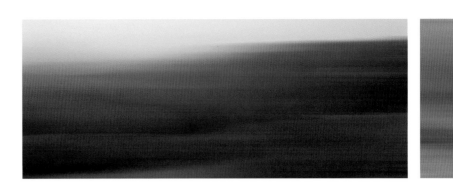

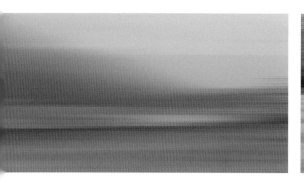

God Almighty first planted a garden; and, indeed,
it is the purest of human pleasures …

FRANCIS BACON, *'Of Gardens'*, Essays, *1625*

WHY DO AUSTRALIANS—rural or city dwellers, men or women—
struggle to raise plants in small, polluted city spaces or, in the country,
against the vicissitudes of climate, coping with plagues of marauding
insects, or the economic vagaries inflicted by distant markets? Why do we
pour our resources, our time and energies into creating them?

The essence of garden making is that it is an act of creativity. Not
everyone can be a celebrated artist, nor collect great art; few can create, or
perform, wonderful music. Few will be acclaimed writers. Each of us is an
artist, however, when we garden, whether we tend pots on a tiny balcony,
cultivate a narrow city plot in the shadow of tall buildings or create landscape parks on expansive hectares in the country.

Gardening is not simply about arranging plants. Garden making
captures the mind, and lifts the soul as its creator watches the changes each
day, and each season, bring. It allows the gardener to nurture plants and
cherish the soil, and to be master of his earth.

Much of the story of European-settled Australia—its history and its
folklore—is that of men. It is the story of the settlement of pastoral runs
by tough, rough men, and of their construction of grand houses in the

young cities and in the bush, as they re-cast themselves into a different class in the new and fluid society. It is also a story of the taking up of mining leases, of land grabs of small selections for mixed farms, a story of mateship and of the creation of empire. It is, largely, a drama where men play the leading roles.

The story of Australia is a boys' tale of daring and hardship, of difficult decisions and brutality—and of the unerring belief that to be white, British and male was to hold power. It is not a story of women and their contribution to the new colony: few of the earliest tales of enterprise are of women. Most of Australia's history, and its literature, pay women scant attention.

But Australia's short European history—its pastoral and economic history, its social history, its cultural history, and its garden history—has been constructed upon, and by, the efforts of strong women. While few of our iconic legends feature women, there is a story to be told of how women carved for themselves a place in a frontier land, how they reacted to the environment that enveloped them, and how they reconstructed the landscape into their own vision of an English Arcadia. The development of an Australian garden style, from settlement in 1788 into the twenty-first century, is their story.

Gardens are not innocent spaces; they mirror the tastes, culture and the intellectual life of a society. They reflect the aspirations, along with the economic, political and social circumstances, of their creators and owners; they provide insights into gender and gender relations, class and geography. In *Remembered Gardens* the significance of the garden in the daily lives of a group of Australian women illuminates a picture of changing demographics, class structure, design and style.

This book describes how privileged women in rural Australia, who at first emulated the styles and tastes of Georgian England, eventually sought—with varying levels of enthusiasm and with mixed success—to develop a garden style unique to the new country. Throughout Australia's history there have been women who have written of their relationship with gardens and gardening. Very few of these records of their hopes, disappointments and memories were published, however. Those stories that were recorded were mainly detailed in diaries and letters, the writing of which was one of a handful of acceptable pastimes for middle-class colonial women.

It is the large country gardens around Australia that feature in *Remembered Gardens*, as extant gardens are more likely to exist in the country, where pastoral properties may have been held by generations of the one family. Rural women are respectful of the gardens their mothers-in-law created, and are often loath to make unnecessary changes. Local communities, also, have a sense of ownership of historic gardens and eschew any changes a new 'custodian' may wish to make. In the case of Edna Walling, the gardens she created and their beautifully executed watercolour designs have been preserved by owners who knew of her fame and value when they commissioned her. In contrast, few historic cottage gardens—more usual in the city due to constraints of space—remain. Where changes in house ownership are frequent, due to urban sprawl, population increases and the resultant pressures of the developer's dollar, varying taste and aspirations result in changes to gardens, along with house colour and interior decoration.

left: Pat and Judy Bowley's garden, Birchbeck, on the New South Wales' Southern Highlands is one of exuberant design and virtuoso planting.

centre: Dalvui, set on the black soils of the Western District of Victoria, was taken up in 1847, and is one of the few surviving private gardens created by the landscaper William Guilfoyle.

right: The garden around Faye's Underground Home. This is just one of the dugout houses that are 'the norm' in Coober Pedy, some 600 kilometres from the coast of South Australia, and where summer temperatures reach 48 °C.

previous pages: Yallum Park, in South Australia's Coonawarra district, was taken up in the 1840s, then developed from 1861 by one of the pioneers of this part of the country, John Riddoch. Today it is home to the Clifford family who bought it early last century.

Settlers have always displayed varied responses to the Australian flora. While some, from Elizabeth Macarthur onwards, expressed their delight in the indigenous plants that they found, such praise was set against a lingering assumption that 'British was best'.

The history of Australia after white settlement begins with the sustenance garden, before gardens were laid out for purely aesthetic reasons. Soon, however, successful settlers were able to create pleasure gardens that exemplified their new pre-eminent position. The creation of a pleasure garden provided some solace for the loss of home and family, and some relief from homesickness. Several stories—such as that of Georgiana Molloy, who was thrust from the soft mists of the Scottish borders into the unfamiliar landscape of Western Australia—are set against the loss of a child in an unforgiving environment; some migrants turned to the garden to create good from bad, beauty from tragedy.

For many of the women illuminated in the story of garden making in Australia, the garden was an attempt to impose a civilising and genteel order on the natural landscape, to familiarise the wilderness; garden making exemplified a rise in colonial taste. An ordered garden remains today a symbol of efficiency, cleanliness, Godliness—and, therefore, womanliness. Botanising, closely related to gardening, was as redolent with imperial messages as the hunt, a pursuit which had been introduced by early settlers to emulate the English gentry, and while the search for horticultural trophies was more often a male pursuit, it provided some women with as much comfort as domestication of the land.

The landholders' ride, aboard the 'sheep's back', provided the women of pastoral families with a life of privilege which did not always, however, quarantine them from tragedy. Gardens provided an acceptable intellectual and creative outlet for such women—in a frontier land where the rule of men mattered. Most of the women discussed in this book saw themselves as occupying a separate sphere from men. Most women looked outward, from the confines of the gardens they created, while 'their' men looked in, to the domestic—garden—scene, from the canvas of a wide landscape. The broader outdoor working environment was the male domain. The house, and the garden, belonged to women and spelled out their success as females: it defined their place in the community as well as intimating the politics of their marriages.

Pastoral wives were often prevented from working alongside their husbands in developing their livestock properties. Frustrated, they turned to garden making as an acceptable outlet for their creativity and capability. It was not only that gardening kept women out of the shearing shed and the sale yard, away from 'men's business', nor simply that it was considered an appropriate 'polite accomplishment'. Gardening allowed—and still permits—each woman to be the artist that the demands of domesticity and child rearing may have denied her. The creation of a garden was one way a woman could demonstrate her abilities and claim some individuality in her life. At the same time, however, women, through gardening, were implicated in the process being carried out by men in following agricultural pursuits—the process of dominating and reconstructing the foreign and threatening native environment.

At the beginning of a new millennium Australian women still bemoan the limitations forced upon them by their gender. They have created, of necessity, power bases in ways different from men, just as they always have. Still, the woman as 'The Angel in the House' remains a dominant image, almost as influential today as it was in Victorian England.[1] Modern advertising confirms this by rarely straying from such a stereotype.

In the city or the country, the garden mediates between the inside space and the outside world. The front garden dresses the homestead and alerts the visitor to a range of characteristics: that the property is successful, that the homemaker is a 'successful' woman. In 1922 *Searl's Key to Australian Gardening*, published by the firm of Sydney florists, seed merchants and nurserymen, Searl and Sons, advised that, 'a properly cared for home is regarded as the highest symbol of civilised society'.

A neat front garden in the city implies a neat home; in rural Australia, a beautiful garden is the presentation to the local community of the status of

At Emu Creek, on the Northern Tablelands of New South Wales, the front garden mediates between the surrounding landscape and the homestead.

the pastoralist. His garden immediately conveys his position and power to those who arrive at the property to conduct business, to purchase stock or to view the quality of the fleece. On the 'Open Days' each autumn and spring, at the famous studs around the country—from Winton and Valleyfield in Tasmania, to Boonoke, Hazeldean and Emu Creek in New South Wales, and Jimbour on Queensland's Darling Downs—the historic and much-photographed gardens provide a silent reminder of the long-established success of the family, and underline and confirm the bloodline of the world-renowned merino rams or stud cattle. A good garden exemplifies order and carries clear messages of power, class and wealth.

Aeonium decorum 'Tricolor'

Women of the pastoral aristocracy derived great pleasure from their gardens, but for early migrants much of the physical work to fulfil their vision was carried out by working-class men. However, by the early twentieth century professional gardening was no longer solely the domain of men: a handful of vocal women pioneered the crossing of the gender barrier at Burnley Horticultural College in Melbourne. At this time trained female horticulturalists, after initially constructing gardens in the English mould for clients, started to write about their respect for the Australian soil and the need to create a garden that honoured the landscape within which it sat. The grandeur and scale of the Australian landscape had begun to capture the women who gardened upon it.

But such admiration did not always translate into a desire to replicate nature with native plantings in their gardens, and the attempts of landscapers like Edna Walling and Kath Carr to develop a unique Australian garden style—one that was less reliant on the mid and deep green exotic trees and shrubs of the northern hemisphere—often conflicted with the desires and aspirations of their clients.

The family records of the women in this book reveal much about their gardening activities. In some cases, however, only the letters and diaries of men, containing detailed accounts of agricultural plantings and costs, staff wages, cattle sales, breeding programs and farm improvements, were kept, while the written thoughts of their wives were lost.

The records of several botanical and historical societies provide details of the horticultural activities of the early decades of the colonies, and the letterbooks of the Royal Botanic Gardens, Sydney, contain details of an exhilarating global botanical exchange. Newspapers, women's magazines and gardening journals, seed and plant catalogues, and photographs also provide important information and context. This book is a culmination of more than 100 000 kilometres of travel throughout Australia, interviews with garden owners, 90 per cent of whom were women, and the stories and photographs of more than 700 gardens. Oral history adds depth to these stories, although, as is the nature of personal recollection, this information was often subjective and sometimes conflicting.

Helen and Bill Richards' garden, Little Riccorang, at Kingscote on Kangaroo Island, is a beautiful, protected garden of water-wise lawns and sweeping beds. Created around Australian native plants, it is always full of birdsong.

Many things distinguish the women in this book from each other—the sum of their lives covers two centuries and they gardened throughout a vast and diverse continent—but they were united by the centrality of garden making to their lives. Each woman has been chosen because she created or maintained exceptional gardens, gardens which were emblematic of the horticultural fashion of the time. It is difficult to 'straightjacket' garden styles, and impossible to identify each decade by a style, but this book illuminates some of the key horticultural features and fashions that have developed over two centuries.

No one book could do justice to all the women who have gardened in colonial and post-colonial Australia. For instance, over the past sixty years Italian, German, Greek, Lebanese and Vietnamese immigrants have changed the way Anglo-Saxon settlers eat and drink, holiday—and garden. Immigrants from Mediterranean countries planted out small suburban plots, both the front garden and the traditionally utilitarian 'backyard', with fruit and vegetables not available in the corner store. The waves of twentieth-century immigrants have created in Australia a vibrant multicultural society, however the focus of this book is on the significant influence of Australia's colonial heritage on our garden making.

Among descendants of British settlers the focus of gardening remains largely British. The voices that today implore Australian gardeners to look to climates similar to Australia's for inspiration are heard, but often go unheeded. Water-wise gardening is still largely academic, even in the midst of a disastrous drought that has seen the implementation of severe water restrictions in most cities. Two hundred years after white Anglo-Saxon settlement, descendants of those settlers—and of the British who came later—while paying some homage to Australia's botanical vocabulary, and admiring its landscape, still look, most often, to the United Kingdom for their inspiration.

BOOK ONE

FROM RELUCTANT SETTLERS TO PASTORAL PRIVILEGE
1788–1900

Prologue

The landscapers 'Capability' Brown and Humphry Repton were among those who created the magnificent gardens at Harewood House, near Leeds in England's Yorkshire. Today the garden encompasses some 60 hectares and is cared for by a team of twelve gardeners.

Modern Australia was built largely on the efforts of a group of settlers who did not want to be here. Convict women—like convict men—had no say in their fate; those women who arrived free in the first decades generally came as the wives of men who chose Australia, out of duty, or because of the chance of a better life. For economic reasons, women had no choice but to accompany their men.[1] But women, like men, quickly set about making the best of their new world.

European settlement of Australia took place in response to several different forces. The earliest engagement with *Terra Australis* resulted from an elitist quest for botanical discovery and learning. Later, in the year that Captain Arthur Phillip led the First Fleet into Port Jackson to create his ramshackle settlement—about where Sydney's AMP Centre stands today—the Linnaean Society was founded in London. At the same time the beautiful and the sublime came together in the Picturesque movement what Wordsworth called 'a strong infection of the age'—the concept of creating landscapes in the manner of pictures. Visions of a Picturesque England, underlined by Romantic writers, fed the aspirations of some of the early settlers.

Europeans had arrived at a land that was fragile, much of it of shallow topsoil covering deep sandstone. It was a land that had been occupied—but not cultivated, as apart from the use of fire to encourage lush new vegetative growth, the Aboriginal people who had roamed Australia for over 60 000 years had not farmed it. While the First Fleet officers had exclaimed in Picturesque language at the scenery they encountered, it was soon evident that the sandy soil around the harbour would not yield a cornucopia. The earliest agricultural endeavours of the settlement failed and it came close to starvation.

An English footprint: Bebeah, at Mount Wilson in New South Wales, was first built in the 1880s for the grazier Edward Cox.

The formal garden at Dalvui today

The colony was saved by exploration further west, in 1788, and the discovery of richer soils at Parramatta, or Rose Hill, as it was first called. And by 1791, as former First Fleet officer, Watkin Tench, found when he visited Rose Hill:

> Vines of every sort seem to flourish; melons, cucumbers, and pumpkins run with unbounded luxuriancy; and I am convinced that the grapes of New South Wales will, in a few years, equal those of any other country … oranges, lemons, and figs (of which last indeed I have eaten very good ones) will, I dare believe, in a few years become plentiful. Apples, and the fruits of other climes, also promise to gratify expectation.[2]

Among the extensive plant collection sent by Joseph Banks with the First Fleet was a wide range of food plants and seeds. On board HMS *Sirius* were 286 bushels of seed for vegetables, herbs, flax and hemp.[3] In addition, the fleet acquired seed and plants en route to Botany Bay: at Tenerife in the Canary Islands, then Rio de Janeiro, where coffee, cocoa, cotton, bananas, oranges and lemons, guava, tamarind and prickly pear were collected, and at Cape Town.

Necessity dictated that the first settlers created food gardens—what historian Victor Crittenden calls The Early Settlement Garden. They considered practicality, not aesthetics, when laying out their gardens: the earliest featured rectangular beds housing vegetables—and perhaps a few flowers—on either side of a path from a wooden picket fence straight to the front door.[4] The colony's first gardening guide, printed in 1806, was a calendar advising on the cultivation of vegetables; flowers were not mentioned.[5]

Bluebells carpet the woodland at Culzean, in northern Tasmania,
that most English of the Australian states.

While the earliest settlers had no choice but to garden for survival, as they established their
wealth, increasing their livestock and their landholdings, many sought to display their success
through building a fine homestead. The role of a wife included the creation of a decorative
garden befitting this new position. Such wealthy landowners sought to create a garden reminiscent of home, or perhaps of a privileged England they had observed. And just as the gardens
designed by the landscaper Humphry Repton were underlining the position of the newly
wealthy in Britain, so those determined to show themselves as the elite in the colony embraced
the English landscape style. This was influenced by the Arcadian idyll depicted in the work of
European Romantic painters—particularly Salvatore Rosa, Nicolas Poussin and Claude
Lorrain—so admired by the British landed gentry. Order, the eulogisation of Nature—even in
its wildest forms—was fundamental to Enlightenment thought.

Settlement continued, undeterred by early failures to impose British agricultural practices on the land, and with relatively little input from women. By 1793 the population of New
South Wales was 3000 but only one in five were women and 75 per cent of the population
were convicts.

For a fortunate minority of the early free settlers the colony provided a quick passage to a
position of landed gentry. Where the colonial officials and free settlers—former small farmers,
tenants and shopkeepers—would have enjoyed no more than a tenuous position in the British
middle classes, they carved for themselves a privileged position in Australia.

Many women—both those who were transported and who came freely—made extraordinary new lives in a country that was as different from 'home' as was possible. However, their
sensibilities, their 'ultra-respectability', was noted with wry wit by Peter Cunningham, surgeon

Swathes of irises and stands of exotic,
cool-climate shrubs at Culzean

The lake at Culzean, in the style of 'Capability' Brown

aboard five convict fleets between 1819 and 1828, in his account of life in the young colony.[6] He observed that the manners of the middle-class free women of the colony became more particular than of those they had left behind, and that an impression of gentility was carefully constructed.

By 1827 one visitor to Sydney was 'scarcely to be sensible that I was out of England'.[7] And William Howitt, visiting in 1852, was struck by the fervour of the re-creation of England:

> … the English stamp and the English character are on all their settlements. They are English houses, English enclosures that you see; English arms, English gardens … English flowers and plants carefully cultivated. You see great bushes of furze, even by the rudest settlers' cottages. There are hedges of sweet briar about their gardens, bushes of holly … there are hawthorns and young oaks in the shrubberies … England reproduces herself in new lands.[8]

FROM THE SURVIVAL GARDEN TO TRANSFERRED VISION

Nature never did betray the heart that loved her.

WILLIAM WORDSWORTH *'Lines Composed a Few Miles above Tintern Abbey', 13 July 1798*

Elizabeth Macarthur 1766–1850

IN 1795, SOME FIVE YEARS after her arrival in the fledgling colony of New South Wales, Elizabeth Macarthur remarked upon the landscape in the evocative language of the Romantic poets:

THE GREATER PART OF THE COUNTRY IS LIKE AN ENGLISH PARK, AND THE TREES GIVE IT THE APPEARANCE OF A WILDERNESS OR SHRUBBERY, COMMONLY ATTACHED TO THE HABITATIONS OF PEOPLE OF FORTUNE, FILLED WITH A VARIETY OF NATIVE PLANTS PLACED IN A WILD IRRE-GULAR MANNER.[1]

It did not take Elizabeth long to create around her a Picturesque landscape of her own. By the turn of the nineteenth century Elizabeth and John Macarthur were among the wealthiest families in the colony and Elizabeth was instrumental in creating elaborate gardens around her home, Elizabeth Farm, near Parramatta, some 25 kilometres west of Sydney. The gardens she planted became renowned, filled with roses, lupins, hollyhocks and northern hemisphere shrubs and trees, some gathered from other prominent settlers, some supplied from the government gardens and others brought on her husband's ship from England and via his contacts in China.

Surveyor-General Thomas Mitchell, who stayed with the Macarthurs at Elizabeth Farm the night before he set off on one of his expeditions of exploration, in November 1831, was effusive in his praise of Elizabeth's garden. He noted in his journal:

THERE I SAW THE FIRST OLIVE TREE EVER PLANTED IN AUSTRALIA; THE CORK-TREE IN LUXURIANCE; THE CAPER GROWING AMONG ROCKS, THE ENGLISH OAK, THE HORSE CHESTNUT, BROOM, MAGNIFICENT

MULBERRY TREES OF THIRTY FIVE YEARS GROWTH, UMBRAGEOUS AND GREEN, GREAT VARIETY OF ROSES IN HEDGES, ALSO CLIMBING ROSES.[2]

The garden, continued Mitchell, was important to the colonist, for 'there he revives the land of his birth, and those associated ideas of earlier years inseparable from the trees, fruits and flowers of his native land.'[3]

For Elizabeth, and for some other early European settlers, the garden exemplified their attempts to re-make themselves into members of the gentry, a class that would not have been open to them in Britain. Elizabeth's garden, now reconstructed to its 1830s incarnation, remains a relic of her ambition to succeed in an environment that was at once both ambiguous and bizarre. Like many women who came to Australia later, her garden must have provided Elizabeth with comfort and solace. She spent many years without her husband, who was twice exiled from the colony, suffered the death of two infants, and lived for long periods without several of her children who returned at young ages to England for their education. While only one letter from Elizabeth to John Macarthur survives, we can piece together from remaining evidence that her garden was a source of joy, and a peaceful escape from a life that was full of challenges and difficulties. But the land had first to provide food to ensure their survival.

~

Elizabeth was born to Grace and Richard Veale, in the village of Bridgerule on the border between Devon and Cornwall, probably on 14 August 1766, and was baptised on 1 October that year. Her father was a yeoman farmer who owned Lodgeworthy, a farm of 35 hectares. After her father died, when

left: The homestead at Elizabeth Farm

centre: The pots that now grace the plant stands in the covered way at Elizabeth Farm are replicas of the originals.

right: The eastern verandah looks onto the garden of China roses, peonies, camellias and pelargoniums.

Elizabeth was six years old, she also lost her home, and was brought up by her grandfather. She spent much of her time with the family of the local vicar, Reverend John Kingdon, whose eldest daughter, Bridget, became her life-long friend. Elizabeth lived with the family during her teenage years; the Reverend Kingdon had been a Fellow of Exeter College, Oxford, and it seems reasonable to assume that Elizabeth was taught by him alongside her friend.

The gardens at Elizabeth Farm are carpeted with oxalis.

She married John Macarthur, a junior officer, and a draper's son—who was later lampooned as 'a Jack Bodice' by his colonial enemies—in October 1788, in a marriage ceremony performed by Reverend Kingdon.[4] Five months later, on 18 March 1789, John and Elizabeth's first son, Edward, was born at Bath, while they were en route to London.[5] Elizabeth brought no dowry to the union and reflected later on the modest beginnings of the marriage: 'I was considered indolent and inactive; Mr Macarthur too proud and haughty for our humble fortune or expectations.'[6]

John arranged to be transferred as a lieutenant into the New South Wales Corps, the new colony of New South Wales attracting the young couple as possibly the swiftest way of bettering themselves. The Macarthurs left England on board the *Neptune* on 17 January 1790, embarking on what was to be an horrific voyage, perhaps an ominous early sign of the difficulties Elizabeth would have to face throughout her life in the young colony. During the voyage her son came close to death, and her husband, as well as displaying early the cantankerous nature that was to cause his family so much trouble in New South Wales, became ill with rheumatic fever. In the terrible conditions that prevailed on the notorious Second Fleet, Elizabeth gave birth to a premature daughter who died within an hour.[7]

Three months after leaving England, and having transferred at sea to the *Scarborough*, the Macarthurs stopped with the Fleet for sixteen days at the Cape of Good Hope. Elizabeth wrote optimistically to her mother:

THE FACE OF THE COUNTRY IS VERY ROMANTIC ... IN EVERY PLANT I SEE SOMETHING NEW; THESE WORKS OF NATURE AT THE FOOT OF THE MOUNTAINS REPRESENT A BEAUTIFUL SHRUBBERY, WHERE INNUMERABLE BEAUTIFUL FLOWERS AND PLANTS DELIGHT THE EYE AND REGALE THE SENSES.[8]

The *Scarborough* arrived at Port Jackson on 28 June 1790, to a colony that was, perhaps, Picturesque—but was housing a settlement on the point of starvation. Although it was midwinter, the Macarthurs landed in a warm and dry June. The officers of the First Fleet had erected their tents close to what was to become known as the Tank Stream, a supply of fresh water that ran into the harbour at the western end of Sydney Cove. The earliest settlers had quickly set about denuding the landscape of its trees and woods to make way for crops and gardens. The giant coastal eucalypts, including the beautiful, pink-skinned angophora, were being felled for houses, fences and boats.

In an early letter from the colony, Elizabeth wrote to her friend Bridget Kingdon:

I HAVE SEEN VERY LITTLE RAIN SINCE MY ARRIVAL, INDEED I DO NOT THINK WE HAVE HAD A WEEK'S RAIN IN THE WHOLE TIME, THE CONSE-QUENCE OF WHICH OUR GARDEN PRODUCES NOTHING, ALL BURNT UP; INDEED, THE SOIL MUST BE ALLOWED TO BE MOST WRETCHED AND UNFIT FOR GROWING EUROPEAN PRODUCTIONS …

The heat, along with the wind, she wrote, 'comes as if from an heated oven'. The garden she was trying to make was 'all burnt up', although, 'On my first land, everything was new to me, every Bird, every Insect, flower, etc; in short, all was novelty around me.'

The carriage loop was added so that Elizabeth could drive through the pleasure gardens in the 'britsha' that John had commissioned in England.

The Ladies' Garden at Broughton Castle, near Oxford, England. The Castle, the home of Lord and Lady Saye and Sele, was originally a medieval manor house, built around 1300 by Sir John de Broughton.

ENGLISH LANDSCAPE DESIGNERS

The work of the landscape designer and architect William Kent (1685–1748), Lancelot 'Capability' Brown (1716–83) and Humphry Repton (1752–1818) provided the background for the gardening aspirations of the more ambitious settlers in the new colony. This trio had been influenced by the earlier aestheticists such as Horace Walpole and William Gilpin, who had declared that the park was 'one of the noblest appendages of a great house'. Nothing, Gilpin wrote, gave 'a mansion so much dignity'.

'Capability' Brown swept away the parterres and formal planting of seventeenth-century designers, damming rivers to create massive lakes, moving land masses to change the contours of the land and planting forests. Repton continued his work, later adding more formal elements into his gardens: terraces, balustrades, steps and flower borders. The first of his four illustrated books on landscape gardening, *Sketches and Hints on Landscape Gardening*, was published in 1795. In 1803 *Observations on the Theory and Practice of Landscape Gardening* was published,

Emotions, feelings and opinions are never black and white; frontier women brought conflicting responses to the landscape they found. While often despairing of her surroundings, Elizabeth, like others, was determined to make the best of her situation, acknowledging in the same letter that the natural vegetation 'is flourishing, even to luxuriance, producing fine Shrubs, Trees, and Flowers which by their lively tints afford a most agreeable landscape'.[9]

The first houses in the colony were made from sods of turf, covered with thatch and plastered and whitewashed, outside and in, with Sydney pipe-clay. The soft trunks of the cabbage-tree palms were also used for the simple houses; once these were depleted, the hard red gum and ironbark trees were felled to make neat, attractive and comfortable houses.[10] Twigs and branches of wattle were woven together and pasted with clay to fill any draughty cracks in the walls.

As she walked around Sydney Cove and Woolloomooloo in those first months Elizabeth saw neat cottages set behind small, fenced gardens divided by a central path to the front door. Vegetables and fruits grew in the front gardens along with edging herbs.[11] Window boxes were burgeoning already with geraniums, which would soon become commonplace, a symbol of the working man's garden.

After the need for survival had become less urgent, vegetables were banished to the 'back yard' and the gardens in front of the whitewashed colonial cottages featured circular or oval beds displaying cottage garden flowers on either side of a straight path. There was no lawn and edgings were of lavender, chamomile and strawberry rather than the difficult to procure and expensive box (*Buxus* spp.).[12] The Cape daisies, veld lilies, watsonias, agapanthus and freesias, collected by travellers as their ships re-stocked at the Cape of Good Hope, were thriving. These plants, along with the lantana that Governor Phillip had brought with him, were so suited to the Sydney climate that they would later be classed as noxious weeds.

The young colony also welcomed ships from India, China, Africa and America. Collections of citrus along with trees like the jacaranda came from the Canary and Cape Verde islands.[13] But it was the first primrose that arrived from England that caused a stampede to the docks.[14] This delicate flower could never have thrived in the hot and humid conditions across much of the colony, but the excitement it created was representative of a yearning for the botanical symbols of the gentler climate of England that plagued many settlers—and that, for many gardeners, continues into the twenty-first century.

Occasionally given to Picturesque expression, Elizabeth described the landscape around her new home as wild and romantic. The Hawkesbury River, she wrote to Bridget Kingdon, was a:

NOBLE FRESH WATER RIVER, TAKING ITS RISE IN A PRECIPITOUS RIDGE OF MOUNTAINS, THAT IT HAS HITHERTO BEEN IMPOSSIBLE TO PASS. MANY ATTEMPTS HAVE BEEN MADE, ALTHO' IN VAIN. I SPENT AN ENTIRE DAY ON THIS RIVER, GOING IN A BOAT TO A BEAUTIFUL SPOT, NAMED BY THE LATE GOVERNOR, RICHMOND HILL, HIGH AND OVER-LOOKING A GREAT EXTENT OF COUNTRY. ON ONE SIDE ARE THOSE STUPENDOUS BARRIERS TO WHICH I HAVE ALLUDED RISING AS IT WERE IMMEDIATELY ABOVE YOUR HEAD; BELOW, THE RIVER ITSELF STILL AND UNRUFFLED—OUT OF SIGHT IS HEARD A WATERFALL WHOSE DISTANT MURMURS ADD AWFUL-NESS TO THE SCENE.[15]

Life in the early days of the colony had many pleasant aspects, particularly for the small circle of settlers close to colonial power. There were parties at Government House, but, noted Elizabeth early in 1791:

I WILL NOT SAY THAT THESE ASSEMBLIES HAVE BEEN VERY SELECT. HOWEVER THERE IS A SUFFICIENCY OF PLEASANT, AGREEABLE PERSONS TO VISIT AND BE VIS-ITED BY, TO SATISFY ONE WHO IS NOT AMBITIOUS TO HAVE A VERY NUMEROUS VISITING ACQUAINTANCE.

followed by a short essay titled *An Enquiry into the Changes of Taste in Landscape Gardening* in 1806, and *Fragments on the Theory and Practice of Landscape Gardening* in 1816.

Repton presented his ideas to clients with a 'Red Book', showing 'before' and 'after' scenes to demonstrate the merit of suggested landscape improvements. His gardens later became ridiculed in some quarters and were said to bear 'the mark of the scissors' due to his habit of removing what others had created. They became a symbol for the pretension of a new wealthy class created by the Industrial Revolution, a class who would commission a land-scaped garden as a sign, it hoped, of its new position in society.

Cottesbrooke Hall: the exquisite house, of pink brick and local stone, was started in 1702, during the reign of Queen Anne and around the time that many other wonderful houses—Chatsworth, Duncombe Park and Castle Howard— were being created. Jane Austen scholars maintain that the house was the setting for Mansfield Park, the author's most 'landscaped' novel. The 3.5 hectares of formal detailed gardens that we see today have largely been developed during the twentieth century, with the help of several distinguished landscape designers including Sir Geoffrey Jellicoe and Dame Sylvia Crowe.

She still had 'no female friend to unbend my mind to, nor a single woman with whom I can converse with any satisfaction to myself'.[16] But she found the native plants and flowers and the landscape, 'charmingly turned and diversified by agreeable vallies and gently rising hills'. She also wrote of the ease with which settlers grew a variety of fruit:

THE GRAPES THRIVE REMARKABLY WELL. THE GOVERNOR SENT ME SOME BUNCHES THIS SEASON AS FINE AS ANY I EVER TASTED, AND THERE IS LITTLE DOUBT BUT IN A FEW YEARS THERE WILL BE PLENTY. WE HAVE ALSO VERY FINE MELONS. THEY ARE RAISED WITH LITTLE OR NO TROUBLE, THE SUN BEING SUFFICIENT TO RIPEN THEM WITHOUT ANY FORCING WHATEVER AND BRINGING THEM TO A GREAT SIZE AND FLAVOUR.[17]

As they grasped the opportunity to reconstruct themselves some 28 000 kilometres from home, the Macarthurs soon established a grand house and garden, set within a thriving farm that was a showpiece of achievement and that determined their position as the first family in the colony. The Macarthurs were given their first land grant in 1793, of

... 100 ACRES [40 HECTARES] OF LAND ON THE BANKS OF THE RIVER CLOSE TO THE TOWN OF PARRAMATTA. IT IS SOME OF THE BEST GROUND THAT HAS BEEN DISCOVERED, AND 10 MEN ARE ALLOWED US FOR THE PURPOSE OF CLEARING AND CULTIVATING IT.[18]

The red-flowering *Aloe* spp. remains from the earliest gardens at Elizabeth Farm and Camden Park.

They called the property Elizabeth Farm. By 1798 it had grown to almost 250 hectares.

Like many other women in Australia—from the settlers in the first decades of the colony to the waves of immigrants who arrived throughout the twentieth century—Elizabeth turned soon after her arrival to both gardening and botanising to sustain her, physically, intellectually and spiritually, and to elevate her above daily cares:

I HAVE MADE A SMALL PROGRESS IN BOTANY. NO COUNTRY CAN EXHIBIT A MORE COPIOUS FIELD FOR BOTANICAL KNOWLEDGE THAN THIS. I HAVE ARRIVED SO FAR AS TO BE ABLE TO CLASS AND ORDER ALL COMMON PLANTS. I HAVE FOUND GREAT PLEASURE IN MY STUDY; EVERY WALK FURNISHED ME WITH SUBJECTS TO PUT IN PRACTICE THAT THEORY I HAD BEFORE GAINED BY READING.[19]

The friendship plant (*Billbergia nutans*) at Elizabeth Farm

Not all colonial settlers immediately established themselves in Georgian mansions surrounded by parks that emulated the British eighteenth-century landscape movement. Some were too busy grasping as much land as they could; others would not have had the means nor the education to aspire to much more than survival. But, for some, the trappings of the landed gentry in an England they had left behind appeared within their reach in the colonies. Through his determination and her skill as a manager John and Elizabeth Macarthur quickly established themselves as one of the leading families of the colony, with a house and a garden—modelled on the English landscape park favoured by the aristocracy—to underline their position. At this early stage of their tenure in the colony, however, the Macarthurs were concerned primarily with establishing and with feeding themselves. Initially there was little time to indulge in the creation of a pleasure garden of the sort that the great landscapers were laying out at stately homes in the United Kingdom.

The homestead at Elizabeth Farm was a long brick cottage, 22 metres by 6 metres, with four rooms, a central hall, a cellar and a verandah. Servants' rooms and the kitchen were separated from the main body of the house. John Macarthur wrote that it was 'a most excellent brick house … surrounded by a Vineyard and Garden of about 3 acres [1 hectare], the former full of Vines and Fruit trees and the latter abounding with most excellent vegetables'.[20]

The Macarthurs' garden at Elizabeth Farm was planted in 1794, the year after their house was built, on the edge of the river at Parramatta. John wrote to his brother stating that his farm was now 115 hectares and describing the flourishing fields of wheat and corn.[21] In 1798 Elizabeth extolled the colony's abundance and its ability to provide food for her family, writing to Bridget Kingdon '… how bountifully Providence has dealt with us. At this time I can truly say no two people on earth can be happier than we are.'[22] A year later Elizabeth told her friend:

WE HAVE AT THIS TIME, ABOUT ONE HUNDRED AND TWENTY ACRES [50 HECTARES] IN WHEAT, ALL IN A PROMISING STATE. OUR GARDENS WITH FRUIT AND VEGETABLES ARE EXTENSIVE AND PRODUCE ABUNDANTLY. IT IS NOW SPRING, AND THE EYE IS DELIGHTED WITH A MOST BEAUTIFUL VARIEGATED LANDSCAPE—ALMONDS, APRICOTS, PEAR AND APPLE TREES ARE IN FULL BLOOM.[23]

left: Camden Park: the view from the house to the surrounding paddocks

centre: Bougainvillea romps through jacaranda

right: The olive tree at Elizabeth Farm, thought to be the oldest in Australia

The farm was now some 250 hectares, bounded on three sides by water, with many hectares under production. There was a dairy to supply the estate, which supported also some forty convict and ex-convict farm labourers, stock keepers, gardeners and domestic servants. By 1800 the Elizabeth Farm estate enjoyed many of the trappings of a gentrified property in England.

Elizabeth was to give birth to nine children in nineteen years. Her third child, a daughter, Elizabeth, was born in 1792, then came John in 1794, and Mary in 1795. Baby James was born in 1797 and lived just ten months; another child, born in 1798, was also named James. William was born in 1800, and then Emmeline in 1808.

In 1801 John Macarthur's avarice for wealth and land, his political recalcitrance and his subversive behaviour toward successive incumbent governors resulted in his being exiled to England. He took Elizabeth, aged nine, and John, seven, with him, to be educated in England; Elizabeth would not see her son again. During her husband's exile, from 1801 to 1805, the management of the pastoral and agricultural estates was left to Elizabeth. By 1805, her sheep numbered 4055, nearly a quarter of all the sheep in the colony. She was obliged to cope with a shortage of labour for, during her husband's absence, fewer convicts had been assigned to her.

But in October 1804 John left England on his own ship, the *Argo*, having, with his customary detemination to achieve his goals, cleared his name and engineered for himself, from Lord Camden, a promise of a further land grant amounting to almost 5000 hectares.[24] Returning with him to New South Wales, on board the *Argo,* were his nephew Hannibal, a wool sorter, skilled mechanics and their families, along with other servants. He also brought home the thirteen-year-old Elizabeth and a governess. And

there was John Lawrence, an experienced English gardener, further demonstrating that the Macarthurs were determined to replicate in the colony the trappings they had observed on the grander estates of home.

Macarthur's return from exile also resulted in the introduction to Australia of some of the botanical treasures that had been exported from China to Britain, as well as from Mediterranean countries. He brought vine cuttings, camellias and roses, and olive trees as a peace offering to some of his detractors, to be planted in the Government Gardens as well as on his Elizabeth Farm estate. He probably also brought 'Slater's Crimson' rose (which had been sent from Canton to London in 1792 by Ambassador George Macartney), along with *Rosa bracteata*, the Macartney rose, and other Chinese plants. It is easy to imagine the joy these exciting new plants must have given Elizabeth.

Elizabeth's reunion with her husband was to be short-lived, however, for John's arguments with Governor Bligh resulted in his return to England, in exile, from 1809 to 1817, and life became more difficult for Elizabeth during her husband's second period of absence. 'Every day I feel such an accumulated weight of responsibility and care, that whatever tends

THE MACLEAYS AT ELIZABETH BAY HOUSE

above: The yellow banksia rose was a favourite with early settlers.

right: The wisteria flowering at Camden Park today

While they may have been many thousands of kilometres from home, the early settlers were not isolated from the horticultural passions in England and Europe. A vigorous intellectual discourse was quickly established between the leading families in the colony, those interested in botany and scientific advancement, the colonial government, and sites of learning around the world. The study of botany, along with engagement in decorative gardening and watercolour landscape painting, soon became an expression of colonial taste.

Lachlan Macquarie (Governor of New South Wales, 1810–21) founded the Botanic Gardens in Sydney in 1816, to acclimatise and assess new plants from around the world, including those from scientific institutions and botanic gardens in India, Mauritius, Britain, Scotland, Ireland and France. By 1825,

about 3000 new food plants and fruit trees had been introduced to Australia. Also among the plants discussed in government correspondence were achilleas, aconitums, alliums, asters, campanula, convallaria, hesperis, hypericum, and many species of iris and liliums. From the Botanic Garden, Edinburgh, came salvias, thalictrums, alyssum, schizanthus, scabiosa; in 1828, from the Botanic Garden, Mauritius, came hibiscus, begonia and rhus. Cytisus, convolvulus, erica and gardenia were brought from the Cape. Montpellier, France, sent anthurium, aster, cynoglossum, geranium, Acer pseudo-platanus, Bellis perennis and Crambe maritima. From the Botanic Gardens in Calcutta came ajugas, bauhinia, buddleia, clematis, ficus and mimosa.[27]

By the 1840s the most beautiful garden in the colony was that at

to lighten any part of it is desirable,' she wrote. Her tranquil garden, which she described as 'so beautiful and verdant', must have provided some calm in the midst of each turbulent day.[25]

Meanwhile, John Macarthur, lobbying those in the Colonial Office in London, finally managed to engineer a reversal in his fortunes and in March 1817, with his youngest two sons, James and William, returned to Australia on the *Lord Eldon* free of charge and with provision made for supplies he wanted to bring with him. A greenhouse was built on deck for his plants. Along with vines, olives and fruit, roses and peonies survived the voyage. He instructed Elizabeth to prepare some 5 hectares at Parramatta to receive his plants and seeds.[26] The party arrived home at the end of September 1817, having added to their horticultural collection at Rio de Janeiro.

Good gardens are a product of leisure. And a beautiful garden—a successfully enclosed space around the house or homestead—soon became a symbol of wealth, status and class in the colony. Within a few years, prosperity allowed Elizabeth Macarthur to turn to more decorative, Picturesque, gardening.

Elizabeth Bay House, created by Alexander Macleay (1767–1848), who arrived with his wife and six of his children in January 1826, to take up the post of Colonial Secretary under Governor Darling. His 2.2 hectare garden, set within his land grant of some 25 hectares on Sydney's harbour, took ten years and more than twenty men employed full time to create. It became the repository for species from around the globe, including China, from where he imported wisteria.

Before the Macleay family moved into the house they gardened at Macquarie Place, now at the centre of Sydney's business district. Macleay's eldest daughter, Fanny, wrote to her brother, William, in England, on 12 September 1826, 'We have now in flower the following beauties' and she itemised:

'Dendrobium speciosum, Diuris 2 species, Blandfordia nobilis, Thelymetra ixiodes, Bignonia Pandora, antirrhinum 3 species, Pelargonium—1 species, Boronia serrulate & paradoxa, Calla lurica Indica, Hyacinthus botryoides … Stenanthera pinifolia, Leucopogon— ericoides, chinensis and fulva, Calytrus ericifolia, Gladiolus 2 species, oxalis … Dianthus Alpinus & caesus, Borago officinalis, Malva Rosea, Sprengelia incarnata, Davallia pixadata, Euphrasia species (most beautiful), Narcissus Macleayi & bulbicodium … Rosa chinensis, Lupinus perennis, Anemone hortens'.[28]

Elizabeth Bay House became a rendezvous for the colony's scientific elite, while the garden, described by Joseph Hooker as a 'botanists' paradise', provided a fitting canvas on which the family displayed their intellectual and aesthetic strength. Elizabeth Macarthur included it in her visits.[29]

The rise in colonial taste was furthered by the formation of the Australian Floral and Horticultural Society, in Sydney in 1836, and in 1839 in Hobart. Tasmania was the first colony to establish a Royal Society in 1842; Victoria's Royal Society was formed in 1859, that of New South Wales in 1866 and South Australia in 1880. The Linnaean Society of New South Wales was incorporated in 1884.

Gardens are ephemeral: no plant stands still and nothing remains the same without the conscious effort of maintenance or preservation. This is particularly true in the Sydney climate, where a growing season of some nine months means that a garden can be lost to weeds in little more than a year. The garden that Elizabeth created in her first decades in the colony no longer exists, although remnant exotic trees remain, now mature. While no plans or sketches of the layout of the first garden at Elizabeth Farm have been found, details contained in her letters reveal that there were English trees, roses and perennials, as well as the bright plants from the warm temperate climates of the southern hemisphere.

The house was set on a gentle slope, looking down upon the Parramatta River. While the entrance to the earliest garden was simple, a carriage loop was later added so that Elizabeth and her daughter could enjoy driving out through the pleasure gardens in the 'britsha' that John commissioned in London, had emblazoned with the Macarthur coat of arms and sent to Sydney, during his second period of exile.

Two hoop pines (*Araucaria cunninghamii*), depicted in an 1859 watercolour by colonial artist Conrad Martens, remain, along with kurrajongs, bunya pines and the exotic trees that Thomas Mitchell had noted. In the shrubbery, which Martens painted from the verandah, were pink China roses, lilies, a bay tree and eucalypts. There would have been flower beds of cannas, dianthus, lupins and larkspur.[30] Elizabeth's letters to her

previous pages: Cottesbrooke Hall, just north of Northampton in the centre of England, is sited looking upon its park, and on an axis with the distant spire of Brixworth Church, which was built in 680 AD. The house is best viewed from the bridge by which you now enter the estate. Camden Park, in a similar fashion, is sited on an axis with St John's Church, built on Macarthur land and with financial aid from the Macarthurs.

below: Camden Park in early spring with the wisteria in full bloom

eldest son Edward are particularly useful in understanding her appreciation of the garden. By 1828, she told him that there was 'a pine and oak on either side [of] the little wicket beginning to look very conspicuous … in the garden we also have a handsome piece of water'. She enjoyed also 'a fine collection of bulbs from the Cape, in addition to those you brought … Amongst these is the celebrated Amaryllis Josephine.'[31] She sent specimens to the Macleays at Elizabeth Bay House, and no doubt received in return some of the thousands of new plants that were being collected by the leading natural scientists in the colony and sent from around the world to the government botanist.[32]

Although the physical work of creating her garden was carried out by a gardening labourer from among the convicts she was assigned, Elizabeth's letters show that she derived great comfort from it. She and her youngest daughter Emmeline took 'carriage exercise' there every day, and walked around it with pleasure.[33] In 1834 she told Edward, 'I have plenty of exercise within the limits of our own estate and looking about the garden and grounds annexed keeps me amused.'[34] The 'China Rose' that John Macarthur had brought back from his first exile continued to bloom:

IN A BLAZE OF BEAUTY AROUND THE GARDEN FENCES … ALMOST IN EVERY COTTAGE—YET THOUGH BECOME COMMON IS STILL A LOVELY PLANT … THE FOLIAGE SOFT AND FLEXIBLE AND YIELDING FLOWERS MORE OR LESS THROUGHOUT THE YEAR. WE HAVE A VARIETY OF OTHER ROSES—SWEET SCENTED AND BEAUTIFUL IN THEIR SEASON—BUT NOT SO ENDURING. [35]

The explorer and naturalist Ludwig Leichhardt, who stayed at Camden Park on several occasions, thanked William Macarthur in June of 1846 for 'Your note and the little box with the two beautiful specimens of Bougainvillea'.

Correspondence reveals that the Macarthur household enjoyed the latest books from England, including those of the Romantic novelists and poets, and was up to date with developments in taste and culture through subscriptions to journals like *The Edinburgh Review* and *The Quarterly Review*. Elizabeth was eager to bring to her surroundings any trends fashionable among the educated at home.

It is likely that the Macarthurs also read the work of John Claudius Loudon (1783–1843), the most influential and fashionable garden writer of the nineteenth century. His huge volumes—*An Encyclopaedia of Plants*, a massive work at 1200 pages, was published in 1829, *The Encyclopaedia of Cottage Farm and Villa Architecture and Furniture* in 1833 and *The*

Suburban Gardener and Villa Companion in 1838—were widely available in the bookshops of Sydney, and much consulted in the colonies. The placement of northern-hemisphere trees at Elizabeth Farm was intended to show each specimen to full advantage, in the Gardenesque manner described by Loudon:

Probably the oldest camellia in Australia, *Camellia japonica* 'Anemoniflora', first taken to England from China in 1806, and still flourishing at Camden Park today

THE PRODUCTION OF THAT KIND OF SCENERY WHICH IS BEST CALCULATED TO DISPLAY THE INDIVIDUAL BEAUTY OF TREES, SHRUBS AND PLANTS IN A STATE OF CULTURE; THE SMOOTHNESS AND GREENNESS OF LAWNS; AND THE SMOOTH SURFACE, CURVED DIREC-TION, DRYNESS, AND FIRMNESS OF GRAVEL WALKS.

Furthermore, he suggested that 'as a garden is a work of art and a scene of cultivation, every plant or tree placed in it should be so placed as never to be placed there by nature or accident or as to prevent the practices of cultivation being applied to it'.[36]

Loudon's instructions no doubt reached a receptive audience among the homesick settlers in the Australian colonies as they viewed what many described as the monotonous vegetation of the new country. Peter Cunningham noted that the gum tree provided 'no rustlings of the fast-falling leaves, nor burstings of the buds into life and loveliness in the spring'.[37]

Like other settlers, Elizabeth Macarthur's appreciation of the native vegetation was often flexible. While Elizabeth and her family may not have been pining constantly for the landscape of home, perceptions of the flora of the colony were set against a greater appreciation of the gardens of England. On 15 July 1818 her daughter Elizabeth wrote to Eliza Kingdon:

ALL OUR DECIDUOUS TREES ARE HOWEVER LEAFLESS ... YET WHEN IN LEAF IT MUST BE ADMITTED THAT THE BEAUTIFUL GREEN OF THE ENGLISH TREES FAR SURPASSES ... THE VERDURE OF OUR UNCHANGING EVERGREENS. WE THEREFORE CONTINUE TO INTERMIX THEM AS MUCH AS POSSIBLE, AND ENJOY THE BEAUTY OF EACH IN THEIR SEASONS.[38]

And, half a century after the colony was founded, the Sydney publisher, James Tegg, wrote in *The Literary News*:

... THE WILD FLOWERS ARE NUMEROUS AND BEAUTIFUL YET FEW POSSESS ANY DELIGHTFUL ODOUR, AND THEREFORE THE COLONIST HAS INTRODUCED AND SUCCEEDED IN NATURALISING MANY OF OUR MOST DELIGHTFUL EUROPEAN FLOWERS AND THEIR FRAGRANCE IS

NOW DIFFUSED OVER EVERY GARDEN. THE HONEYSUCKLE, SWEET PEA, JONQUIL, HOLLYHOCK, SINGLE AND DOUBLE STOCKS, MIGNONETTES (THAT DELIGHTFUL WEED ORIGINALLY A NATIVE OF EGYPT) ARE ABUNDANT AND ROSES ARE NOW SEEN IN PROFUSION UNFOLDING THEIR PALE CRIMSON LEAVES IN EVERY GARDEN; AMONG OTHER VARIETIES THE PRETTY ROSA FLORIBUNDA MAY BE SEEN CLUSTERING AROUND THE WINDOW FRAMES OF SOME PRETTY COTTAGE, ITS BUNCHES OF SMALL WHITE OR CRIMSON, GLITTERING WITH DEWDROPS AND DIFFUSING THEIR FRAGRANCE AROUND THE DWELLING.[39]

During the 1820s, after John Macarthur's return to New South Wales, Elizabeth Farm was enlarged to a more prestigious establishment, but John was dreaming of an even grander residence, Camden Park, at Menangle, on the southern outskirts of Sydney, to better display the family's pre-eminent position in the colony. However, he was declared insane in 1832 and died two years later; his vision for an impressive mansion at Camden Park was completed by his sons.

By 1838 the Macarthurs' land, at both Elizabeth Farm and Camden Park, had grown to over 12 000 hectares. There was no greater example of the aspirations of the nineteenth-century colonial gentry than Camden

The Clivea Walk at Camden Park

Park. Except for the presence of convict labour—fifty per cent of the 110 employees were convicts—the property was reminiscent of the great estates of England. 'To complete the transplanted vision', writes historian David Day:

THE MACARTHURS BUILT A VILLAGE COMPLETE WITH CHURCH FOR THEIR WORKERS. A VISITOR IN 1842 REMARKED ON HOW 'THE HOUSE, PARK, THE WATER, THE GARDENS, THE STYLE OF EVERYTHING AND OF EVERY PERSON, MASTER AND SERVANT, RESEMBLED SO MUCH WHAT ONE MEETS WITH IN THE OLD COUNTRY'[40]

William Macarthur's horticultural collections at Camden Park were nurtured in a series of glasshouses.

William Macarthur, John and Elizabeth's youngest son, was largely responsible for the estate's extensive gardens. He became part of the next generation of the colonial elite, where power was not just afforded to those who had grasped great tracts of land, but also to those whose position was underlined by a quest for intellectual endeavour and learning.[41] While

William's knowledge, skill and passion for botanical matters far surpassed those of his mother, Elizabeth derived great pleasure from the gardens he created. She wrote to Edward in 1830, expressing the importance she placed upon William's horticultural pursuits:

I CANNOT BUT FEEL ASTONISHED AT THE PERSEVERING INDUSTRY OF YOUR BROTHER WILLIAM WHO HAS SO BENEFICIALLY DEVOTED HIS TIME AND BEEN SO SUCCESSFUL IN PLANTING AND PROPAGATING TO A VERY GREAT EXTENT—TREES, PLANTS, FROM ALMOST EVERY PART OF THE WORLD. IT WOULD DELIGHT YOU TO OBSERVE THE CARE HE HAS TAKEN OF EVERYTHING HE HAS INTRODUCED BY YOUR SELF—AND AS SUCH I ASSURE YOU MAKE NO INCONSIDERABLE FIGURE IN THE GARDEN AND THE PLANTATIONS AND IT IS WITH SWEET RECOLLECTION AS WE PASS EACH TREE OR FLOWER OF YOURS THAT WE CONVERSE WITH YOU ...[42]

And at the height of her husband's insanity Elizabeth had found some peace by walking in the Botanic Gardens, close to where she had alighted four decades earlier:

... I HAVE HAD THE PLEASURE OF A VISIT HERE FROM YOUR SISTER ELIZABETH SINCE MY LAST—THEY STAYED TWO NIGHTS AND WE WALKED TO THE BOTANIC GARDENS TOGETHER WITH MARY AND MR B. I BELIEVE WE SAUNTERED ABOUT THREE HOURS OR MORE LOOKED AT MANY THINGS YOU HAD CONTRIBUTED TO THE COLLECTION, AND AMONGST THE NUMBER THE ARBUTUS—THERE IS A NEW GARDEN FORMED CONTIGUOUS, BETWEEN THE OLD—AND 'FARM COVE' WHICH IS THE BOUNDARY OF THE NEW—IT IS LAID OUT AFTER THE PLAN OF THE 'GLASGOW BOTANICAL GARDEN' OF DR. HOOKER—AND WILL BE VERY BEAUTIFUL.[43]

Elizabeth lived out her days at Elizabeth Farm, often staying at Camden Park, as well as at Woolloomooloo, close to the city centre, and at Watson's Bay, on Sydney Harbour, with various of her children. The garden continued as part of her daily life until her death in 1850.

Elizabeth Macarthur's garden was a clear statement of her success, and confirmed her social status by transplanting a vision of Englishness, in the image of an eighteenth-century landscape park. For Elizabeth the garden was a tranquil place to which she could escape the heavy duties with which she was burdened; it offered companionship after the separation from her husband and children. She shared her affection for her garden and the botanical world with at least two of her children, her son William and her daughter Elizabeth.

HUNTERS AND COLLECTORS

And God blessed them, and God said unto them,

Be fruitful, and multiply, and replenish the earth,

and subdue it: and have dominion over the fish of the sea,

and over the fowl of the air, and over every living thing

that moveth upon the earth.

GENESIS *1:28*[1]

Georgiana Molloy 1805–1843

'LANGUAGE REFUSES TO UTTER what I experienced when mine died in my arms in this dreary land with no-one but Molloy to comfort me,' wrote the young Georgiana Molloy in a letter home after the death of her first child, born in May 1830, in a tent and under an umbrella held against the driving rain, not three months after her arrival in the new colony of Western Australia.[2]

The death of her baby was to be just the first tragedy in a land that was to provide a life very different from that she had imagined when she confided her hopes and dreams to the diary she kept aboard the ship on which she set out for the colony with her new husband, Captain John Molloy, some twenty-five years her senior. Perhaps no story is more illustrative of the hardships early women settlers faced than that of Georgiana Molloy, one of the first white women to travel south of the Swan River settlement.[3] Tragedy and hardship were to be constants in her short life, and she turned for comfort to horticulture in various forms.

Georgiana's story demonstrates that garden making was an essential act of colonisation. It was an act of domestication, as frontier women settlers sought to familiarise and humanise the wilderness in which they found themselves. In addition, along with the comfort derived from gardening, for a few educated women, isolated from the social and cultural circle to which

The borders of Scotland from Scott's View: soft countryside familiar to Georgiana Molloy

they were accustomed, the added intellectual endeavour of botanising—of the chase for horticultural bounty—provided a life-saving fascination. For some, horticulture was the only common ground between the old country and a life of disappointments in the new land. Georgiana, conventionally brought up as a member of the gentry, was one such woman.

~

Born on 23 May 1805 into a life of middle-class expectations, Georgiana Kennedy grew up at Crosby Lodge, an ivy-clad two-storey country house set in spacious gardens, close to the medieval castle town of Carlisle, in the English county of Cumberland, near the Scottish border. She was descended from old border families, the daughter of well-to-do parents who had inherited property. Her father, David Kennedy, lived, according to Georgiana's biographer, the life of a country gentleman.[4] When Georgiana was sixteen, her father was killed in a hunting accident. Mrs Kennedy moved her family of three daughters and two sons to Rugby, on the border of Warwickshire and Northamptonshire, to further the boys' education, and, perhaps, to better the girls' prospects of achieving good marriages.

England's Lake District provided much of the vision that our early settlers—who were well versed in the Romantic poets of the area—attempted to transfer to the Antipodes as they constructed a new life for themselves, and a new garden, in the colonies.

As a genteel girl in Carlisle Georgiana enjoyed private classes in the 'polite accomplishments' of pianoforte and harp, in singing and dancing, embroidery, literature, scripture and botanising, the last having been made fashionable by Queen Charlotte, wife of George III.[5] It is reasonable to assume that she would have read the Romantic poets, including William Wordsworth, who at that time were eulogising the lakes and mountains not far south of her home. Her greatest friends were the deeply religious Dunlop sisters—Mary, Margaret and Helen—with whom she often stayed at Keppoch House, their 130 hectare estate just over the Scottish border. The Dunlops had a scholarly background, were educated in law and divinity, and were increasingly caught up in the religious fervour that was sweeping Britain after the defeat of Napoleon, and in the aftermath of the Industrial Revolution.

Georgiana, of all the Kennedy siblings, was most affected by the new religious mood, her piety no doubt deepened by her friendship with the Dunlops. In 1829, Helen Dunlop married the Reverend Robert Story, and moved the short distance from her home to Roseneath, a village between Loch Long and the beautiful Gare Loch, in the south-west of Scotland. Ben Lomond towers 1000 metres above the village; in the background are Ben Bheula and the Argyll Forest. In 1829 the district was at the centre of religious revival and Georgiana and her friends were deeply engaged in discussing questions of Faith and Belief.

Rydal Mount, just beyond Ambleside on the northern tip of Lake Windermere, was home to Romantic poet William Wordsworth for almost four decades, from 1813.

The large garden at Roseneath was filled with violets and primroses; the pillars on the verandah supported climbing roses. Bound up with the theological fervour was a rise in the study of botany and Georgiana and her friends spent hours roaming over fields, heaths and moors, collecting and observing examples of God's work exemplified in nature. Georgiana's diary of Saturday 5 July 1829 records in Romantic language the picturesque landscape of her friend's home: '… this evening was particularly bright the [fertile?] print of Roseneath formed a rich contrast to the grey parts of the mountains …'[6]

It was during her stay at Roseneath that Georgiana received a letter from Captain Molloy, requesting her hand in marriage. He also asked if she would venture with him to the Swan River settlement, a promised land free of convicts and with land grants available for all.[7]

Georgiana and Captain John Molloy, a decorated veteran of the Napoleonic wars and the Battle of Waterloo, were married on 6 August 1829 at the church in Roseneath. After their wedding the newlyweds travelled to London, and there was more than a hint of the frontier in the language the 24-year-old Georgiana used when she wrote to her friends in Scotland of her adventure to a new world, a 'promised land'. It is easy to imagine—and her sentiments would have echoed those of frontier women in other settlements throughout the New World—that the pious Georgiana saw herself in biblical terms, as a pioneering woman seeking paradise.

Wordsworth designed his 2.2 hectare terraced garden, Rydal Mount, to afford views of the misty and ethereal waterway. It remains today largely as he created it, and is home to his descendants.

On 19 October 1829, after weeks of frustrating and expensive delays—for they had to maintain their newly acquired household—the Molloys sailed from Portsmouth on the *Warrior,* with five servants and three children, a large collection of horses, pigs, sheep, cattle, stocks of food and household goods, as well as seeds, both ornamental and culinary, cuttings, plants and garden tools.[8] Among Georgiana's shipboard luggage were her diaries, in which she recorded her fears and her dreams for her new home. Mary Dunlop had given her a potted geranium which, she noted in her diary, was flowering in December that year.[9] She also recorded her disappointment with her shipboard companions. On the second day of her journey she told her diary that she, 'went on Deck, it was rather rough and things still in confusion, the people all appear most ordinary … We dine at [paper torn] and afterwards I withdrew to my cabin and thought of all my dear friends.'[10]

The South African arum lily (*Zantedeschia aethiopica*), collected by early settlers en route to the colonies, has made itself too much at home in the favourable conditions of Western Australia.

She also wrote nostalgically of the landscape of Roseneath, of the soft mists that hovered around the lochs and the mountains behind. She thought of the picturesque scenes romanticised by the Lake poets as they yearned for the purity of pre-industrialised Britain, of her home further south at Rugby, and for the vistas created by Repton who had taken his scissors to so many of the estates close by. Her memory was perhaps sharpened by the cramped conditions on board, made even more uncomfortable by the fact that she was now pregnant, and although accounts of the Swan River settlement gave her courage, she wrote daily of how ill and weak she felt.

On Monday 4 January 1830 she wrote longingly of the comfort and security of home: 'Not very well. Worked and wrote up this journal. This day last year I planted some Rose trees Helen sent from Roseneath before the dining room windows. I remember every little incident so well, this is not in the "Red Book".'[11] Families such as the Kennedys and the Dunlops would have been well aware of Repton and his work: his name had entered the lexicon of Georgian Britain's gentry.[12] For Georgiana, Repton and his Red Books could well have been the epitome of graciousness, exemplified by a beautiful, extensive pleasure garden and parkland. The garden at Roseneath, in its picturesque setting, burgeoning with softly blooming roses, was the embodiment of the gentility and peace that she assumed would epitomise her own marriage. Georgiana's attitudes to garden making, expressed throughout her letters home during her fifteen years in the colony of Western Australia, show that she was very much informed by Repton and his ideas on landscape. Her shipboard experiences, with travelling companions she felt were irreligious and coarse, were not an auspicious beginning. One passenger on board the *Warrior* was Charles Bussell who, with his three brothers, was to be so much part of the development of the colony. He noted:

MRS MOLLOY HAS ALL THE AIR OF A LADY WELL BORN AND WELL BRED WITHOUT HAVING MIXED MUCH IN THE WORLD, AND THERE IS CONSEQUENTLY A GREAT DEAL OF INTEREST ABOUT HER. SHE IS RATHER INCLINED TO THE ROMANTIC AND IS DELIGHTED TO HAVE ANYONE WITH WHOM SHE CAN CONTEMPLATE THE SUBLIMITY OF A NIGHT SCENE OR EXPIATE UPON THE BEAUTIES OF THIS OR THAT PIECE OF POETRY.[13]

On 12 January, twelve weeks after leaving Portsmouth, the *Warrior* reached Cape Town and Georgiana could be among women she felt were of her own kind, the Governor's and the Colonial Secretary's wives. Georgiana invoked the activities of the plant hunters when she proclaimed the Cape wildflowers, the bulbs and the succulents 'a botanical domain without compare'.[14] She convinced her husband to spend £7 7s 6d on seeds, including oleander, Cape gooseberry, and the pink-flowered watsonia, to transport to her new home.

Georgiana and Molloy arrived off Rottnest Island on the coast of Western Australia on 11 March 1830, assuming they could transplant an Anglo-Saxon way of life from the northern hemisphere into this land of sand and heat. Georgiana described for her diary their arrival in the new colony:

ROTTNEST IN VIEW AND WE SHORTLY ANCHORED AT SWAN RIVER. MOST HAPPY OUR TEDIOUS VOYAGE IS ENDED I AM VERY GRATEFUL TO GOD FOR HIS MERCIFUL PROTECTION DURING ALL OUR DANGERS.[15]

The *Warrior* passengers were landed at Fremantle, the port for the colony, on 13 March. Settlers were mostly housed in tents erected on the brilliant white sands, under an intense sun. One observer said that it was:

A BARREN-LOOKING DISTRICT OF SANDY COAST; THE SHRUBS CUT DOWN FOR FIREWOOD, THE HERBAGE TRODDEN BARE, A FEW WOODEN HOUSES, MANY RAGGED-LOOKING TENTS AND CONTRIVANCES FOR HABITATIONS—ONE HOTEL, A POOR PUBLIC-HOUSE INTO WHICH EVERYONE CROWDED.[16]

Georgiana's naïve and hopeful entry for 13 March again assumes her new life would parallel that which she had left behind: 'Did not go to Church it is so warm … How strange we should be so soon domesticated in an unknown Land.'[17] The next day the travellers embarked upon the 7 kilometre journey up river to Perth. 'We set off for Perth Town and were delighted with the country most beautifully wooded with magnificent aromatic trees and shrubs,' she wrote optimistically. Perth, even after just a few months, was a growing town with three hotels. A wide main street, St George's Terrace, had been cleared. There were a few houses, chiefly for the officers, and a temporary residence for the Governor had been erected. A church had been built next to the parade ground of the 63rd Regiment, most of whom were housed there in tents. Perth society was made up mostly of retired naval and military officers and their wives, all members of the landed gentry in England.

THE PLANT HUNTERS

above: The coveted Himalayan blue poppy, *Meconopsis betonicifolia*

right: Rhododendron Loderi Group

facing page, left: Treasures at Doshong La, in Victoria's Dandenongs. The garden was named by owner Otto Fauser after the mountain pass in South Eastern Tibet where the legendary plant hunter Frank Kingdom Ward found twenty alpine *Rhododendron* species.

facing page, right: Fritillary, *Fritillaria pontica*

The nineteenth century saw an energetic search for botanical booty in the Far East and the Americas, and specimens collected by British plant hunters found their way, of course, to the colonies. Leading British families, including the Devonshires at Chatsworth, in Derbyshire, competing with each other for botanical trophies, sponsored plant-hunting expeditions and received in return 'dividends' of plants and seeds.

Although some plants had reached the West from China in the seventeenth century, the hunt intensified after Joseph Banks sent William Kerr to Canton to collect for Kew Gardens in 1803: *Rosa banksiae* was among the prizes. By 1800, about 200 nurseries had been established in Britain.

China was further opened up for trade after its defeat by Britain in 1842, and the Horticultural Society lost no time in sending plant hunters to search for botanical treasure. Robert Fortune spent two years travelling and collecting in China and Japan, and in 1844 Thomas Lobb sent orchids and rhododendron to England from Java, India, Burma, Malaya and Borneo. The *Ceanothus* and the conifer *Cupressus*

Sandflies and the heat aside, Georgiana could be forgiven for assuming that her life might return almost to the gentle pattern she had left at Roseneath Manse, for Governor Stirling and his 23-year-old wife, Ellen, were sociable and energetic. 'Friday 22 April. Left our tents at Freemantle [sic] and went to Perth to attend the dance [?] at which there were 58 Gentlemen and 8 Ladies,' she recorded in her diary.[18] A Literary Society, albeit short-lived, was established, as were agricultural and horticultural societies. By 1831 there would be plans to establish a botanical garden with help from the Horticultural Society of London, which had sent out fruit trees, vegetables, flower roots and cuttings with the botanist James Drummond, who had accompanied Stirling to the new colony in 1829 and was now superintendent of the government gardens.

The promised grants of good land, however, turned out to have been something of an exaggeration. The land along the Swan and Canning rivers had been taken up by the officers and settlers who had arrived on the first ships, but they soon found that this was very different from farming land in Britain. The sandy soil was often barren, and the vast tracts taken up required great numbers of workers, none of whom came free, as in the other colonies.[19] These travails, along with the difficult climate and living conditions, and Stirling's enthusiasm for the land further south, convinced

macrocarpa arrived in Britain from California.

In Britain the cultivation of tender and exotic plants became more widespread after the price of glass fell dramatically with the repeal of the glass tax in 1845. With advances in glasshouse design and the widespread use of water heating, glasshouse production of exotic fruits and flowering plants thus became accessible to many.

In 1899 the Veitch nursery family employed Ernest Wilson to collect maples and davidias in Burma. In 1903, Wilson was in China, again collecting treasure for the Veitch nurseries. The most intrepid of the plant hunters was perhaps George Forrest who, in July 1905, based himself at the French Catholic Mission at Tzekou, 3000 metres up in Yunnan province at the point where China, India and Tibet meet. He recorded that the alps were clothed with rhododendron, primulas, gentians, saxifrages and lilies, 'a veritable botanists' paradise'. Frank Kingdom Ward was in China in 1913 and the following year Wilson was in Japan collecting for the Arnold arboretum. All the specimens were avidly sought by plantsmen and

botanists in the Australian colonies, and soon found their way into the gardens of the privileged families.

Match stick banksia, *B. cuneata*

the Molloys to take the Governor's advice to establish a settlement on the Blackwood River. Stirling had observed breathtaking scenery of majestic forests and beautiful beaches as he had sailed along the south coast; sealers had reported a large river, land more fit for farming and a cooler climate.

The Molloys' possessions were loaded onto the *Emily Taylor* and, with the Bussells and several other settlers and their servants, they set sail on 29 April 1830. John Molloy had already been allotted 5000 hectares of land, on the basis that property he brought to the colony was valued at £960 10s.

The settlers rounded the wild and beautiful Cape Leeuwin at the base of the continent, and pulled in to Flinders Bay on Sunday 2 May: from here the group could observe their new Arcadia. The Southern Ocean broke upon white sands and the beach gave way to a heavy covering of stringybark and red gum forest. Behind were the straight grey-white trunks of the karri trees (*Eucalyptus diversicolor*), towering to some 90 metres, many of them hundreds of years old.

Disembarkation, with an assortment of animals, and possessions in packing cases and barrels, took three days. The small group set up camp on the western shore of the river mouth, their tents thin and incompetent in the face of the constant driving rain and the onset of Antipodean winter weather. It was decided this was where the town, to be named Augusta, would be established; the Governor had appointed Molloy as Resident Magistrate.

Little more than a week later Georgiana's first child, Elizabeth Mary, was born. No doctor was among the settlers, nor a midwife, and Georgiana was attended only by her maidservant, Anne Dawson, who had lost her own baby on the voyage from England. The baby lived just a few days. Georgiana recorded the child's short life in her diary. 'On Monday the 24th May 1830 Elizabeth Mary the only child of John and Georgiana Molloy was born …' Then follows daily description of the progress and regression of the baby: 'Wednesday 26. I gave her a little magnesium … Her feet and legs were icy cold …'[20]

In the midst of this bleak account Georgiana tells of unpacking a small box of seeds that had been given to her: '… little did I expect to open it at such a time.'[21] But the unpacking of the seeds was a turning point for Georgiana, the beginning of her efforts to domesticate her new land, and the beginning of a passion for botanising. With a desperate need to turn death into rebirth, to force good from tragedy, to create something living from destruction, Georgiana recounts her husband placing the baby in its tiny grave, with:

RYE GRASS AND CLOVER OVER IT AND HAS RECENTLY PUT SOME TWIGS OVER IT TO FORM A SORT OF TRELLIS WORK WITH THE SURROUNDING CREEPERS WHICH IN THIS COUNTRY ARE VERY NUMEROUS. I HAVE ALSO SOWED CLOVES AND … PLANTED PUMPKINS WHICH WILL RAPIDLY CREEP ON THE TWIGS OVER IT AND FORM A SORT OF DOME … '[22]

Like frontier women before her and since, Georgiana sought through garden making to fashion beauty from emptiness, to create some good from unspeakable sadness, to bring softness and gentleness to a harsh environment. The renewal that is evident in a growing garden is one aspect of garden making that provides comfort and solace: the seasons will go full circle and spring must follow winter. The need to nurture is a part of the female psyche that is fulfilled through gardening, and is one of the reasons that women take a different approach from men to garden making.

The days were much cooler than in Perth and driving winter

Honey myrtle (*Melaleuca fulgens*) is visited by native bees.

previous pages:
Pear-fruited mallee,
Eucalyptus pyriformis

rains had already set in. The settlers' first task was to build houses, preceded by that essential first act of occupation, the conquering of the alien bush by stripping bare the land, echoing settler activity since pre-Neolithic Britain. Settlers soon found the Augusta area anything but an Eden, for while the aspect and the scenery were beautiful, the massive forests that covered the surrounding land were almost impenetrable. Their main enemy was the giant karri, among the hardest timber in the world; it took days to fell one tree. A dense understorey of vines, of native clematis and wisteria, of ferns and shrubs, made their work even more difficult, and by August that year a total of less than 4 hectares had been readied for planting.

For Georgiana, the most civilising of activities was the creation of her garden: 'The flower seeds are a great treasure, and I am having my garden enlarged on purpose for them. I highly value those gathered from my poor Eliza …'[23]

The attempt to feminise and familiarise the landscape was a practice common to women in frontier, patriarchal settlements; for Georgiana Molloy, garden making was also symptomatic of her faith. Although her religious beliefs must have been tested by the tragedy of her child's death she would have been mindful of God's work, close by, manifest in nature, and perhaps drew considerable comfort from it.

John Molloy had taken up a block of 7 hectares for his household on the edge of the Blackwood River; the Bussells pegged out a block on one side and another settler, James Turner and his large family, the block on the other. The Molloy residence was erected near to the water's edge: it was a two-storey, rectangular building built of stringybark slabs with a verandah running along the front. There were several outhouses, including a kitchen and scullery and sleeping quarters for their servants—Molloy's valet, Elijah Dawson, his wife Anne and the gardener Staples. Georgiana quickly set about reconstructing, as best she could, the rough environment. By 1832 she could write home to her sister, Elizabeth:

I AM SITTING IN THE VERANDAH SURROUNDED BY MY LITTLE FLOWER GARDEN OF BRITISH, CAPE AND AUSTRALIAN FLOWERS POURING FORTH THEIR ODOUR (FOR THE LARGE WHITE LILY IS NOW IN BLOOM).[24]

As well as the tall-growing highly scented lily, *Lilium candidum*, her garden was filled with the sweet, clove-like scent of *Dianthus*. There were orange and red nasturtiums and sweet peas, and brilliantly coloured geraniums. The scent of Virginia stock, of the mignonette and of evening primrose reminded her of home. The verandah was adorned with a purple creeper which also covered 'most attractively', she wrote, the side windows. From

the Cape she had brought pink gladiolus, watsonias and oleander, so suited to the West Australian climate. She could also have brought the heavily scented freesia that now covers fields in the area, taking over from the native flora and, along with the Cape daisy and the white arum lily, classed today as a noxious weed.

Under her direction, Dawson and Staples created an orchard which flourished in the warm temperate climate, with fig trees grown from slips, 'from the specimen which gained the prize from the Horticultural Society at Winchester'. She enjoyed grapevines raised from seed, and an abundance of the Cape gooseberry and peaches grown from stones carried with her from Cape Town. But she still viewed her new home with eyes that remembered the ever-changing landscape of England and Scotland, coping with the surrounding bush only because she had challenged it by making a garden around her house. 'If it were not for domestic charms the eye of the emigrant would soon weary of the unbounded limits of thickly clothed, dark green forests,' she later wrote.

In July, the bush surrounding her garden bloomed purple with the native wisteria and in August the bright red 'running postman' added its own brilliancy. But she sought to harness the wilderness that surrounded her house at Augusta by describing it in a familiar lexicon:

Freesias, collected by early settlers as they stopped at Cape Town en route to the Swan River colony, soon became 'garden escapes'.

IN THESE MONTHS THE WILDERNESS INDEED BEGINS TO BLOSSOM AS A
ROSE. THE PURPLE CREEPER ALONE HAS CONSENTED TO BEING DOMES-
TICATED AND HAS ASSOCIATED ITS BEAUTIFUL PURPLE FLOWERS WITH
A VERY ELEGANT PINK CLIMBING PLANT FROM THE MAURITIUS ... IN
THE BACKGROUND IS THE BOUNDLESS AND EVERGREEN FOREST ...

Winter-flowering scarlet banskia,
Banksia coccinea

The garden she created at her home in its isolated cove provided great
solace, and she constantly referred to it in her letters to England. But
Georgiana, like Elizabeth Macarthur on the other side of the continent,
found the lack of suitable female company difficult: her loneliness is palpable in her letters. And this was no Macarthur household with plentiful
servants to smooth the way to a life as refined as the one she had left. When
Georgiana wrote to her friend Helen Story about the loss of her child she
felt compelled to talk of her own loneliness, 'I thought I might have had one
little bright object left to solace all the hardships and privations I endured'.

The new settlement was completely isolated from Perth. That, cou-
pled with the difficulty of procuring domestic servants, meant that
Georgiana found herself removed from almost all female company, let
alone women of her own class. She would later write to Helen Story of 'this
strange life':

IN MARCH OUR SERVANTS' INDENTURES ARE UP, AND WE ARE LITERALLY
EXPECTING TO BE WITHOUT AND WE SHALL BE UNLESS SOME VESSEL MOST
UNEXPECTEDLY BRINGS PEOPLE HERE ... LET THEM BE SUPPLIED WITH
WOOLLEN GOODS OF DARK COLOUR. SHOES AND EVEN CLOGS WOULD BE
GOOD HERE IN THE WINTER ... IF EVER WE LEAVE AUSTRALIA, I THINK IT
WILL BE TO SETTLE IN BONNIE SCOTLAND. I OFTEN DREAM OF THE GARDEN
OF THE MANSE. I USED TO TAKE SO MUCH INTEREST IN IT ...[25]

Georgiana's second child, Sabina, was born at Augusta on 7 November 1831; a third daughter, Mary, on 16 June 1834. Settlers had to be prepared to turn their hands to any task, however menial. 'My head aches,' Georgiana wrote in January 1833 to her childhood friend Margaret Dunlop:

Bell-fruited mallee,
Eucalyptus preissiana

I HAVE ALL THE CLOTHES TO PUT
AWAY FROM THE WASH, BABY TO
PUT TO BED, TO MAKE TEA AND
DRINK IT WITHOUT MILK AS THEY
SHOT ONE COW FOR A TRESPASS,
READ PRAYERS AND GO TO BED,
BESIDES SENDING OFF ALL THIS
TABLE FULL OF LETTERS ... WHAT
GOLDEN DREAMS WE USED TO HAVE ABOUT YOUR COMING TO STAY
WITH ME! HOW WOULD YOU LIKE TO BE NEARLY THREE YEARS IN A
PLACE WITHOUT A FEMALE OF YOUR OWN RANK TO SPEAK TO, OR BE
WITH YOU WHATEVER HAPPENED.[26]

The difficulty of her situation, and the indignities of frontier life for women, is again vivid in her words:

LITTLE SABINA ... 14 MONTHS OLD ... I CANNOT WEAN HER HAVING NO
ONE TO TAKE HER FROM ME FOR THE TIME, FOR I NEED NOT BLUSH TO
TELL YOU I AM OF NECESSITY MY OWN NURSERY-MAID IF I COULD
AFFORD TO KEEP ONE THEY ARE SO EXCEPTIONABLE I DURST NOT TRUST
MY CHILD WITH THEM ... TO WEIGH OUT RATIONS, ATTEND TO BABY
AND ... NEEDLEWORK OF EVERY KIND BOTH FOR HER, MOLLOY AND
MYSELF AND SERVANT IS REQUIRED ... I HAVE NOT TOUCHED A NEEDLE
FOR THIS WEEK I AM NOW EXHAUSTED THE DAY UNCOMMONLY HOT.[27]

But, like settlers before her, Georgiana never gave up hope of a more civilised life and wrote to her mother from Augusta on 4 January 1835:

CPT. MOLLOY DESIRES ME TO REQUEST YOU WILL PURCHASE FOR US FROM THE 35 POUND BILL PLAIN REAL SILVER SOUP LADELS TO MATCH OUR SPOONS WHICH ARE OLD FASHIONED PLAIN HANDLES ...

Comfort could also be taken from her garden, as she told her mother, 'The prunus are growing very fast and I think will soon flower.' [28] On 4 June 1833 she recorded in her diary that 'Staples sowed carrots, turnips, spinach'. By August she could record that it was 'Fine. Sowed many garden seeds. Rain at night,' and then, a few days later, 'Beautiful day. Dawson planting potatoes'. But while she found companionship in her bush surroundings and the garden she was creating, she often hankered for the colours and the scents of home:

OH! MY DEAR AND LOVELY ROSENEATH! MY HEART BLEEDS WHEN I THINK OF ALL THE HAPPY, CELESTIAL DAYS I SPENT THERE; AND ALL THE VIOLETS AND PRIMROSES ARE FRESH IN MY MEMORY. HOW DOES YOUR GARDEN GET ON? AND DID THE AYRSHIRE ROSES ENTWINE ROUND THE POLES AT THE END OF THE GARDEN?[29]

There was never simply one response to any one set of circumstances. Georgiana Molloy, while coming to terms with her bush environment, and later writing of the glorious climate and sweetly scented native flowers, still constantly framed her praise within the assumption that European plants were more likely to please and comfort.

While Augusta turned out to be no Arcadia, Georgiana could empathise with the natural beauty of the south-west corner of the country, even if the heavily forested region afforded the settlers little hospitality. While later she would express her memories of the settlement along the Blackwood River in Picturesque terms, she was constantly reminded of how different the reality of her life had transpired from her romantic, newly married aspirations. The circumstances in which she found herself in the colony threw into question all she had taken for granted. Her home was the site of endless menial and manual work: it was not a place where class distinctions were clearly defined and maintained, without question. In this, the most remote part of all the Australian colonies, and where land was cheaply available to all, the class structure taken for granted in Roseneath had been swept away.

While the challenges of settler life continued to present themselves without respite, Georgiana was to find, to her surprise, that the bush that surrounded her could also be her companion. She received in April 1836—the same month that a baby boy, John, her fourth child, was safely delivered—a letter that was to change what was left of her short life. The letter was from Captain James Mangles, RN, a cousin of Lady Stirling, the Governer's wife. Mangles, an amateur botanist, was a colleague of Dr John Lindley, who was Professor of Botany at the University of London, former assistant to Joseph Banks at Kew Gardens, author of *Ladies' Botany* and organiser, in 1830, of Britain's first flower show. Mangles exchanged horticultural treasures with Joseph Paxton, the Superintendent at Chatsworth, and with aristocratic families throughout the United Kingdom.

Accompanying Mangles' letter to Georgiana in her remote corner of the globe was a box of 'many long-wished for seeds', along with the request that she refill the box with seeds and specimens of her region, and return them to him. Whether out of good manners, curiosity, or because she saw a chance for intellectual companionship at some level, she accepted Mangles' challenge, and wrote to thank him on 21 March 1837, telling him that while she was busy with 'domestic drudgery', she would collect the seeds, as well as leaves and flowers. She set about the task with determination, involving her two young daughters in her work.

And, like any proper obsession, Georgiana's forays into the bush started to consume most of her time. While she had previously accepted that her 'chief pleasure' was her garden, she now found the orderly collecting, pressing and mounting of species completely new to her provided an intellectual challenge that was both addictive and comforting. She

The orange flame pea, *Chorizema cordatum*

previous pages: The rare
black kangaroo paw,
Macropidia fuliginosa

collected the plant material, carefully cleaned and conserved the seeds—
harvested at just the right time to ensure viability. She pressed the leaves
and flowers of each specimen, mounting them, all correctly labelled, as a
Hortus Siccus—a collection of dried plants—in the books that Mangles
regularly sent her. Georgiana's surviving diaries and letters show that this
scientific endeavour brought as much joy and solace as the creation of her
garden and the domestication of the space in which she found herself.[30]
For women like Georgiana the hunt for botanical specimens was not
intended to portray success and prowess, as it may have been for men, but
rather it was a journey to an intellectual and creative place.

As well, the association with key scientific figures and institutions
must have provided Georgiana with a link to a more civilised world. There
was the joy to be found in discovery and intellectual pursuit and the satisfaction in finding an interest that belonged to her rather than an activity that
was required of her as a wife. The garden was not simply, therefore, a place
where a 'polite accomplishment' was performed, but part of an intellectual,
scientific institution, and a site that provided a sense of self.

In November 1837, however, her new-found joy was brutally inter-
rupted by the drowning of her eighteen-month-old son, John, who was
found dead at the base of the household well at Augusta. 'The fatal truth
stole over me,' she wrote to Mangles of the moment the dreadful realisation of the tragedy came to her. 'As the little body was pulled from the well,'
she continued, somehow able to describe her desperation to a man she had
never met:

THAT DARLING PRECIOUS CHILD, LIFELESS, HIS FLAXEN CURLS ALL DRIPPING, HIS
LITTLE COUNTENANCE SO PLACID HE LOOKED FAST ASLEEP BUT NOT DEAD, AND
WE DO NOT BELIEVE HE IS SO UNTIL SOME MINUTES AFTER ... THAT LOVELY,
HEALTHY CHILD WHO HAD NEVER KNOWN PAIN OR SICKNESS AND WHO HAD
BEEN ALL MIRTH AND JOYOUSNESS ...[31]

Illness overcame her after little John's death, but botanising provided some
small respite from her grief. Within a month she was making daily excur-
sions into the bush, immersing herself in the daily changing beauty of the
natural world. She filled Mangles' *Hortus Siccus*, but wrote of her concern
at the inferiority of the plants she was sending to him in return for the
seeds of precious northern hemisphere trees she requested from him. The
plants of her new world did not compare favourably with those of home
and she yearned for a 'large flower':

I AM OF THE OPINION THAT THESE FLOWERS ARE NOT SO INTERESTING AS OUR
OWN, AND, AFTER THE NOVELTY HAS PASSED, SOON CEASE TO PLEASE. THESE

POSSESS NO ASSOCIATIONS, NOR DOES ANYTHING ABOUT THEM ATTRACT BUT THE LUSTROUS COLOUR. VERY FEW HAVE ANY SCENT, AND I QUARREL MUCH WITH THEIR EXCESSIVELY MINUTE COROLLA IN THIS ... DEAR AUGUSTA IS QUITE OUT OF THE WORLD AND EVEN THE LIMITED SOCIETY OF S. W. AUSTRALIA AND VERY FEW BESTOW A THOUGHT ON FLOWERS.[32]

'What could have led you, my dear Sir,' she wrote in the long letter to him, posted in January 1838, 'to have selected me as a collector, much more to imagine I had botanical knowledge, I cannot devine.' In the same letter she wrote further of the burdens endured by the wife of a settler:

GRUBBING, HOES, BEEF, POTATOES, ONION, ANCHORS AND ANCHORAGE, WHALING, HARPOONING, ARE THE CHIEF TOPICS OF CONVERSATION. I MUCH FEAR I SHALL BE SO MUCH EMPLOYED IN THE ODIOUS DRUDGERY OF CHEESE AND BUTTER MAKING THAT I SHALL NOT BE ABLE TO ATTEND TO THE FORMATIONS AND CULTURE OF MY FLOWER GARDEN, FOR I AM MY CHILDREN'S SOLE INSTRUCTRESS, SEAMSTRESS ... [33]

The difficulty of life aside, it is likely that Georgiana was following with attention the rise in colonial taste—evidenced by the development of a keen interest in such pursuits as botany and landscape painting—that was taking place in the eastern colonies. She would have sought news from the schooners that called at Augusta, through her husband's correspondence with the Governor's office, and from colonial officers and their wives in Perth. She kept up to date with English horticultural fashion by receiving notes from the British Horticultural Society and through Loudon's monthly magazine, *The Gardener*, first published in 1826.

She soon acknowledged that her botanising came to provide such a diversion from the vicissitudes of her life that she was neglecting the duties prescribed for her as a woman and a wife. 'Often had Molloy looked at a buttonless shirt,' she later told Mangles, 'and exclaimed with a Woebegone Visage, "When will Captain Mangles' seeds be sown?"'

INDEED, MY DEAR SIR, I HAVE BEEN MORE FREQUENTLY FROM MY HOME THIS YEAR IN MAKING UP YOUR COLLECTION THAN IN THE WHOLE OF THE NEARLY EIGHT YEARS WE HAVE LIVED AT AUGUSTA ... I HAVE SPARED NEITHER TIME NOR TROUBLE IN SERVING YOU.[34]

Whatever he thought of the flora of the colony, Mangles could have been in no doubt that collecting plants and seeds for him had become for Georgiana something of a salvation. And there is no doubt that her work provided valuable additions to the Kew herbarium. In 1839 Lindley wrote to Mangles:

YOUR FRIEND MRS MOLLOY IS REALLY THE MOST CHARMING PER-
SONAGE ... THAT MANY OF THE PLANTS ARE BEAUTIFUL YOU CAN SEE
FOR YOURSELF, AND I AM DELIGHTED TO ADD THAT MANY OF THE BEST
ARE QUITE NEW ...'[35]

above: Chatsworth, the Derbyshire
estate of the Duke of Devonshire

opposite: One of the glasshouses
at Chatsworth, where many of
Georgiana's Western Australian
treasures found a home

Joseph Paxton was also delighted with the hundreds of specimens and
seeds that Georgiana sent. There were seeds of the native climbers, there
was wattle as well as the vibrantly coloured kangaroo paw. There was the
beautifully scented native bush, a boronia, the only plant that was to be
named after Georgiana. He would later write to Mangles:

THERE ARE SOME SPLENDID THINGS IN THE *HORTUS SICCUS* OF PORT
AUGUSTA, COMPRISING MANY NEW SPECIES OF HOVEA, CHORIZEMA,
DAVIESIA, BORONIA, EPACRIS, AND KENNEDYA ... THERE APPEAR TO BE
MANY OTHER FINE PLANTS WHICH APPEAR TO BE NEW. THIS LAST
COLLECTION OF SEEDS YOU WERE SO KIND AS TO SEND US ARE FAR
SUPERIOR TO ANY THAT WE HAVE RECEIVED AT CHATSWORTH.[36]

Eventually, however, the Molloys acknowledged that the unforgiving
Augusta landscape would not yield a prosperous life. 'I have not even had
time to say my prayers tonight,' she wrote home. 'This life is too much for

either dear Molloy or myself, and what I lament is that in this decline of life, he will have to lead a much more laborious life than he did in one and twenty years service.'[37]

They realised they must follow in the footsteps of the Bussells who, along with other Augusta settlers, had sought easier pastures some 80 kilometres north, where the Vasse River flows into the sea at Geographe Bay, around the area that is today the town of Busselton, and a three-hour drive south of Perth, and where Molloy had been appointed police commissioner. Their large grant of land there was, Georgiana wrote to her friend Margaret Dunlop, in 'most pleasing country and answering with truth to the description given of its park-like appearance with long waving grass'.[38]

The Molloys left Augusta on 5 May 1839 to travel to the Vasse, to the property they had named Fairlawn. 'My feelings on leaving my much beloved retreat are best expressed in those beautiful lines of Milton, when he represents Eve driven from the garden of Paradise,' Georgiana told Mangles. No letter remains to give us an insight into how she felt when she arrived at Fairlawn, but it must have come as something of a disappointment after the house at Augusta, with its backdrop of majestic karri and its front garden looking on to the reflective Blackwood River. The land around the brackish Vasse River is flat, the vegetation scrubby. But

Albany daisy bush,
Actinodium cunninghamii

Georgiana's dream of softening the landscape again became her focus as she imagined the new garden she would create.

Georgiana was able to begin her garden at Fairlawn in 1841, after the soil had first provided for the family. 'Our operations begin next month in the garden,' she wrote to Mangles in January that year.

For Georgiana the garden was the exemplification of an idealised married life, where any situation, even a home in 'this alienated land', as she described the colony to Mangles, could be made right. So much hope was vested in the garden, and even the dreaming and the planning must have been therapeutic:

WE INTEND HAVING A WINTER AND SUMMER GARDEN ... I INTEND, PLEASE GOD, TO CULTIVATE CHINA ASTERS ACCORDING TO THE CHINESE MODE. THE RICH CARPETS THEY PRESENT TO THE EYE WILL BE PLEASANT TO LOOK UPON FROM THE DWELLING ...[39]

Her gardening kept her company during her husband's frequent trips away on duty. She planted anemones, peonies, pinks and admitted to having 'a preponderance of flowers'. The house that was built at Fairlawn was a fine two-storey building. The purple-flowered snapdragon vine (*Maurandya barclayana*) from South America, which had been sent by Mangles as seed

Rice flower (*Pimelea spectabilis*), which is found throughout Western Australia

to Augusta, was festooned along the verandah, which faced the river. There was also another exotic vine, *Cobaea scandens*, with its large lilac flowers, that she had carried from Augusta.

Her great pride was the bookshelves which she had built in the sitting room and which were laden with the many books that Mangles had sent her. There was Marnock's horticultural magazine which, she told him, was extremely useful, along with the long-wished-for *The Language of Flowers* and *The Greenhouse*. There was Major Mitchell's *Australia* for Molloy. 'Words fail me when I attempt to return you my grateful thanks and acknowledgments for its useful, beautiful and handsome contents,' she wrote on 31 January 1840 after a box of books and gifts arrived from Mangles. There was also a lady's rake, a watering can and other garden tools. There were seeds of sweet peas and of the magnolia tree, only recently found in America. 'I only wish you could witness the unbounded pleasure that is evinced on the opening of a box all the way from England,' she wrote. There was also an early, publisher's proof of Jane Loudon's *The Ladies' Companion to the Flower Garden* which was to go to nine editions and provided households in the United Kingdom and the colonies with all the advice necessary for laying out a garden, carpet bedding, ribbon gardening and perennial borders. Georgiana described it as beautiful beyond description.

Three more daughters were born to the Molloys: Georgiana's sixth daughter and seventh child was born in December 1842. She never regained her health and suffered until her death in the April of the following year. She was thirty-seven years old.

Garden making and plant collecting played a pivotal role in the colonial life of Georgiana Molloy as she sought to feminise and domesticate the landscape in which she was placed. In a short and difficult life amid a harsh and alien landscape, the hunt for botanical treasure, along with the planning of her garden, was part of an intellectual and creative process that brought Georgiana much-needed solace during years of depredation and tragedy.

While the earliest stories of Australia are most often of pioneering men or of convict women who made for themselves a better life, Georgiana Molloy's story was to be one of the most poignant. A sense of disappointment pervades her correspondence: despite her participation in the intellectual hunt of botanising, hers was a life unfulfilled. Only one plant has been named after her: *Boronia molloyae*, a small pink-flowered bush indigenous to the land south of Perth through which she searched for specimens for her receptive colleague some 28 000 kilometres away.

Boronia molloyae, from the south of Western Australia, the only plant named for Georgiana Molloy

ENGLISH BLUEBELLS ARE BETTER

The droughts to which we are so continuously subject render
abortive all attempts at maintaining a garden in the English style;
and point out to me, that stonework, and terraces, and large shady
trees, the characteristics of Hindostanee gardens, are more suited
to our climate than English lawns and flowerbeds.

JOHN THOMPSON *Chief Draftsman, Surveyor General's Department, Sydney, 4 May 1839, to his friend J. C. Loudon*[1]

Louisa Anne Meredith 1812–1895

IN HER ACCOUNT OF HER FIRST FEW WEEKS in the colony of New South Wales, in September 1839, Louisa Anne Meredith wrote, 'I confess my thoughts were wandering in search of some gum-tree likeness of the stately aisles of elms and limes that I loved so well at home.'[2] Ten years later, long after she had set up her home and garden in Tasmania, that most English of the colonies, she was still mourning the 'un-English' aspect of the native trees, bemoaning:

FORESTS OF STRAGGLING DINGY GUM-TREES (*EUCALYPTUS*) WERE HERE AND THERE MINGLED WITH AN EQUALLY DINGY GROWTH OF WATTLE AND HONEYSUCKLE-TREES (*ACACIA AND BANKSIA*); THE GROUND BORE VERY LITTLE HERBAGE ... [3]

The story of Louisa Anne Meredith reveals that while some early nineteenth-century settlers saw great value in their surroundings, writing of the abundance that could be wrested from the soil, their praise was most often set against the more luxuriant landscape of home. There was no single, simple, response from settlers to the scenery they found; their sentiments were constantly ambiguous. While Louisa Anne Meredith was critical of the environmental devastation caused by successful settlers seeking to demonstrate their new-found position with extensive English-style gardens, she also constantly compared, unfavourably, the local flora with that she had left behind.

Marlbrook, at the foothills of the Tasmanian midlands, on the Midlands Highway (now known as the Heritage Highway), was built early in the 19th century on a land grant that dates to the first settlement of the colony. If Louisa ever visited the 'Midlands Gentry' (also known as the 'Shepherd Kings', the prosperous families who owned large properties between Kempton and Launceston), she would have passed this convict-built, sandstone house. The wonderful garden we see today has been created by owners Mary and Richard Darcey.

~

Born Louisa Anne Twamley in Birmingham in 1812, Louisa had been rigorously educated by her mother and, by twenty-five years of age, was already a published writer, political journalist and artist. Her friends included the poets William and Mary Howitt, she quoted the poet William Cowper in her publications, and one of her early books of poetry was dedicated, with his permission, to Wordsworth. In her later writings of colonial life, the work of Dickens provided a context for her commentary.

Clematis 'William Kennett', flowering today at Spring Vale. Bred in Surrey in England in 1875, this clematis must have been planted since Louisa's short tenure.

Louisa's father had been a tradesman, often out of work, and money had been short; her mother, who claimed descent from the kings of Wales, had, her family felt, married beneath her. Louisa's had been a life of relative poverty, removed from the privileges of her mother's wealthy and powerful legal family.[4] George Meredith, her mother's brother, had emigrated with his family to Australia in 1821 and had settled on the east coast of Van Diemen's Land, as Tasmania was known until 1856, around what is now the town of Swansea on the western shore of Oyster Bay, adjacent to the Freycinet Peninsula. Through grant and acquisition, he had quickly accumulated large land holdings; his stock was renowned throughout the island, he set up whaling stations on the islands off the Tasmanian coast and built trading vessels. His success was such that he had become known as the 'Squire of Swanport'. In 1833, pitying Louisa's impoverished situation, George offered his niece the position of governess to the children of his second marriage to his former maid, Mary, at his Tasmanian home, Cambria. Louisa had refused the offer, responding indignantly:

WHERE WOULD MY LITERATURE BE IN VAN DIEMEN'S LAND? WRITING SONNETS TO WHALES AND PORPOISES, CANZONETS TO KANGAROOS, MADRIGALS TO 'PRIME MERINOS' AND DIRGES TO BLACK SWANS, ILLUSTRATED BY PORTRAITS OF THE ENGAGING AND LOVELY NATIVES? [WHERE] WOULD BE ALL THE LITERARY PAPERS, PERIODICALS, NEW MUSIC, NEW ENGRAVINGS, ETC. ETC, WITH WHICH I AM NOW ENLIVENED, AMUSED AND EXCITED TO 'GO AND DO LIKEWISE?'[5]

In 1838, after an absence in the Australian colonies of some eighteen years, her 27-year-old cousin Charles, George Meredith's second son, returned to his home town of Birmingham as a handsome and successful pastoralist. Louisa was at the height of her literary success, at the centre of a politically active literary group, and writing for the radical *Birmingham Journal.* Louisa and Charles, one year her senior, married the following year, on 18 April 1839, and ironically Louisa found herself, in June, en route to Sydney on board the *Letitia.* They sailed into Sydney Harbour on 27 September 1839.

By the time the Merediths arrived at Port Jackson, the earliest settlers had staked their claims throughout much of New South Wales. The Macarthurs, for instance, had been in the colony for four decades and their grand house at Camden had been completed in 1835, creating an estate in the English style and cementing their position as the colony's leading family. John Oxley, Surveyor-General under Governor Macquarie, had first set eyes upon the rich Northern Tablelands area of New South Wales in 1818 and the district was first settled in 1832 by Hamilton Collins Sempill, followed by William and Henry Dumaresq in 1834, the Dangar brothers, and then Gilbert Elliot, who took up the Emu Creek pastoral run in 1837.

Further afield, the Leslie brothers had just taken up the first property in Queensland and families such as the Whites, the Duttons, the Angases, the Riddochs and the Falkiners had arrived to seek and make their fortunes. The Faithfulls, who had sailed with the Second Fleet, now owned vast tracts of land on the Southern Tablelands of New South Wales.

In Tasmania the Taylors had arrived in 1821, quickly acquiring land and stock, building grand colonial Georgian residences and laying out landscape parks. Along with George Meredith, Joseph Archer had

commissioned the *Emerald* to bring him to the colony of Van Diemen's Land in 1821, and now owned the estate of Panshanger, overlooking the South Esk River in Northern Tasmania. The house is today described as Tasmania's finest Georgian building.

Settlers—the majority of whom had arrived as convicts, but some of whom, like George Meredith, had chosen to take their chances in a new community—were seeking to re-construct themselves, along with the khaki-coloured landscape, into their own vision of the English Arcadia they had left behind. Landowners in Tasmania and New South Wales yearned for Picturesque scenes of home, reminded of an Arcadia not only by the works of the English Romantics but by the travelling colonial artists who represented the antipodean landscapes as a paradisiacal cornucopia.

When Louisa Anne Meredith arrived at Sydney on that spring day in 1839 she enthusiastically noted the beauty of the settlement around the harbour. Her attitude was perhaps softened by her expectation that she and Charles would remain in the colony for just five years, reaping the profits from their pastoral estates in New South Wales before returning permanently to England. Louisa quickly resumed her writing, making notes on the gardens and houses she found in Sydney, and on the abundance of produce available. In *Notes and Sketches of New South Wales* she acutely observed the behaviour of the settlers, their treatment of the land, their houses, their gardens, their dress and manners, and their aspirations. The book sold well in England and remains one of the most important chronicles of life in the colony.

Upon arriving in New South Wales she had expressed her delight at how the public and private gardens in the colony had been laid out. She noted approvingly the acclimatised plants from other parts of the world

left and centre: Just after their arrival in New South Wales, Louisa and Charles travelled over the Blue Mountains to Bathurst, where Louisa admired the landowners' estates. One may have been Blackdown, established by Elizabeth and Thomas Hawkins. The Hawkins had arrived in Sydney, with their seven children and her mother, on 11 January 1822.

right: Another important estate was Winton, in central Tasmania.

that were now common in Sydney gardens. Rarities confined to greenhouses in England were commonplace in the colonies: there were vineyards, orchards of pomegranate and loquat and groves of oranges with their fragrant blossom.

Louisa delighted in the collections of exotic plantings—trophies, perhaps, of imperial success—held in the Botanic Gardens. Like settlers before her, however, she noted the superiority of the English landscape:

above: Mugga ironbark, *Eucalyptus sideroxylon* 'Rosea'

opposite: Louisa wrote nostalgically of 'stately aisles of elms and limes'. She would have felt at home at Duneira, in Mount Macedon.

A GROUP OF GRACEFUL WEEPING-WILLOWS OVERHANG A PRETTY SHADY POOL, WHERE A STATUE, BY AN ENGLISH SCULPTOR ... IS NOW ERECTED ... THE FIRST SPECIMEN OF HIGH ART THAT THE COLONY HAS OBTAINED.[6]

One indigenous plant, *Doryanthes excelsa,* won Louisa's approval: 'That magnificent indigenous flower the gigantic lily is often and easily cultivated in gardens, and well deserves a place in the stateliest'.[7] She was, however, often somewhat dismissive of most native plants:

THE TREES ARE CHIEFLY DIFFERENT SPECIES OF EUCALYPTUS, OR 'GUM-TREE' ... THE LEAVES ARE MOSTLY OF A DULL GREEN, WITH A DRY SAP-LESS LOOK ABOUT THEM, MORE LIKE OLD SPECIMENS IN A HERBARIUM THAN FRESH LIVING AND GROWING THINGS, AND BEING BUT THINLY SCATTERED ON THE BRANCHES, HAVE A MEAGRE APPEARANCE. THEY ARE, HOWEVER, 'EVERGREENS', AND IN THEIR PECULIARITY OF HABIT, STRONGLY REMIND THE OBSERVER THAT HE IS AT THE ANTIPODES OF ENGLAND, OR VERY NEAR IT, WHERE EVERYTHING SEEMS TOPSY-TURVY ... AT FIRST I DID NOT LIKE THIS AT ALL.[8]

Not surprisingly Louisa's observations were set within the context of the plants she knew and loved at home. In the first days of her stay in New South Wales, she made constant comparisons:

GERANIUMS THRIVE AND GROW VERY RAPIDLY, BUT I DID NOT SEE ANY GOOD ONES; NONE THAT I SHOULD HAVE THOUGHT WORTHY OF CULTIVATING IN ENGLAND. A HORTICULTURAL SOCIETY HAS NOW BEEN ESTABLISHED SOME YEARS, AND WILL DOUBTLESS BE THE MEANS OF MUCH IMPROVEMENT.

She wrote also of the gardens of the villas and cottages built around the harbour, 'their adjoining gardens making a pleasant green contrast with the uniform brown hue of the scrub'.[9]

She wrote admiringly of the houses facing the Domain, at Woolloomooloo, which had been built by the city's successful residents, and reminded her of the elegant Nash Terrace in Regent's Park, in London. 'It is a very large busy town,' she wrote, 'reminding me of portions of Liverpool and Bristol with many good buildings though few have any pretension to architectural beauty.'[10]

After resting in Sydney for two weeks, Louisa and Charles set out to inspect his pastoral runs, west of the 'grand and dreary' Blue Mountains that had been crossed by Blaxland, Lawson and Wentworth in 1813, opening up the fertile plains beyond to a thriving grazing community. Louisa, at the age of twenty-seven now pregnant with her first child, rested with her sister-in-law at Bathurst, some 400 kilometres west of Sydney, while Charles travelled on to inspect his sheep stations along the Murrumbidgee River. Their first child, George Campbell Meredith, was born at Bathurst on 1 July 1840.

The gardens Louisa found in the colony often provided the framework for her opinion of New South Wales. At Bathurst, she described the 'unpleasing' landscape that she found, and longed for 'green, beautiful old England':

In Tasmania, Louisa found fine Georgian houses on vast estates. One, Brickendon, at Longford, was built in 1829 by William Archer and remains in the Archer family today.

EVERY GREEN THING LOOKS AS IF A SALAMANDER HAD BEEN OVER IT, EITHER
DROOPING AND DYING, OR DRIED UP LIKE HALF-BURNED PAPER. I HAVE SEEN
LARGE TRACTS OF CULTIVATED LAND, COVERED WITH LUXURIANT GREEN CROPS
OF WHEAT, BARLEY, OR OATS JUST GOING INTO EAR, SCORCHED, SHRIVELED,
ABSOLUTELY BLACKENED BY THE HEAT AND FIT FOR NOTHING BUT TO CUT
AS BAD LITTER. LESS IMPORTANT,
THOUGH EXTREMELY VEXATIOUS, IS
THE DESTRUCTION CAUSED IN GAR-
DENS, WHERE THE MOST DELICATE
AND BEAUTIFUL FLOWERS ARE EVER
THE FIRST TO WITHER UNDER THE
BURNING BREATH OF THIS FERVID
AIR-KING.[11]

But Louisa was complimentary of the
success of the pastoralists; for her,
their distinction was underlined not
only by the size of their landholdings
but also by the orderliness of their gardens and vineyards:

THE CHIEF INHABITANTS OF BATHURST LIVE AT SOME DISTANCE FROM
IT; MANY OF THE WEALTHY, AND ALSO HIGHER CLASS OF SETTLERS,
HAVING FARMS AND GOOD RESIDENCES WITHIN A FEW MILES, WHICH
RENDERS THE SOCIETY SUPERIOR TO THAT OF COLONIAL SETTLEMENTS
IN GENERAL. NEARLY ALL ARE SITUATED ON THE VERGE OF THE PLAINS,
COMBINING BOTH THE FLAT AND HILLY COUNTRY IN THEIR SUR-
ROUNDING SCENERY, AND THEIR GARDENS AND VINEYARDS ... SEEMED
MORSELS OF A BRIGHTER WORLD, WHEN COMPARED WITH THE ARID
WASTE AROUND THE TOWNSHIP. [12]

The mill at Riversdale still
stands, although in need of
restoration. Louisa Anne and
Charles lived at Riversdale
while waiting for Spring
Vale to be built.

On her return from Bathurst, after only some seven weeks in the colony,
she again linked good garden keeping and superiority when she noted of
Parramatta, 'Some of the cottages and villas on the banks are very prettily
situated, with fine plantations, gardens, and orange-groves around them,
and nice pleasure-boats moored beside mossy stone stops leading to the
river'.[13] She commented on the gardens 'richly tapestried with jasmine,
woodbine, roses, and climbing plants of every description'.[14]

Louisa Anne Meredith is the settler most often cited by environmental historians to exemplify a more recent notion that not all early settlers abhorred the indigenous flora they found.[15] But while she criticised
the destruction of the native vegetation in order to create landscapes in the

English manner, an example of settler pretensions, Louisa often framed her faint praise of the local flora in the assumption that British was better. At Homebush Bay, where the Merediths settled after their trip to Bathurst, renting a house from the surgeon D'Arcy Wentworth, Louisa loved the native climbers, including the native wisteria *Hardenbergia comptoniana* and the *Kennedia*. The shape of the blue flowers of the trumpet vine, *Bignonia australis*, reminded her of foxgloves. 'Various kinds of epacris also abounded, with delicate wax-like pink and white flowers,' she wrote. And she commented on the environmental devastation caused by the early settlers in the area:

THE HOUSE STOOD ON THE HIGHEST GROUND IN THE ESTATE, AND FOR SOME HUNDREDS OF ACRES ALL AROUND NOT A NATIVE TREE NOR EVEN A STUMP WAS VISIBLE, SO COMPLETELY HAD THE LAND BEEN CLEARED, ALTHOUGH NOT WORTH CULTIVATION.'[16]

She vigorously criticised the colonial habit of razing the vegetation in order to reconstruct the landscape into a vision of an Arcadia transplanted from 'home':

THE SYSTEM OF 'CLEARING' HERE BY THE TOTAL DESTRUCTION OF EVERY NATIVE TREE AND SHRUB, GIVES A MOST BARE, RAW, AND UGLY APPEARANCE TO A NEW PLACE. IN ENGLAND WE PLANT GROVES AND WOODS AND THINK OUR COUNTRY RESIDENCES UNFINISHED AND INCOMPLETE WITHOUT THEM; BUT HERE THE EXACT CONTRARY IS THE CASE, AND UNLESS A SETTLER CAN SEE AN EXPANSE OF BARE, NAKED, UNVARIED, SHADELESS, DRY, DUSTY LAND SPREAD ALL AROUND HIM, HE FANCIES HIS DWELLING 'WILD AND UNCIVILIZED'.[17]

But, comparing them to the English, Louisa found some Australian plants too bright:

IN THE SAME BARREN SPOTS, TOO, I FOUND A LIKENESS OF ANOTHER OLD FRIEND, THE SMALL MEADOW CONVOLVULUS, THE NEW ONE BEING FAR BRIGHTER IN HUE THAN THE SLY, MISCHIEVOUS LITTLE SPRITE THAT FRISKS OVER OUR ENGLISH FIELDS ... [18]

While 'The honeysuckle-tree (*Banksia latifolia*) is so unreasonably named,' she reasoned:

THAT I MUST NOT PASS IT BY WITHOUT A REMARK; NOR HAVE I QUITE FORGIVEN IT FOR DISAPPOINTING ME BY BEING SO *VERY* UNLIKE ANY SORT OR SPECIES OF THE SWEET OLD FLOWER WHOSE NAME IT SO UNFITTINGLY BEARS. I CANNOT REMEMBER ANY OLD WORLD TREE TO WHICH I CAN IN ANY WAY COMPARE IT ...

And then, 'the old pear-tree shone out like a beautiful vision of home'.[19]

The Merediths' plan of returning to England after just a few years in the colony was thrown into disarray by the almost immediate collapse of Charles' businesses in New South Wales and, according to Louisa, by 'the loss of all we owned in that colony'. In 1840 they were forced to relocate to Tasmania, to stay with George Meredith, from whom Louisa had so scornfully refused help less than a decade earlier.

Colonial life among those who had reconstructed themselves as the elite in the new society did its best to imitate that of the landed classes in England. The frontier settlements held endless opportunities for self-betterment, the only obstacle to establishing a setting reminiscent of English life being the lack of water. English customs set the standard, and the success with which settlers paralleled the manners of home was noted by visiting English writers and adventurers. Some settlers, Louisa Ann Meredith found—and as ship's surgeon Peter Cunningham had observed a few decades earlier—were desperate to recast themselves into a class to which they would not have had access at home. Louisa's accounts of life in the colony provide ample evidence of the attempts to emulate genteel British life: 'Dinners and balls of course form a part of the arrangements for the races and hunts, and everything is conducted in as English a manner as can be attained by a young country imitating an old one ...'[20]

The pear trees that flourish today at Spring Vale were brought by Louisa from her father-in-law's home, Cambria.

previous pages: Rosa 'Duchesse de Buccleuch', bred in France in 1837. The Duchess was Lady Charlotte Anne Thynne, daughter of the 2nd Marquess of Bath and wife of the 5th Duke of Buccleuch. Old roses were available in Tasmania, imported by the officers of Port Arthur, who were in touch with the botanical institutes in England and Europe.

She complained that colonial women had few interests beyond gossip while their husbands' conversations rarely extended beyond wool and money. They hardly read, she observed, although, the Australian Library contained an excellent selection of books for so young an institution. And, compared with their English contemporaries, Australian women were brash. 'Not a question is heard,' she wrote:

RELATIVE TO ENGLISH LITERATURE OR ART; FAR LESS A REMARK ON ANY POLITICAL EVENT ... BUT ALL ARE DRESSED IN THE LATEST KNOWN FASHION, AND IN THE BEST MATERIAL, THOUGH NOT ALWAYS WITH THAT TASTEFUL ATTENTION TO THE ACCORDANCE OR CONTRAST OF COLOUR WHICH AN ELEGANT ENGLISHWOMAN WOULD OBSERVE.[21]

The Merediths' removal to Tasmania after the reversal in their fortunes in fact brought some relief to Louisa. She and Charles, along with a nursemaid for the baby George, arrived in Hobart on 21 October 1840 and rested for several weeks in the homes of Charles' two sisters and their husbands. After the heat, the dust and the flies of the 'ever-brown land', New South Wales, Tasmania felt comfortingly familiar, 'as being so much more

CLASS IN THE COLONIES

above: The opulent fountain at Seven Creeks Estate, in north-east Victoria, one of the earliest properties in the state. It is now home to Dennis and Margaret Marks.

right: The delicate summer house at Nooroo, in April, is surrounded by the colours of autumn. The garden, at Mt Wilson, in the Blue Mountains west of Sydney, was started in 1880.

Surgeon General Peter Cunningham made detailed observations on the aspirations of the new Australians. These reveal how determined some settlers were to empower themselves by transferring to the colony the class systems of England. Cunningham wrote in 1827:

'One sub-division of the emigrant class alluded to is termed the *exclusionist* party, from their strict exclusion of the emancipists from their society ... Etiquette is, if possible, more studied among our *fashionable* circles than in those of London itself. If a lady makes a call, she must not attempt a repetition of it until it has been returned, on pain of being voted ignorant of due form ... while cards are ceremoniously left, and rules of precedence so punctiliously insisted on by some of our *ultras,* that the peace of the colony was placed in imminent jeopardy only a few years

back by the opening of a ball before the leading lady of the *ton* made her appearance ...'[25]

Louisa Meredith also questioned the manner in which many new settlers rigorously maintained distinctions among the new classes:

'The distinctions in society here remind me of the 'Dock-yard people,' described by Dickens, that keen and kindly satirist of modern follies. Thus—Government officers don't know merchants; merchants with 'stores' don't know other merchants who keep 'shops'; and the shopkeepers have, I doubt not, a little code of their own, prescribing the proper distances to be observed between drapers and haberdashers, butchers and pastrycooks. The general character of the invitations to the entertainments at Government House has caused much discussion and animadversion; the citizens who drive chariots not liking

English than in the larger colony, and I could fancy myself some degrees nearer home'. The climate was kinder; while annual rainfall in Hobart and along Tasmania's east coast was not particularly plentiful, at 600 millimetres, high summer temperatures rarely exceeded 22 °C. There were familiar white-flowering hawthorn hedges, verdant valleys and sheets of water to remind her of the Lake District. 'It seemed,' she wrote, 'like being on the right side of the earth again'.[22] And:

THE LITTLE GARDENS BEFORE AND BETWEEN MANY HOUSES IN THE MIDDLE OF THE TOWN, WITH THEIR GREAT BUSHES OF GERANIUMS IN BLOOM, WERE ALL FULL OF SWEET ENGLISH SPRING FLOWERS, LOOKING HAPPY AND HEALTHY, LIKE THE STOUT ROSY CHILDREN THAT EVERY-WHERE REMINDED ME OF HOME.[23]

'In the Tasmanian gardens,' she continued 'are mulberries, cherries, currants, raspberries, strawberries, gooseberries, apples, pears, quinces, medlars, plums of all kinds and peaches in abundance, growing well and luxuriantly.'[24]

to be mingled in company with their tradespeople who only keep gigs ... English customs and fashions are carefully followed, and frequently outdone by the more wealthy and (if I may be allowed the phrase, in speaking of commoners) *aristocratic* of the colonists.'[26]

'Such inconsistencies perpetually struck me,' she wrote of colonial women and their aspirational behaviour, 'showing the general preference for glitter and show, rather than sterling English comfort'.

Anthony Trollope was among several English writers to comment a few decades later on the good prospect for social mobility in the colonies, but also that some things—like the difficulty of finding good servants—rather spoiled the illusion. In his book *Australia,* he wrote admiringly,

'I imagine that the life of the Victorian landowner is very much as was that of the English country gentleman a century or a century and a half ago ... They shot over their own lands, and hunted over their own land ... The ladies stayed at home and looked after the house, and much that is now trusted to domestics and stewards was done by the mistress and her

daughters, or by the master and his sons. The owners of these country houses were Tories, aristocrats, proud gentlemen— but they were not fine gentlemen, nor, for the most part, were they gentlemen of fine tastes in art or literature.'

'In the far Antipodes,' he continued, 'Loyalty is the condition of the colonist's mind. He is proud of England—he always speaks of England as home ...' However, Trollope found the colonies very comfortable:

'It was impossible not to love the public gardens at Sydney ... You may lie there prostrate on the grass, with the ripple close at your feet within a quarter-an-hour of your club. Your after-dinner cigar will last you there and back if you will walk fairly quickly and smoke slowly.'[27]

No state in Australia preserves the paradigm of transferred vision better than Tasmania. Settlers quickly took up land grants and, with a little help from well-cultivated connections with colonial power, increased their holdings, building—with abundant convict labour until transportation ceased in 1853—fine Georgian houses on vast estates that provided an appropriate base for their newly pre-eminent positions. As soon as they had established their pastoral interests, paddocks enclosed by hedges 'laid down' in the traditional English manner and expansive gardens and parks were set out, emulating those of home. The writer Anthony Trollope noted that if he were to live in the colonies, he would:

PITCH MY STAFF IN TASMANIA ... THE CLIMATE IS FAR PLEASANTER THAN THAT OF ANY PART OF THE MAINLAND. THERE ARE, ONE MAY ALMOST SAY, NO MOSQUITOS ... EVERYTHING IN TASMANIA IS MORE ENGLISH THAN IS ENGLAND HERSELF.

Such transplanted English-ness was particularly evident on the grand estates that were being created in 'the afterglow of the English Georgian period'.[28] The owners of these properties—Panshanger, Valley-field, Woolmers, Brickendon and Winton—created botanical gardens of new introductions as showpieces of their achievements. The broadleaf trees of England, along with conifers from Europe and North America, were imported in various ways, from the newly designed Wardian case to

The picturesque view from George Meredith's home, Cambria. Louisa finally felt more at home here— on the 'right side of the earth'.

the pocket handkerchiefs of settlers.[29] Tasmanian settlers continued to emulate English gardens for longer, with greater determination and with greater success, than their counterparts in New South Wales. Such colonial gardens today remain the important front face of the island's successful pastoral enterprises.

In such an environment Louisa Meredith was filled with renewed hope for the future: 'The Government Gardens,' she wrote, 'charmed me by their verdant and shady aspect. They are—for I must again repeat my oft-used term of praise— *English*-looking gardens … with sweet homely faces and perfumes'.[30]

In Hobart she spent two weeks happily engaged in sightseeing and social activities and in the artistic and intellectual climate that the Governor, Sir John Franklin, and his wife were attempting to foster. She loved the situation of the city, on the Derwent River, with Mount Wellington towering behind, creating a sublime and beautiful tableau.

The Spiky Bridge was built by convicts in 1843 to cross a terrifying ravine in the notoriously difficult road from Hobart, along Tasmania's east coast, to Swansea. It is thought that the jagged rocks, which gave the bridge its name, were designed to prevent cattle (and perhaps carriages) from falling over the sheer sides.

following pages: Joseph Archer, who arrived in Van Diemen's Land with George Meredith, built Panshanger. Today Panshanger is among the finest of colonial Georgian houses in Australia.

When the time came to leave Hobart for George Meredith's estate at Oyster Bay the family were obliged to travel overland, by hazardous roads, due to Louisa's fear of sea travel. But the journey, rather than stimulating any Romantic or Picturesque musings, was terrifying:

MOUNTAIN, HILLS, VALLEYS, RAVINES—ALL ARE WILD AND TRACKLESS AS THEY WERE THOUSANDS OF YEARS AGO, EXCEPT WHERE A RUDE FENCE OF BRUSHWOOD INDICATES THE BOUNDARY-LINE OF DIFFERENT PROPERTIES … I WAS COMPELLED TO CLING TO THE CARRIAGE—I CANNOT SAY I SAT IN IT, BUT CROUCHED ON THE FOOT-RUG, CLASPING BABY IN ONE ARM, WHILST I HELD TIGHTLY ON WITH THE OTHER, NOT DARING TO GLANCE BEFORE ME AT THE ABYSS BELOW …[31]

Six days later, after covering a distance of 160 kilometres—only a two-hour journey today—the family arrived at Cambria, George Meredith's expansive east coast estate, to stay with him, his second wife and five children. The house was sited to command views over its beautiful gardens, over tracts of the bushland, and across to Oyster Bay and Schouten Island with its 'lofty picturesque outline'. French doors fed onto a 'noble veranda' on which pillars were wreathed with roses and jasmine. Geraniums, poppies, stocks, hollyhocks, marigolds and wallflowers flourished in the garden and

hawthorn hedges neatly delineated the paddocks.[32] Louisa noted approvingly the orderliness of the estate. Here were plants with which she was familiar; here was a language she understood:

A LARGE GARDEN AND ORCHARD, WELL STORED WITH THE FLOWERS AND FRUITS CULTIVATED IN ENGLAND, WERE NOT AMONG THE LEAST OF THE CHARMS CAMBRIA POSSESSED IN MY EYES; AND THE GROWTH OF FRUIT TREES IS SO MUCH MORE RAPID AND PRECOCIOUS HERE THAN AT HOME ... THE ORCHARD PRODUCES SO GREAT AN ABUNDANCE, AS TO AFFORD A CONSIDERABLE QUANTITY OF CIDER EVERY YEAR ... JUDGING FROM THE REMARKS ON CIDER-MAKING IN 'LOUDON'S ENCYCLOPAEDIA OF AGRICULTURE', I CONCEIVE THAT OUR TASMANIAN CIDER IS FERMENTED TOO MUCH.[33]

With servants to look after her, and in more recognisable territory, Louisa was able to recover from the journey.

But the Merediths' life in Tasmania was to be anything but settled and ordered. They were forced, either by bad luck or by Charles' mismanagement of his affairs, to move several times. On each occasion, Louisa created a garden around her new home. Their financial affairs were not advanced when Charles, against his father's advice, bought 5000 hectares of unimproved land, Spring Vale, a few kilometres inland and some 4 kilometres north of Cambria, and took out a large mortgage at 10 per cent.[34] While a residence was being built at Spring Vale, George offered the family the use of a house nearby, Riversdale, and Charles and Louisa moved there in May 1841.

Louisa's second son, Charles Henry, was born 1 November 1841 but, due to a bout of diarrhoea that saw the doctor called sixteen times, the baby died in March 1842. After his death Louisa nursed her grief, often alone, for her husband spent long days clearing and fencing the Spring Vale property. She comforted herself with plans for the creation of a house and garden there, the first home that she could call her own, dreaming of establishing a familiar order.

Years later, when the family returned to rent Riversdale, the only immediate solace Louisa could grasp again was the creation of some order in her environment. 'Once again I was busily and pleasantly occupied in making a place look as much like an old home as possible,' she wrote. 'I could not possibly sit down quietly to write whilst I had my new garden entirely to remodel.'[35]

The Merediths moved into Spring Vale in August 1842, and Louisa set about stamping her own mark on the landscape. The garden she created over that summer and the autumn of 1843 was resplendent with familiar plants from home—with geraniums, with crimson and pink China roses that grew over arches and bowers, with fuchsia, pansies—and, she noted 'every new arrival flourishes most satisfactorily in this fine climate'.[36] Borders were edged in thyme rather than the 'bright, clean, neat box-edging used in England', walks were smooth and neat and the lawns were sown with English seed. 'In looking *at* the house,' she wrote:

WE KNEW EXACTLY WHERE THE VERANDA WOULD 'COME IN,' AND WHERE THE CLIMBING ROSES, AND VINES, AND CLEMATIS, WOULD BE TRAINED OVER IT; AND WHEN WE SURVEYED THE VIEW FROM THE WINDOWS, THE

left: The Spring Vale house and garden today

centre: The stables at Spring Vale now house the cellar door sales.

right: The Gallica *Rosa* 'Charles de Mills', bred in France in 1790

COARSE REALITY OF SCRUB AND LOG-FENCE WAS NICELY SOFTENED BY
THE 'MIND'S EYE' VIEW OF THE SLOPING GREEN LAWN, AND NEAT WELL-
LAID OUT GARDEN BEYOND, WHICH FORMED PART OF OUR ARRANGE-
MENTS, AND WHICH WAS ALREADY WELL STOCKED WITH CHOICE
FRUIT-TREES FROM THE CAMBRIA ORCHARD.[37]

But by 1844 Charles' financial problems had brought them close to
bankruptcy, unable to pay their mortgages, and in May that year he
accepted a post as police magistrate at Port Sorell, a bleak village on
Tasmania's north coast. The family—with a new baby, Charles Twamley,
born that April—moved to a damp and depressing cottage that Louisa
dubbed 'our Castle Dismal'.

Even though his post at Port Sorell was tenuous and Louisa could
find no congenial company among her neighbours, Charles purchased
land nearby to build another house, to be named Poyston after his birthplace in Wales. In 1846 Louisa again planted a garden, familiarising the
spaces around her with rose cuttings, trees obtained from neighbours, and
flowerbeds of hollyhocks, carnations and tiger lilies, edged in herbs. A
fourth son, Owen, was born on 6 April 1847. But Charles resigned his post
in 1848 and with his wife and three young sons returned to manage his
father's properties, again renting Riversdale.

While Louisa may have been at pains to deride colonial women and
their desire to appear gracious and well bred, she herself was concerned
with symbols of gentility. The theme of the garden as a symbol of a good
housewife featured throughout Louisa's first colonial publication, *Notes
and Sketches*, and was a recurrent theme in her second book, *My Home in
Tasmania*. She believed that a good garden demonstrated womanly success. She noted with opprobrium the slovenliness of the 'working classes',
admonishing that no attempt had been made to create a garden:

THE HABITATIONS OF THE WORKING CLASSES, FOR *POOR* THERE ARE
NONE, ARE THE LEAST PLEASING OBJECTS ONE MEETS WITH IN THIS
COLONY. INSTEAD OF THE NEAT CLEAN COTTAGE OF AN ENGLISH
LABOURER ... ITS SMALL GARDEN-PLOT OF VEGETABLES, POT-HERBS,
AND SWEET FLOWERS, AND CHEERFUL, THOUGH HUMBLE ASPECT,—
HERE YOU MUST PASS A WRETCHED HUT OR HOVEL ... NOT A HERB, NOT
A CABBAGE IS TO BE SEEN; NO ATTEMPT AT MAKING A GARDEN,
ALTHOUGH A FENCE MIGHT BE HAD FOR THE TROUBLE OF CUTTING IT,
AND, BY VERY LITTLE LABOUR, ABUNDANT CROPS OF VEGETABLES AND
FRUIT PRODUCED.[38]

Rosa 'Charles de Mills' and
wisteria clamber up the old
verandah posts at Spring Vale.

Louisa continued to comment on the colonial desire to emulate the
English landscape. 'We proceeded to Richmond,' she wrote, 'a place named,

I imagine, in true Antipodean fashion, from its utter lack of all likeness to its charming old-country namesake.'[39] And again:

ENGLISH TOWN AND COUNTRY NAMES ABOUND, AND THE PLAIN FARM-HOUSES OF SETTLERS ARE OFTEN CALLED AFTER SOME OF THE MOST MAGNIFICENT PALACE-SEATS OF ENGLISH NOBLES, MAKING THE CONTRAST, WHICH CANNOT FAIL TO OCCUR TO ONE'S MIND, LUDICROUS IN THE EXTREME ... RIDICULOUS COMPARISON.[40]

Good gardens rely on a ready and regular water supply. Away from the coastal belt water was a major concern in most regions throughout the colonies. Then, as today, a lack of water played a vital role in the character and the imagination of the country. Louisa Anne Meredith soon commented on this, writing in *Notes and Sketches*:

THE *WANT OF WATER* IS A DRAWBACK OF WHICH NO DWELLER IN ENGLAND CAN IMAGINE THE CURSE. I WELL REMEMBER MY HUSBAND'S ADMIRATION OF OUR ENGLISH RIVERS, BROOKS AND THE LITTLE NARROW, TRICKLING LINES OF BRIGHT WATER THAT TRAVERSE OUR MEADOWS AND GARDENS; AND WHEN I USED TO LAUGH AT SO MUCH GOOD ENTHUSIASM BEING THROWN AWAY ON A *DITCH*, HE WOULD SAY,

The Riversdale house and garden today

'AH! ONLY WAIT UNTIL YOU HAVE LIVED A FEW YEARS IN A DRY COUNTRY, AND THEN YOU WILL BETTER UNDERSTAND THE INESTIMABLE VALUE OF SUCH *DITCHES*!'[41]

Water became a recurring theme in her writings:

GARDENS IN THIS NEIGHBORHOOD MIGHT BE SMALL EDITIONS OF PARADISE, HAD THEY SUFFICIENT AND REGULAR MOISTURE; BUT THE UNCERTAINTY OF THE SEASONS, AND THE IMPOSSIBILITY (NOT TO MENTION THE EXPENSE) OF SUPPLYING THE DEFICIENCY BY ARTIFICIAL MEANS, RENDER THE MOST INDUSTRIOUS AND ANXIOUS ATTENTION TO THEM A SOURCE OF ANNOYANCE RATHER THAN PLEASURE.[42]

For all Louisa's faults—she was dogmatic, patronising and unsympathetic, and became a figure of fun to her husband's half-sisters—she, like so many settler women, suffered great hardship. While the men may have seen the challenging landscape in the Picturesque terms favoured by Walter Scott in his popular Waverley novels, many women must have found nothing romantic in the wild landscape that threatened the safety of their families. And they endured loneliness and danger that would be unbearable today. Among all her artistic pursuits it was Louisa's gardening that provided her with greatest comfort and companionship.

Louisa no doubt spent many hours by this window, looking onto the garden she was creating at Riversdale.

The golden age for the Merediths arrived after Louisa decided that Charles, at forty-four years of age and with neither property nor savings, should become a politician. He was elected to represent the County of Glamorgan and took his seat in Tasmania's parliament on 17 July 1855; this turned out to be a profession at which he excelled. He served, somewhat ironically, as Colonial Treasurer under three governments and held the portfolio of Minister for Lands and Works, among other senior positions, until his death in 1880.

As well as keeping a cottage near Oyster Bay, the Merediths took a house in Hobart, and Louisa immersed herself in activities at Government House, to which she had entrée through her friendships with successive Governors and their wives. Coincidental with the Merediths' move to Hobart came the development in the colony of an appreciation of nature and landscape. Louisa was at the forefront of the move to engage the settlers in aesthetic interests. She had kept up her painting, executing depictions of the landscapes as well as of the houses and gardens that she created:

SOMETIMES I ADDED TO MY LITTLE COLLECTION OF PORTRAITS OF THE PRETTY NATIVE FLOWERS, OR IMPROVED MY SELF IN SKETCHING GUM-TREES, WHICH I FOUND DEMANDED FAR GREATER CARE IN THEIR DELINEATION ... SOME OF THE *EUCALYPTUS* TREES GROWING ON THE RICH LOWLANDS ARE REALLY VERY BEAUTIFUL, AND WOULD BE DEEMED SO EVEN AMIDST THE MAGNIFICENT PATRIARCHAL OAKS OF AN ENGLISH PARK ...[43]

She attended the theatre, painted both the flora and fauna of Tasmania, and wrote several more books to literary and public acclaim, along with articles for journals and magazines in the colonies and in the United Kingdom. She also immersed herself in work for the conservation of Tasmanian flora. Her book *Tasmanian Friends and Foes—Feathered, Furred, and Finned* (dedicated to the children of a former governor of Tasmania) was published in 1881, and contained skilfully rendered, detailed watercolours of indigenous flora and fauna.[44] Like many settlers, as Louisa matured and her eye became more sensitive to the muted colours of Australian flora, she appreciated its subtle beauty even more.

There is no evidence, however, that she considered the space within her garden fence to be the appropriate place for its cultivation. England remained the reference point, even for artists such as John Glover, the English watercolourist who had arrived in Tasmania in 1831 in search of 'the Arcadian rural felicity created in painting by Claude Lorrain in Rome', and who later became well known as a result of his depictions of the Australian landscape.[45] While Glover set out to accurately portray

A red-flowering gum, in the garden at Spring Vale today

Australian colours and shapes, the arrangement of his subjects and the shape of his trees was derivative of a romanticised Europe, reflecting the Romantic sensibilities that grew up around the Lake District that he loved so well. Glover's paintings represented the humanising of an aggressive landscape by placing exotic botanical trophies in burgeoning borders of English perennials.

The Merediths shared the fate of many settlers in Australia: even after several decades in Tasmania Louisa framed any praise of her new home with reminiscences of England. While she continued to paint and write about Australian flora and fauna, she always compared the plants she admired with those she loved 'at home'.[46] She became an influential member of Hobart society, continued her writing and water-colour painting and worked for the conservation of indigenous fauna. She died at the age of eighty-three, while staying with friends in Melbourne, on 21 October 1895.

The story of Louisa Anne Meredith demonstrates how rigorously and how successfully some colonists, particularly in Van Diemen's Land, emulated British habits, design and taste. Her story shows that while the rise in colonial taste provided for an understanding of local flora, most appreciation of indigenous plants was set against the assumption that the British counterpart was superior.

BOOK TWO

Prologue

Jimbour, the Darling Downs' home of the Russells,
one of Queensland's early pastoral families

The first decades of the twentieth century brought great opportunities for women in Australia. Change had begun in the previous century, however. In 1881 the University of Sydney had accepted women as students; Louisa Lawson launched her feminist magazine, *The Dawn*, in 1888. One of the world's first Married Women's Property Acts, and female suffrage, had passed through the South Australian Parliament at the end of the nineteenth century. As the new century dawned, in 1900—the year that the influential English garden writer, designer and artist Gertrude Jekyll published her book *Home and Garden*—Vida Goldstein launched in Australia a suffragist journal with the ironic name of *The Australian Woman's Sphere*, committed to attacking and resolving inequities for women.

The federated nation was just a year old, and the world's youngest, when, in 1902, Australia became the first country in the world to allow women to vote for, and to stand for election to, the national parliament. In 1922 Edith Cowan became the first woman elected to a state Australian Parliament, Western Australia, where she successfully introduced the *Women's Legal Status Act*.

But the first half of the twentieth century will be remembered most for the two devastating world wars that shaped the mood of the new nation and set the stage for ongoing questions of identity. The Great War of 1914–18 changed forever Australia's aspirations and demographics, but also changed the opportunities available to Australian women—as well as their expectations of themselves.

World War II also saw women encouraged to work outside the home. Magazines like *The Australian Women's Weekly*, launched in 1933 to a first-issue circulation of 120 000, while extolling the domestic skills expected of women also supported the mobilisation of the

Sunrise lights the
bougainvillea at Jimbour.

The detailed parterre and fountain
in the front garden at Jimbour

Women's Land Army. However, equality for women only went so far: women were expected to
return home once the wars were over and men returned to seek employment.

Men were free to move in an outside world where aggression and combativeness were considered acceptable, but no 'lady' earned a living. 'Hearth and home' continued to be promoted
as the rightful place for successful examples of womanhood. In an article titled 'Marriage Wins
over Her Career', *The Sydney Morning Herald* reported, as late as 1945:

> Miss Frances Hackney announced her engagement to Mr Walter Frohlich a few hours
> before she received her Doctorate of Science for her thesis 'Studies in the Metabolism of
> Apples', at Sydney University yesterday. Miss Hackney said that she had no plans apart
> from her marriage, which will now have precedence over her career. 'I don't think I will
> continue with my career. My fiancé, who is an engineer, is not a bit impressed by me.
> He'd rather have me as a wife than as a doctor of science.'[1]

And while gardens perceived at their most light-hearted—in their role to provide pleasure—
may appear to be the least gendered of spaces, they can also represent places of conflict, where
questions of power and of disempowerment are addressed within the seemingly innocent
boundaries of high hedges, voluptuous perennial borders and scented rose gardens. Prestigious
scientific bodies, such as the Horticultural, Linnaean and Acclimatisation societies, were still
dominated by men, but the garden represented a sphere that separated women from more
empowering, male, pursuits. The garden—at least in Victorian and Edwardian Australia—was
often a private space to which women could be safely relegated, to indulge in garden making:

The Federation flirtation with 'Australiana' decoration
and plantings was brief. Here, the bird's nest banksia,
B. baxteri (*left*); willow hakea, *H. salicifolia* (*centre*)
and heath banksia, *B. ericifolia* (*right*)

a site in which female roles and activities took place. Gardening at an amateur level was an
acceptable, exemplary, 'ladylike' pursuit.

And while the celebrations in 1888 for the Centenary of Phillip's landing and then Federation
in 1901 had translated, briefly, into a fashion for 'Australiana' decoration and a surge of national
pride, Australia's loyalty to the mother country remained strong and mostly unquestioning. In
the same way that the earliest English tenant farmers who had settled in the new colony
embraced a mantle of respectability which they constructed into a colonial aristocracy, so post-
colonial Australia looked to Britain for approval. The United Kingdom still provided the blue-
print for appropriate behaviour, manners, dress—and good garden design.

Australia's wealth was built upon the sheep's back. Riding there also were the pastoral dynasties that had pioneered the country during the nineteenth century—the Collins and the
Russells in Queensland; the Gordons, Falkiners and Faithfulls in New South Wales; the Duttons
in South Australia; the Chirnsides, Hentys and Manifolds in Victoria and the Taylors and
Archers in Tasmania. The wealth of these families had been laid down in the 1840s and consol-
idated in the 1880s, the height of the squatter era, where properties could run to tens of thousands of square kilometres in size.

An acclaimed garden—along with such British indulgences as hunting on horseback,
playing polo, tennis and croquet, travelling the world and being presented at Court—exemplified position, privilege and social and economic success. And for many pastoralists' wives, the
garden was one of the limited sources of creative pleasure available to them. Often living on
vast properties, isolated from family and the cultural events they had enjoyed as young women
growing up in the city, these women had few peers with whom they shared a background or

history living close by, or to whom they could confide hopes and dreams or turn to in times of loneliness or loss.

Their duty was clearly defined: as wives, mothers and hostesses. They automatically received *Tatler, Queen* and *Country Life* magazines direct from England by subscription and continued to replicate England in their endeavours to be conventional, respectable wives. *Country Life*, launched in England in 1897, was an essential addition to the décor of the Australian drawing room, providing advice on the lifestyle and behaviour of wealthy Edwardian families. Descriptions and photographs of the latest fashion and correct form in dress, the furnishing of the reception rooms and the appropriate layout of the grounds and gardens, made this icon of English middle and upper-class life required reading for 'genteel' Australian women.

THE GARDEN POLITICAL

We dream our dreams

What should we be without our fabulous flowers?

The gardener dreams his special own alloy

Of possible and the impossible

VITA SACKVILLE-WEST *1946*

Una Falkiner 1881–1948

ON 22 SEPTEMBER 1921 Una Falkiner wrote in her diary, 'gardened and set seedlings, and sketched and took my sweet wee Diana round to see the flowers. She does love them so'.

Gardening was central to Una Falkiner's life. Diary keeping was another constant. Hardly a day passed during her 38-year marriage to the pastoralist and sheep breeder Otway Falkiner that she did not record her thoughts on the garden in her diary. Una's diaries, which she kept from before her marriage, draw a thread through the decades of her married life until her death in 1948. They allow us to construct a picture of Una as a woman, as a wife and as a member of the ruling pastoral elite. She writes not of business or politics, nor records any comments her husband may have made to her about the running of the properties, but of her gardens, her children and society matters.

Like many women Una Falkiner used her talent for garden design and planting to convey clear messages of position and rank. Gardens are zones where issues of class, gender and economic power are canvassed. But even for women of privilege, the garden could represent bounded space, where they were safely detained in acceptable, 'ladylike' pursuits, unlikely to challenge established gender roles in a patriarchal society.

~

Una Le Souef (pronounced *swef)* was twenty in 1901, the year of the Federation of the colonies, the year that Queen Victoria died, the year that the Australian population reached 3.7 million and the first year for which her diary survives. The daughter of Albert A. C. Le Souef, the founding director of the Melbourne Zoological Gardens, Una was born into the social and botanical elite of Melbourne's golden age and lived within the 30 hectares of Royal Park. The gardens, under the patronage of the Governor, provided a popular outing for Melburnians, and were laid out with ferneries, rose gardens, flower beds and well-kept walks. The family frequently holidayed at the 272 hectare property at Gembrook—in the Dandenong Ranges east of the city—that Albert Le Souef, as Director of the Victorian Zoological and Acclimatisation Society, had bought to house the partridges and pheasants that he was hoping to introduce into the Australian way of life.

The Le Souefs were descended from exiled French Huguenots who had lived in Britain since 1645. Albert Alexander Cochrane Le Souef was born in Kent in 1828 and arrived in Melbourne in 1840, at the age of twelve, with his parents.[1] He married Caroline Cotton in 1853 and together they had nine children, of whom Una was the youngest. Albert was appointed Secretary of the Zoological Gardens in 1870 and Director in 1882.

Una lived a life typical of a young woman from a privileged background. From a young age she loved flowers and gardens and displayed an early knowledge of horticulture. She painted and sketched landscape scenes and wrote of the beauty of nature, as was expected of gently raised young women of the day. Her diary speaks of visits to Daffodil Shows, and describes one garden she visited as 'a bower of flowers'. Her 1901 diary, illustrated with amusing sketches and caricatures, tells of singing lessons and visits to the art gallery, of picnics in the Botanic Gardens and boating expeditions with her mother as chaperone. She describes farewelling friends leaving for Europe on the *Arcadia,* of playing tennis on the lawn with a young man called Teddy and boys 'calling loudly for tea', and of balls and dances.[2] On 19 September 1901 she wrote that she 'Went to the Gallery, per usual, and on to singing … We painted pear blossom; it was beautiful'.[3] A few days later she wrote that 'All the *Spirea* (may) bushes were in full swing and all the foliage vivid green'. She referred to her visits to various properties named after estates in England: antipodean success stories still sought to be associated with the symbols of success and wealth at 'home', as Louisa Anne Meredith had noted so disapprovingly some sixty years earlier.

Una, aged twenty-eight, married Otway Falkiner (1874–1961) on 15 November 1910 in St John's Church, in Melbourne's affluent suburb of Toorak. She immediately returned with him to live at Boonoke, one of several properties held by the family in the Riverina district of New South Wales—by 1930, described as 'by far the largest merino stud in Australia, and therefore the world'. The Riverina district, today about a ten-hour drive south-west of Sydney, was renowned by the 1870s for its rich pastoral industry. Producing some of the best wool in the colonies, the area was, however, among the last to be settled in the state, being considered barren and inhospitable, comprising vast, treeless plains supporting just a smattering of tough

A camellia from an old garden, *Camellia japonica*

ACCLIMATISATION SOCIETIES

Acclimatisation Societies were established in the colonies in the mid nineteenth century—around the same time as the Royal Horticultural Societies were being formed in New South Wales, Tasmania, Victoria and South Australia—to introduce species from home into the Antipodes, at the same time anglicising, it was hoped, the indigenous fauna.

The Victorian Zoological and Acclimatisation Society was formed in 1860; in 1871 Albert Le Souef became its Honorary Secretary—there were no women listed among the members. Its mission was to 'enrich the colony by stocking its broad territory with the choices and products of the animal kingdom, borrowed from every temperate region on the face of the globe …' Deer, along with ostrich, were introduced to the Society's gardens at Royal Park, and rabbits, carefully nurtured in gentlemen's houses since five survived the First Fleet, were thriving and would soon become a pest across the country.

saltbush. The area receives about 400 millimetres of rain in a good year, and is often in drought. But the mighty watercourses of the Darling, Murrumbidgee and Lachlan rivers that cross the Riverina were waiting to be discovered, and by the 1840s the best land along the river banks had been seized by squatters.

Una lived as an Edwardian aristocrat; due to the rural location, the size of her garden and the number of her staff, she was aloof from the demographic changes occurring in Australian cities. With the exception of an occasional attempt to break free of the constraints placed upon her by her position, she played the role of the dutiful wife of a successful pastoralist without protest. Una and Otway had three children: Lawre was born in 1911, John Alexander in 1918 and Diana in 1920.

Una's diaries indicate that the garden was her reference point; its needs shaped each day and its seasons framed her life. If her marriage provided the grounding for her social position, the garden was both the repository and the result of her creative soul. She would come to rely on the solace that could be gained through garden making.[4]

The Boonoke pastoral estate was a self-supporting village, as stations had to be in those days. Meat was butchered on site, hams and bacons were cured, butter was churned and cheese made, cases of fruit were dried and stored; there was even a mould for making candles. The inside house

Nindooinbah House, west of Brisbane, was home to the Collinses, among the first families to settle in Queensland. They lived in a similar fashion to the Falkiners of Boonoke.

staff consisted of a housekeeper, a Chinese–Australian male cook, a laundress and four housemaids. The household ran as smoothly as a good hotel. And Una's gardens—seemingly innocent spaces between the homestead and the paddocks beyond the barbed-wire fence—first at Boonoke and then at Widgiewa, where she and Otway lived from about 1915, set the scene, helping to ensure the property was the showpiece of the district.

The beauty of the garden both exemplified and confirmed the success and prosperity of the property—it was reported in a daily paper that by 1954 almost 50 per cent of the 130 million-odd sheep in Australia were of Boonoke lineage. Buyers came from throughout the world to stay at the Falkiner properties, particularly Widgiewa and Boonoke, to buy the prize stud merino rams. They stayed where the setting was most pleasant, where they felt most welcome and were made most comfortable.

Vice-regal patronage served to determine further the pre-eminent place the Falkiners held in post-colonial society: Una noted in her diary the various invitations she and Otway enjoyed. When the Governor General visited in 1930 Una recorded in its pages on 29 August:

ALL THE HOUSE AND GROUNDS IN APPLE PIE ORDER & THE GOVERNOR GENERAL LORD STONEHAVEN ARRIVED BY OTWAY WHO WENT TO MEET THE TRAIN. THE DAY WAS PRETTY & SUNNY & HIS EX. ENJOYED THE TRIP ACROSS THE FLOWER STREWN PLAINS.[5]

Edwardian gardens flirted with the exotic and were influenced by the Orient. This tea house at Nindooinbah House was designed by the artist the late Patrick Hockey.

Regal representatives of Great Britain must have felt very much at home in the surroundings Una had created at her homes in the Riverina, with their deference—in the décor of the houses, and the layout, planting and meticulous maintenance of the gardens—to English taste and imperial superiority. Governors stayed with the Falkiners at Boonoke and Una felt at liberty to write to the Prime Minister in 1948 offering accommodation at Widgiewa during an upcoming Royal Visit.[6]

The garden, and the joy gained from its creation, is a theme running through the lives of each of the women discussed in this book, and the garden provided the context for Una's life. Her garden at Widgiewa, about a hectare in size and set on the banks of the Colombo Creek, a tributary of the Murrumbidgee River, was laid out with English-style perennial borders burgeoning with Michaelmas daisies, zinnias, chrysanthemums, stocks, lilies and iris, which when picked for vases would be arranged in a room devoted to that purpose in the homestead. There were roses, including the latest releases from Europe, such as 'La France' and 'Elise Polso', flourishing in the hot and dry climate of the Riverina, where summer days reached 40 °C and the annual rainfall was not much more than 400 millimetres. Swathes of English bulbs 'pushed their brilliant green spikes up through

EARLY TWENTIETH-CENTURY GARDENS

above: At Nindooinbah House subtropical plants were redolent of the privileges of the Raj.

centre: The Alister Clark rose 'Golden Vision'

right: The Alister Clark Memorial Garden at Bulla, near Melbourne, honours the work of this Australian rose breeder. Alistair Clark's home, Glenara, was close by.

Gardens created in the colonies during the reign of Queen Victoria (1837–1901) displayed all the plants popular in Britain. In towns and cities, the front gardens of the less wealthy continued to feature circular and oval beds surrounded by upturned rock or glazed tiles; often a circular bed was centred on the front door. Gravel still filled the spaces between the beds, and paths were of gravel. Gardens of the wealthier settlers now featured edgings of box, introduced to the colony in about 1828, and even carriage circles. A typical front garden for a large Victorian terrace house might have a parterre of box hedges encasing standard roses. In both Victorian and, later, Edwardian gardens, particularly large country gardens, rockeries were popular.[7]

Edwardian gardens flirted with the exotic, fuelled by the imagery of

colonial outposts such as India. Grand country gardens, like Nindooinbah at Beaudesert, west of Brisbane, maintained features with many aspects of orientalism, the height of fashion. Subtropical plants such as frangipani, bamboos and palms from Asia and the Indian sub-continent proved popular, not because they bore a resemblance to the indigenous plants of northern Australia, but because they spoke of the exotic Far East, which

the warm damp earth'. There were groundcovers of violets. Vast, mani-cured lawns—some 30 metres by 15 metres—rolled out from the entrance gate to the brick, U-shaped homestead. On either side of the entrance was a massive Moreton Bay fig tree, probably the largest in Australia. To one side was a mature monkey puzzle tree (*Araucaria araucana*), native to Chile and prized by plant hunters. White-painted seats surrounded jacaranda trees.

Una loved flowering fruit trees and family pictures were most often taken beneath them. The gardens that spread out from the two long wings of the house were heady with the scent of the orange blossom that drenched the air, and with the fragrance of magnolia and other exotic trees from China and America imported by well-known nursery firms in Melbourne. Una's diary, which provides the canvas upon which the minu-tiae of her daily life as the wife of a pastoralist is drawn, is itself set against, and framed within, the life of the garden. On 20 June 1920 she wrote, 'sit-ting on the verandah in the sun with Diana—and being brought roses by John; loving life'.

The early years of Una Falkiner's married life coincided with a ten-sion between loyalty to England and to the newly federated Australia. This

following pages: The bull-bay magnolia, *M. grandiflora*

was redolent with messages of col-onial privilege and power. Decorative woodwork featured on verandahs, in fences and gates; woven wire gates were used in simpler gardens from 1900 to about 1940.

The turn of the nineteenth century to the twentieth century saw a brief republican flirtation with indigenous plants. Flannel flowers, waratah, wattle and Christmas bells all adorned pressed metal ceilings, porcelain,

furniture, silver and even wash bowls and chamber pots. The popularity of native plants in gardening was short-lived, however, as they proved difficult to cultivate, needing the precise repli-cation of their habitats' climate and soil to thrive.

During the first decade of the twentieth century the Arts and Crafts Movement, promoting the integrity of materials, converged with an emerging Queen Anne revival and Old English style; this combination of craftsman-ship and architectural styles of the past was reflected in decorative and complex gardens. Gertrude Jekyll's fascination with plant combinations and the intricate weaving of colour, texture and shape—itself influenced by the Impressionist painters of the era—suited this style of architecture and became popular in Australia.[8]

Roses bred by the Aust-ralian breeder Alister Clark (1864–1949) at his home, Glenara at Bulla, near Melbourne, were popular, particularly the climbing rose 'Black Boy', the apricot-pink 'Lorraine Lee' and 'Sunny South', bred in 1918. Climbers often seen in gardens between the world wars included the coral vine (*Antigonon leptopus*), bougainvillea, Virginia creeper and wisteria. Lawns of couch and buffalo were popular in warm climates and, in cool climates, 'English' grasses—bent, rye, chewings fescue and Kentucky blue—were desirable.[9] While these changing and evolving fashions were most noticeable in the cities, their best elements were replicated in rural gardens.

THE DUTTON FAMILY

The Falkiners were not the only family
who, having won their land early, lived
royally and accepted without question the
trappings of British imperialism. In South
Australia's Clare Valley another great
pastoral family, the Duttons, was living
in much the same fashion.

Anlaby, the Dutton property, had been
established in 1839 and perhaps reached
its height under Henry Dutton in 1890,
when thirty men sheared 60 000 sheep
annually. The house was extended to
the grand Victorian homestead that it
remains today, and an Italianate façade,
descending by a flight of stone steps to
a generous grass terrace, was added.
The gardens were likewise extended, to
18 hectares, and became world-renowned.

In an antipodean parody of the
Grand Tour of eighteenth-century English
noblemen—who would bring 'toy' painters from Italy to re-create images of a
Claudian Arcadia—gardeners were often
brought to Australia from England to work
on the large gardens around homesteads.
Fourteen gardeners, some from England,
were employed to maintain the terraces,
lawns, flower gardens and parkland at
Anlaby. Conservatories were built for
camellias, orchids and vegetables; there
were lily ponds and more than 6000 roses
in several rose gardens.

ran parallel with a tension between the demands for
equality for women and the lingering notion that a
woman's only power was transmitted via a husband. In
the country an upper-class woman's rightful place was
supporting her husband's pastoral endeavours by maintaining the family's superior position in society. Una
found herself caught between both the privileges and
the impositions of Empire and a yearning to explore a
wider frontier.[10] Families like the Falkiners, privileged
and still prospering courtesy of the wool boom,
remained entrenched in the trappings of Empire and,
along with them, Australians at large still looked to
Britain to dictate acceptable standards.

Upper-class Australian women were presented at
Court, the ultimate symbol of the aristocracy. Una was
presented in April 1929 during a tour to Europe and
Britain: '… most excited to see our beloved England,' she
wrote in her shipboard diary in March. Her daughter
Lawre, who was educated at the elite Clyde girls' school
and 'finished' in Paris, was also presented, at the com-
mencement of her European tour. British was still
best—and that included British gardens.

Early settlers encountered a landscape that
challenged their resolution to plant an English footprint upon the space into which they entered, and
waves of immigration pre- and post-World War II
brought garden influences from non-English parts of
the world, but many gardeners continued to replicate
England 150 years after the first colonist stepped ashore
at Sydney Cove. In Una's garden Jo, the English gardener, had, she wrote, 'planted the bed in the proved
English style, all in rows and spaces'.

Una Falkiner, like many women, rarely challenged accepted male superiority. Otway's successes at
merino breeding are well documented, but Una's life
remains largely confined to her diaries, only available to
those who seek them out in the Mitchell Wing of the
State Library of New South Wales.

And like many women of her time, Una's position was also delineated by that of her husband. To

flaunt his wishes would be to stand alone, without the protection afforded to her as his wife. Suzanne Falkiner, Una's great-niece and the author of several books on the Falkiner family, notes the place the Falkiner women held within the family:

THE GIRLS WERE COMELY, BUT THEY WERE ALSO THE PRODUCT OF A FAMILY ATTITUDE WHICH WAS TO CONTINUE THROUGH TO THE NEXT GENERATION. IN BETWEEN THEIR SCHOOLING, THEY RODE HORSES, WORKED SHEEP WITH THE MEN, AND HUNTED KANGAROOS, TAKING EQUAL PLACE WITH THE BOYS. BUT THEY WERE ALLOWED NO SHARE IN THE MANAGEMENT OF THE BUSINESS, A POLICY BASED PARTLY ON FRANC'S [OTWAY'S FATHER] BELIEF THAT WOMEN WERE NOT GENERALLY BUSINESS-MINDED, AND PROBABLY TO DISCOURAGE SUITORS WHO WERE INTERESTED IN THEIR PROPERTY ALONE.[11]

Hanging in the bar of the pub at Conargo, just north of Deniliquin in the Riverina district, is a photograph captioned 'The Falkiner Family 1939' which shows thirteen men of three generations, but no women.[12] So, Una's sphere was clearly defined by her gender, her place bound by being Otway's wife. His wishes took precedence over hers, and she was as financially powerless as any other woman in Australia.

The mobility and liberty of such men was exemplified by Otway Falkiner, who was often absent from home, moving freely between his estates, spending a great deal of time indulging his racing interests in Sydney and Melbourne in the company of a diverse range of acquaintances and friends.[13] Una's movements, on the other hand—while she did seem to travel between the Falkiner properties, to race meetings and social events in Melbourne and, less frequently, Sydney—were restricted, notably by her husband. 'Affairs were arranged for me, I was only the vessel they passed <u>through</u>!!', she wrote in her diary. On 13 July 1922 Otway prevented her from taking part in a riding expedition:

In 1905 Henry Dutton's son, Henry Hampden Dutton, married Emily Martin; the iron fountain set in the main grass terrace was made in her family's foundry. She was a passionate gardener, a noted concert pianist, violinist and an artist. Many cold-climate trees planted by Emily remain at Anlaby, including bur oaks and five enormous Chinese elms. Throughout the gardens, collections of her roses remain: in the wild garden is the single-flowered white Banksia rose, as well as *Rosa* 'Trigintipetala', the ancient Damask used for the production of 'attar of roses'. In the lower rosary is a hedge of the spinosissima rose, with its single flowers and black hips. There are massive examples also of the Cherokee rose and *R.* 'Mermaid', both planted by Emily.[14]

Emily's children were born at about the same time as Una's; her son, Geoffrey Dutton, summed up his family's position in his autobiography, *Out in the Open*:

People like my grandfather, rich from Australia's wool, modelled themselves on landholders in the Mother Country, which of course was always called home. They surrounded their large houses with conservatories and shade-houses.[15]

The music studio at Anlaby, where the writer the late Geoffrey Dutton worked.

I WAS ALL READY TO GO OUT RIDING WITH MADGE AND LAWRE & HAD
THE HORSES UP, BUT OTWAY WOULD NOT LET ME GO. THOUGHT IT TOO
ROUGH FOR ME. I WAS SO DISAPPOINTED AS I AM LONGING TO GO
POKING ABOUT THE CREEKS & PRETTY PLACES.

The garden provided Una with a buffer, whether or not she welcomed—or needed—it, between the outside world and the intimate space
of the household. In addition, the creation of a genteel environment, most
emphasised by her admired house and garden, was a construct into which
she could retreat; a survival technique perhaps. There Una, like many
women, was able to imagine that all was in order in her world. The garden
was the personification of a successful
life and provided her with a safe haven;
its beauty and peace were restorative,
and she could please herself with how
she spent her time. On 11 April 1930 she
wrote that she, 'went into the lovely
soul soothing garden and seated in a
comfortable cane chair … I painted the
blue border of Mich daisies!'

Una positioned herself, publicly
at least, alongside her husband, attach-
ing herself to the rule of financial and
social superiority. Her response to the
labour unrest of 1921 and her proud
description of Otway's role in breaking
the 1922 shearers' strike is clearly
aligned to her class. The year, she noted, in a rare comment on matters
other than gardening or society—although she raised the concerns primarily because her holiday plans had been thrown into disarray—'has not
begun very happily, with its labour troubles & strikes. No one can go holi-
daying in our coastal steamers, as they are not running!'[16] Fifteen months
later she complained:

A HORRID DAY, EVERYONE IS FEELING UNCOMFORTABLE WITH THE
ATTITUDE THE MEN ARE TAKING UP ABOUT SHEARING & PRACTICALLY
ALL THE STAFF IS LEAVING, THRO' HAVING YOUNG MEN ON THE PLACE
& STANDING BY THEM, & THE GIRLS WERE HORRID TO THE NICE LAD
I BROUGHT UP FROM THE SHED, HE IS FROM THE NAVY & MOST HANDY
& OBLIGING.

above: John and Rosamund
Wallinger's restored garden at
The Manor House in the Hampshire
village of Upton Grey. Gertrude
Jekyll's intricate weaving of colour
and texture influenced many
Australian gardens.

opposite: The quintessential South
Australian landscape: river red gums
(*Eucalyptus camaldulensis*) shade
the paddocks.

Wisteria, one of Una's favourite plants. Here, *Wisteria floribunda* 'Macrobotrys', photographed at Kew Gardens, London

and:

… HERE THEY ARE FEEDING 5,400 UNEMPLOYED IN MELBOURNE AND WE CANNOT GET A COOK & LAST MONTH THE SAME WITH A LAUNDRESS. THEY WILL NOT COME INTO THE COUNTRY, LET'S HOPE THE IMMIGRANTS WILL POUR INTO AUSTRALIA.[17]

A drought and the Depression of 1929 combined to have a disastrous effect on the wool industry—Boonoke stud sales slumped in 1930 and further in 1931, to just half the turnover of 1928. In June 1930 Una wrote, 'we went second class as times are so bad'.[18] The disempowered position she held within her marriage was exemplified later, when a shortage of funds for staff meant that economies were introduced to the garden. Una confided to her diary how bitterly she understood her position of powerlessness in the subordination of her needs to male interests, writing after the laying off of one of the gardeners at Widgiewa:

OTWAY SEEMS TO THINK THAT LITTLE WAGE NEED NOT BE, BECAUSE IT IS A DROUGHT. I BET THEY DO NOT ECONOMISE ON GARDENERS AT … BOONOKE OR ZARA … THERE ARE 200 BAGS WAITING TO BE TIED ON THE GRAPES AS THE STARLINGS ARE ON THEM LIKE ANTS.[19]

The garden determined Una's day, as much as her position in society: 29 September 1922 was

A BEAUTIFUL DAY. A FULL DAY WAS WAITING FOR ME. GETTING OUT LINEN, STORE DAY, COOKING, CHICKENS COMING OUT. EM. LEFT FOR JERILDERIE TENNIS. LAWRE, JOHN AND I GARDENED. I NEVER HAVE SEEN THE GARDEN SO FULL OF SWEET SMELLING IRIS AS IT IS & STOCKS & POPPIES. THE WISTERIA THAT I TOOK MY SWEET DIANA'S PHOTOGRAPH UNDER LAST YEAR, THIS YEAR IS BLASTED, ALL ITS FLOWERS HAVE DROPPED OFF IN THE BUD.

Una made some attempts to step outside the boundary of what was acceptable for women of her position, however. In 1929 she sailed for Paris and London to sightsee, to visit gardens and to be presented at Court, as was customary for wealthy women of her class. But she was also in London looking for a distributor for a film she had produced on life on an Australian outback station. An Australian newspaper clipping reported:

MRS FALKINER IS NOW IN LONDON, AND IS ARRANGING WITH THE ALL-BRITISH FILM COMPANY FOR THE GENERAL RELEASE OF HER FILM 'THE LIFE OF A JACKEROO' IN WHICH ALL THE SCENES WERE 'SHOT' AT WIDGIEWA.[20]

Una also contributed to the liberation of women from the domestic grind that delineated their day if they were not in a position to hire staff: she invented a trolley to cart the laundry to the clothes line. To her bitter regret Otway would not let her market her invention, and she saw it manufactured by and sold under the name of a large company.[21] It appears that creative activities, such as small-time film making and writing children's books, along with her professed interest in conservation and preservation of plantings along railway lines, were acceptable for women of Una's class as they were not likely to upset the status quo. Money-making enterprises would not be condoned, being considered beneath the family and demeaning of a husband. They would also have given women a measure of independence that would have undermined male rule.

Una constantly referred to her husband in her diary, sometimes wryly, realising her place was bound up in his position, that her position was dependent upon him. The daily menus of the household were dictated by her husband's tastes, and it was only when he was away that she could rebel and follow a less formal timetable. On 25 July 1920, she told her diary, '… so we had a lovely manless time—did what we liked and eat what we liked, no old joints! But minces, and stews and savouries and coffee to our tea'.

The next day he—'my darling Otway'—had returned, and she wrote:

HE'S HOME. SO ONCE MORE WE REPAIR TO DECENT LEGS OF MUTTON AND SOUPS AND GENTEEL LADYLIKE CONVERSATION ATTIRED MODESTLY AS BECOMES OUR STATIONS.[22]

Ten years later, she wrote, on 14 March 1930, 'Oh what a heavenly day! As Otway is away still in Sydney I am taking it up in bed! As I am tired to distraction! or was!'[23] And a decade later:

A GLORIOUS AWAKENING IN MY DELICIOUS DOUBLE BED WITH LAVENDER SCENTED SHEETING AND OUTSIDE AS LONG SHADOW STOLE ACROSS THE JADE LAWN, BIRDS MELODY MADE THE AIR RING. SOON STARS OF COLOUR SHOWED WHERE FRESHLY OPENED ROSES HUNG ...[24]

The lilac *Syringa vulgaris* 'Mme Lemoine'

So, a beautiful garden was the epitome of respectability, just as important in the twentieth century as it had been in the early days of the colony, when Surgeon General Peter Cunningham noted in 1790 how careful Sydney's hostesses were to appear ultra respectable and ultra domesticated. In 1893, Mrs Rolf Boldrewood had published *The Flower Garden in Australia*, the first Australian gardening book to be written by a woman. 'From a child I was always fond of a garden,' she writes in the introduction and continues, a model of respectability:

THERE ARE FEW PEOPLE WHO WILL NOT AGREE WITH ME THAT NOTHING IS MORE DELIGHTFUL THAN THE FRESH SCENT OF FLOWERS IN THE EARLY MORNING ... MY CHIEF ENJOYMENT, HAS EVER BEEN IN THE CARE OF MY GARDEN. IN MY VARIOUS HOMES I HAVE ALWAYS SUCCEEDED IN SURROUNDING MYSELF WITH FLOWERS. FURTHERMORE, THE MORE WORK ONE DOES IN A GARDEN, THE MORE LOVELY AND SATISFACTORY IT BECOMES, WHILE THE INTEREST ALWAYS APPEARS TO INCREASE FROM YEAR TO YEAR ... HOW ONE IS REPAID, TOO, BY SEEING THE SEEDS SOWN IN AUTUMN COMING UP AND PRODUCING FINE PLANTS! IN THE SPRING TIME WHAT MANIFOLD BLOOM AND LOVELINESS O'ERSPREAD EVERY NOOK AND CORNER![25]

Upper- and middle-class women in Australia, as in Britain, were occupied with the decorative, rather than the useful. The garden was not

where Una laboured physically, but rather another genteel realm in which she demonstrated her position and into which she poured her creative energies. The garden was where she painted in watercolour, and on 1 October 1930 she wrote:

THE GARDEN IS TOO LOVELY FOR WORDS. AM PAINTING THE WISTARIA AND LILAC AND SCARLET FLOWERING PEACH. EVERYWHERE IS HUMMING WITH BEES AND GLOWING WITH COLOUR AND WAFTING OUT EXQUISITE SCENTS.

When she took part herself in the physical work of gardening it was as an indulgence, out of choice, not necessity. 'Jo and I are doing the pruning,' she writes on one occasion. 'It is a lovely place to be! Snipping away and Jo bursting into song, all the latest love ditties.' (And at Nindooinbah, Margaret Persse Hockey remembered her grandmother, who designed the Nindooinbah garden: 'Granny used to garden in all her rings. She would bend from the waist; she would never crouch.') The serious daily toil of the garden was left to employed males: Una instructed the gardeners

The 'Amy Johnson' rose, bred by Alister Clark in 1931

following pages: Dizzy (Ann) Carlyon grew up on Boonoke in the 1950s. Her father, Basil Clapham, was manager of the Falkiner properties. Here, in Dizzy's Mornington Peninsula garden, the rose 'Albertine' creates a cool, shady arbour.

on planting, pruning and distributing manure. On 29 September 1921 she wrote, 'it poured last night, anyway I washed my head and packed and talked to Charley about the garden'. [26] On another day, 'I went down at dusk—my faithful old Jimmy was raking his piles together of dead vegetables; getting all ready to put on the manure tomorrow.' On 15 March she was:

UP & GOING VERY BUSILY & AFTER JO AND JACK IN THE GARDEN. EXQUISITE! I FINISHED UP PAINTING IN JIMMY'S GARDEN, ON AN UPTURNED BOX, THE PUMPKINS, & BRILLIANT GREEN BEANS & ARTI-CHOKES, AGAINST THE WHITE AUTUMN GRASS.

The garden also provided solace, often needed in the midst of what might seem to those observing from outside a golden life. She sought comfort in the garden after the deaths of two children. Her fifteen-month-old daughter Diana died on 30 January 1922, after what appears to be a mystery illness. 'Another lovely mocking day,' she told her diary. 'The nights are too lonely for words.' On 23 February it was 'A cold and icy day … I felt too miserable for words … I dread the nights.' But soon, on 26 March, she could glean some joy from the garden:

A LOVELY DAY … WE ARE ALL SITTING OUTSIDE THIS AFTERNOON ON THE LAWN, ENJOYING THE SUN & TWITTERING BIRDS & I HAVE FINISHED OFF SWEET DIANA'S CARDS & LETTERS.

Una loved the iris, with its scent of early summer.

Una also turned to the garden when she received the terrible news of the death of her adored son John Alexander on 22 September 1942, when his aircraft crashed at Casterton in England. He was twenty-four years old.[27] Over two decades Una had lovingly told her diary of the charms, schoolboy escapades and successes of her beloved son. Her adoration was returned. In one of John's letters from the war he wrote of how he treasured the image of her walking in her garden smelling the flowers and 'throwing her arms in the air in joy'.[28]

The cable telling of John's death reached Otway two days after his plane crashed. When Una was told, she wrote, 'Life has stopped for me today! & henceforth I shall go through my time left, with the blinds drawn down … The sun and the radiance has ceased to sparkle.' When she then wrote, 'Then out to the garden,' the reader is thankful that she could at least immerse herself in the beauty and purity of the garden on which she had always relied. In the depths of her grief the garden provided some light. On 2 October 1942 she wrote, 'The sun shone & the Spring flowers opened but I still think I will wake up soon & find this all a nightmare.' And the next day, '… we talked out on the verandah as it was coming up very thundery & hot. The port wine magnolia & wisteria were too delicious. How John loved them!' On 26 December 1942 she told her diary, 'the first Christmas without my beautiful John Alexander, for 24 years, and so few days I have had the delight of being with him! All radiance has flown from life!'[29] Una died on 23 December 1948, aged sixty-seven years.

The garden provided the overarching framework for Una Falkiner's life, and a reference for her moods and her health, for the changing seasons and the shifting fortunes of the Falkiner properties. It provided the canvas upon which her passions and disappointments were articulated. The source of comfort, a yardstick for taste and beauty, the garden also provided Una—like other women of her time and class—with agency in her marriage, in her community and in her life.

At the same time, however, the garden was a clearly gendered space where women could be elegantly corralled, away from positions of responsibility and power. It was a separate—female—sphere. Una's life reveals how English manners and customs, culture and experience provided the background to her life. Her garden, created in the image of England, despite the realities of the Riverina climate, demonstrates that her life was enacted within a framework of imperial constraints and privileges.

THE GARDEN — A WAY OF LIFE

It is not the gardeners who count, but God who makes it grow.

We are God's fellow-workers, and you are God's garden.

WINIFRED WEST *in her address to Frensham School, 17 July 1963*[1]

Winifred West 1881–1971

LESS THAN A TWO-HOUR DRIVE south of Sydney by modern motorway—140 kilometres—lie the Southern Highlands of New South Wales. Some 300 metres above sea level, winter can often bring snow, and even in midsummer swirling mists descend in the late afternoon. The soil is deep, rich, red volcanic basalt loam in many parts and the annual rainfall can be as high as 1500 millimetres. Cold-climate gardens of exotic autumn colouring trees, English-style, wide borders of perennials and scented northern hemisphere shrubs flourish. Colonial Governors holidayed there from the mid nineteenth century. And, since then, the area has been the site of extensive summer retreats—'Hill Station Gardens'—for successful Sydney professionals. This is a region vastly different from most of Australia, and this was the environment in which, in 1913, an Englishwoman, Winifred West, established Frensham School for girls.

Winifred West encouraged women to express their individuality and creativity through gardening. She saw gardens as an integral part of the education of young women; the gardens she created around her school were the canvas upon which her ideals were demonstrated. Her influence came about not by lessons in garden design, however, but by her use of the garden to exemplify her philosophies of shared information and service to others, taught in a spirit of Christian love and non-competition. For West

Winifred West's father was warden at St Mary's, the Anglican church in her village of Frensham, in Surrey, England.

the garden was a metaphor for living, demonstrating that the presence of beauty was possible—indeed, essential—through every aspect of life.

Few records remain of Winifred West's early life. A great deal of her story is told by Priscilla Kennedy, her niece. Some aspects have been gleaned from the published diaries of West's cousin, the writer George Sturt.[2] Cynthia Parker, headmistress of Frensham from 1968 to 1993 and another admirer, also takes up the story.[3] West left no diaries and just a few letters; the scant records that remain are held in the Mitchell Wing of the State Library of New South Wales. It is impossible, then, to fill in the gaps in the story of West's life without a certain amount of supposition.[4]

It is possible to comment with greater certainty on West's philosophy of education for young women, and for living, as she regularly presented her ideas to the students, staff and parents. These talks and speeches have been published and clearly indicate values she held dear.[5] Interviews conducted with alumni concur with Kennedy's and Parker's opinions that West was an enlightened educator and a woman of enormous character and charisma. These recollections also show that the garden provided a platform upon which West set out her ideology.

Winifred attended Queen Anne's School, in Caversham, Surrey.

Winifred West was born in the pretty English village of Frensham, near Farnham in the affluent county of Surrey, on 21 December 1881. Frensham is a quintessential English village of stone houses and beautiful gardens, with a palpable sense of quiet affluence. Winifred was the second child of Fanny Sturt and Charles West; her father was headmaster of St Mary's, the local school, as well as warden at the village Anglican church and organist. In her biography of West, Priscilla Kennedy describes a family who loved books and music, gardening and walking, animals and the countryside that surrounded their home. Tragedy struck when Winifred was ten: her father, aged fifty, died from pneumonia. Fanny West, then just thirty-six years old, was left with little income and six children to support. Showing a strength of character, determination and practicality that became evident in Winifred, Fanny took in lodgers to help support her children, who all won educational scholarships.[6] The eldest child, Charles, became a chorister at Winchester Cathedral School, while Winifred was a boarder at Queen Anne's School, Caversham, for six years from its inaugural year, 1894. She would later recall fondly the influence of those years:

The sunken rose garden at Newnham College, Cambridge

GAMES AND OUT-OF-SCHOOL ACTIVITIES—LONG WALKS ESPECIALLY IN THE AUTUMN ARE VERY HAPPY MEMORIES AND THE THOUGHT OF THEM FILLS ME WITH NOSTALGIA FOR THE ENGLISH COUNTRYSIDE ... MUSIC IN THE SCHOOL WAS A GREAT JOY ... OUTSIDE CONCERTS AND ENTERTAINMENTS WERE HIGHLIGHTS.[7]

In 1900 Winifred West went up to Newnham College, Cambridge, where she read medieval and modern languages for three years. Degrees— and even then titular degrees only, without voting rights at the university—were not awarded to women at Cambridge until 1921, however. We might imagine that this experience influenced West's later attitudes to the limitations placed upon women. While Australian universities had granted women full degrees since the 1880s, several Australian graduates remember the discrimination they experienced in English institutions.

Teaching was one of the few careers that were open to women, and, after university, West taught for four years at the Guernsey Ladies' College, where, according to family history, she met an Australian to whom she

became engaged. Priscilla Kennedy writes that her aunt travelled to Australia in October 1907, to marry him. On board ship, however, West met one of the Shackleton explorers, a meeting that changed the course of her life. She apparently fell in love, leaving her, she believed, no choice but to break off her engagement when she arrived in Sydney.

It is also possible that, during the voyage, with further time spent in reflection, West realised that she could only achieve her full intellectual potential by remaining single. This was a time when educated women were obliged to choose between marriage and a career. Evidence across Britain, the United States and Australia reveals that notions of the feminine ideal prevalent at the time made it almost impossible for a woman to have both.

Early feminist M. Carey Thomas, from 1894 to 1922 president of Bryn Mawr, the academically rigorous American college for women, wrote to her niece, 'but my choice was made easy by the fact that in my generation marriage and an academic career was impossible'. Nor was Thomas encouraging the choice of marriage over career for her students, telling her niece, 'Our failures only marry'.[8] George Sturt's diaries also reveal something of the prevailing attitude toward women, education and marriage. Upon being told of Winifred's engagement, he wrote:

Seven Irish yews, planted to commemorate the first seven pupils at Newnham College, form the gardens' southern boundary.

THINKING OF WINIFRED AND HER ENGAGEMENT (SINCE I SPOKE OF IT WITH HER LAST NIGHT) I HAVE GROWN WHOLLY CONTENTED WITH IT. AT FIRST IT SEEMED LIKE THE BREAKING OFF OF HER CAREER. ALL THINGS, UNTIL THIS WAS ANNOUNCED, HAD SEEMED POSSIBLE FOR HER: THEN THIS CAME—LIKE SHUTTING UP ALL THE DOORS. BUT NOW I SEE IT OTHERWISE ... *A DIFFERENT, AND PERHAPS BETTER, KIND OF CAREER POSSIBLE FOR HER IN MARRIAGE ...*[9]

Wherever the truth lies, after West arrived in Sydney, now alone and independent, she taught private female students each morning at her home, to support herself. This was a common practice, particularly before 1920, when many 'private venture schools', often run by newly arrived female immigrants from the United Kingdom, operated.

Winifred West may have discussed with her students the subjects they were being taught, and was perhaps horrified that education for girls at this time still often concentrated on the 'refined' accomplishments, preparing them only for the career of homemaker. It might have been that West saw that the influence of small academies run by enterprising women was on the decline, noted the unbalanced, gender-based, curriculum offered by the state system and, responding to her experiences at Cambridge, wanted to ensure a more complete education for Australian girls. It is also likely that West, living at Rushcutters Bay and experienced as a teacher, observed the example of these nearby private girls' schools and saw an opportunity not only to further the education of young women, but for a business adventure that would provide her with a fulfilled intellectual way of life, allowing her to choose independence and a career over marriage.

below and following pages:
The Gertrude Jekyll garden: The Manor House at Upton Grey, meticulously restored by John and Rosamund Wallinger, is close to Winifred's West's English village of Frensham.

After her arrival in Sydney, as well as taking on private students, West herself took lessons in the evenings from the acclaimed artist Julian Ashton, and soon became a skilled botanical watercolourist, working each afternoon as an illustrator at the Australian Museum.[10] Each Monday afternoon was reserved for hockey practice, and West met Phyllis Clubbe at a hockey game at Rushcutters Bay in Sydney in 1908; the two soon became firm friends and instigated the first women's interstate hockey matches. Clubbe was also enthusiastic about the idea of starting a school. Mary Perry, a close friend of Clubbe and also in the hockey team, had been left £1000 in her grandfather's will; she offered it to West to start a school. While this may appear strange and an enormous leap of faith on the part of Perry, those who knew West tell of her charisma, her strength of purpose and her ability to captivate others with her ideas.

West established Frensham in the Southern Highlands, leasing a large house in the small town of Mittagong from the businessman Arthur Tooth. She chose the location as she believed that everyone had a right to be educated in beautiful, quiet surroundings, out of the city, and that 'Quietness is necessary for inner growth—that we may discover and express ourselves.'[11] It is also an area reminiscent of her home village in Surrey.

It is not apparent that the curriculum was much more rigorous than that offered at any of the other private schools for girls. The first lesson, singing, was given on Monday, 21 July 1913. There were three pupils. The prospectus West issued in 1912 for future parents demonstrated that, for West at least, 'Anglo-dominance' was the suitable framework for many aspects of post-colonial life. 'Miss West (Newnham College Cambridge),' it announced:

At Frensham School, the iris is awarded
for achievement and contribution.

WOMEN'S EDUCATION

At the end of the nineteenth century girls
from the middle and upper classes were
still educated, either at home or at private
schools, in 'polite accomplishments' and
domestic skills, to befit them for their role
as society's moral arbiters.[14]

Most Australian private schools had
been started, and were controlled, by single
women—many of them English—until into
the twentieth century, when they were
taken over by school councils. In Sydney,
St Catherine's was established in 1854,
Abbotsleigh in 1885 and Ascham in 1886,
all assisted by the boom times of the 1880s.
Although the Abbotsleigh curriculum included English, French, sciences and Latin,
there was still considerable emphasis on
the social graces. Ascham was bought by a
Mr Carter in 1902 but while he placed new
importance on mathematics, music and natural history, the school also taught dress-
making, needlework, singing and dancing.

Meanwhile, in the public system, the
new syllabus for boys introduced in 1905
included English, mathematics and nature
knowledge. 'In girls' schools, lessons in
household economy, food, clothing,
domestic hygiene and care of children
should form the greater part of the year's
course,' the syllabus advised, 'Matrimony
[being] the ultimate goal of nearly every
girl'. Neglect of such training would leave a
mark 'not only upon the home, but [also]
upon the national life'.[15]

WILL BE OPENING A BOARDING SCHOOL FOR GIRLS.
THE AIM OF THE SCHOOL IS TO PROVIDE A THOR-
OUGHLY SOUND EDUCATION ON MODERN ENGLISH
LINES; TO DEVELOP TO THE FULL THE CAPACITY OF
EVERY GIRL AND HELP HER TO BECOME A USEFUL
AND GRACIOUS WOMAN IN WHATEVER POSITION SHE
MAY HAVE TO FILL.[12]

Her cousin, George Sturt, with the same assumption
that British was best, had told her that he was convinced that she was to be 'the future Pioneer of Austral
Culture!', presumably implying that she would bring
her English education and experiences to improve the
education of colonial girls.

Within a few years, through West's good management, determination and a great deal of her persua-
sive charm, Frensham was financially sound enough to
afford the purchase of the Tooth house, along with
more buildings and a substantial amount of land.

From the moment she arrived in Mittagong, on
3 June 1913, West set about gardening. It is interesting to
reflect that, even for women, the creation of a garden,
while assumed to be the most feminine of activities,
signifies the imposition of their will upon the landscape. Perhaps West's experience of the ways in which
her world had been controlled by men—her time at
Cambridge is one example—resulted in not only the
establishment of her school but also her desire to dominate her immediate landscape by the creation of the
garden upon it.

Photographs of Winifred West reveal a striking
woman, and students and staff speak of her vision,
strength of character and physical beauty. Many who
knew her commented on her prowess in the fields of
sport, drama, music, art and scholarship. Her students
recalled her ability to draw out the best in them, often
finding talents of which they were unaware.

Winifred West's tenure as headmistress of
Frensham School, between 1913 and 1938, spanned
twenty-five tumultuous years for Australians, through
World War I and the years of the Great Depression.

While women were graduating from Australian universities, many continued to choose marriage over career; gardening was one activity that continued to provide women with some agency after the return of the men from war robbed them of their new-found independence. West, no doubt aware of these different forces at work in the community, also understood that attitudes would not be the same again.

The main house at Frensham, on the New South Wales Southern Highlands, photographed from the secret garden

In her first address to the school community, on 1 June 1914, when the student body numbered twelve, West noted that Australia was on the brink of a new phase in its history, 'and in the history of women'.[13] She must have found herself caught amidst the tension created by her desire for equality of opportunity for women, the realities of Australia of the time, and the aspirations of the parents of her charges. She felt keenly that the Australia of the time did not make opportunities for women available and her tireless work for her girls is well recorded.

Plants are still allowed
to spill over stone walls
at Frensham School.

Like other women in this book, West did not set out to emulate
nature. Her garden was English, although set against a background of
soaring eucalypts and the Australian landscape that she came to love. Her
garden reinforced all that West had brought from the privileged green
fields of England to Frensham, and the climate and soil of the Southern
Highlands provided the perfect conditions for creating such a garden. But
she also chose the Southern Highlands for her school for aesthetic reasons,
to live in balance with nature and because she believed engagement with
the soil was central to spiritual development.

It is impossible to discuss the life of Winifred West and her contribution to the lives of the women she taught and influenced without
contemplating questions of beauty. Education and aesthetics were combined, irrevocably linked, in the garden West created, and, in turn,
reflected her appreciation of beauty. She employed the language of
beauty in her regular addresses to the school community. Her speech to
celebrate Frensham's fourth birthday, in 1917, was emblematic of her philosophy, and revealed how pivotal to her style of education she believed
surroundings to be:

CHILDREN SHOULD BE BROUGHT UP TO LOVE BEAUTY AS THEY DO OTHER VIRTUES—ESPECIALLY IN A COUNTRY WHERE THE TENDENCY IS TO BE UTILITARIAN AND TO GIVE BEAUTY A VERY LOW PLACE IN THE SCALE OF THINGS NECESSARY OR DESIRABLE. BEAUTY MUST HAVE A GREAT EFFECT ON OUR DEVELOPMENT.[16]

She hoped that, through gardening, her students could connect their lives to an idealised past, an undefiled Arcadia. West's aesthetic sense and her assumption that beauty was superior to utilitarian concerns becomes immediately apparent upon viewing the garden at Frensham. It comprises wide, open spaces, terraces supported by stone or brick walls over which English-style perennials fall freely, and private, enclosed areas. No paths were laid out at the time the gardens were first built. West believed in allowing the students to make the paths—the goat tracks—as need dictated. Around the main house she created stone-edged beds of flowering English perennials, spring-flowering bulbs and the dark purple iris. Balancing the restful spaces was a large area of wilderness still known as 'The Holt'. This word—still in use in the English village of Frensham today—means a wood or wilderness, and it is an area of bushland that West purchased for games, walks and exploring. The main lawn at Frensham, on which an original eucalypt remains, providing a shaded gathering place for students, is integral to the sense of peace that pervades this garden and which was so important to West. To her, an uncluttered space was central to the notion of beauty.

May hedges were much loved.

At the end of the garden at Frensham is a small, secluded, rectangular garden surrounded by a high hedge of may (*Spiraea* spp.). It was designed by West for seclusion—but not exclusion—a quiet place of solitude for reflection and contemplation, themes integral to her ideals of beauty. It was filled with roses, their scent adding to the beauty of the space, and with flowers and spring-flowering bulbs from West's English heritage which the younger girls were allowed to pick to make garlands to adorn the heads of friends who were celebrating birthdays. One student recalls:

ONE ALWAYS CONNECTS GARDENING WITH ... MISS WEST. ONE PART OF THE GARDEN WAS ALWAYS 'MISS WEST'S GARDEN'—I THINK IT WAS USUALLY THE MOST COLOURFUL PART ON ACCOUNT OF HER UNFAIL-ING KNACK WITH FLOWERS. WE ALL HAD FORM GARDENS & WERE EACH SUPPOSED TO HELP IN THEIR UPKEEP.[17]

A study of her speeches reveals that West hoped the Frensham gardens would underline her belief that engagement with the mythical and the spiritual was essential for emotional wellbeing. Reduction of life to the mere factual was unhealthy. She set out to achieve a magical, enchanting garden at Frensham. Lessons—which in the early days of the school, ended at lunchtime—were often taught in the garden; performances and celebrations were conducted in special areas in the grounds. Secret hideaways were created in the garden to encourage a spiritualism in the girls; 'Thursday Island' was built in Nattai Creek, which runs through the lower part of the grounds. An open-air theatre, with benches dug into a grassy slope, was formed for performances and for Sunday services, including the

HILL STATION GARDENS

Mount Macedon gardens are replete with autumn-colouring plants: the gardens of Penola (*above*), Ard Choille (pron. 'Ard Hilly') (*centre*), Glen Rannoch (*far right*) and Alton (*following pages*).

Hill Station Gardens in cold-climate areas such as the Southern Highlands of New South Wales have a rich and privileged tradition, of which Frensham was part. The term 'Hill Station Garden' is laden with messages of privilege and exclusivity and recalls the mountain estates constructed under colonial rule in India or Sri Lanka (then Ceylon). There, English civil servants and representatives of British mercantile companies could retreat with their families for respite from the shimmering summer heat suffered on the plains. The privileged could holiday in close proximity to the Governor and look down, from the cool of the mountains of Simla, Darjeeling and Newara Eliya, upon the general population.

In Australia, successful colonists—merchants, pastoralists, and later city professionals—emulated such behaviour. They bought country houses in the mountains behind the eastern

seaboard cities, close to the Governors' holiday houses, to remain close to colonial power. The grand mountain garden, replete with horticultural bounty from around the world, provided the essential backdrop. The gardens of the Southern Highlands of New South Wales, and those of Mount Macedon, north of Melbourne, best exemplify the Hill Station Garden, the ultimate aspirational garden.

Names evoked the mist-shrouded mountain passes of the subcontinent— Kirami, Kuranda, Tanahmerah, Darjeeling and Doshong La. These gardens were not always sites of creative endeavour and solace for the womenfolk, instead often being repositories of male prowess, male spaces planted with treasures from around the globe and housing collections of botanical excellence. Perhaps it was only due to climate that they were filled with horticultural bounty from the northern hemisphere, rather

blessing of the animals, for girls were allowed to bring their pets, from horses, dogs and cats to snails, to school. Close by is a cypress grove where outdoor ballets and dances were performed. Along with The Holt, this innocent space that harks back to unspoiled nature was central to the spiritualism invested in the gardens that West created. (At the same time, however, she exerted her power over this landscape by clearing sections of The Holt for sites on which games of cricket—that most imperial of sports— and hockey, would be played.)

A child who came to Frensham in 1927 reiterated the affection that many students felt for the school, for all it taught and the ideals it represented. She said of her reasons for loving the school, 'Wattles in The Holt seemed to me a pretty good reason. We could climb trees, make a noise, and we never wore gloves.'[18]

And whatever West may have felt about education for girls when she arrived in New South Wales in 1907, academic work at Frensham was handled with a light touch. Clubs were a central part of school life. The Gardening Club was considered as important as the Pen and Ink Club, the

than with the sub-tropical tapestry of the gardens of the sub-continent, whose messages of power and success they sought to emulate.

Mount Macedon was settled in the 1870s; its desirability was confirmed when the Victorian Governor, Lord Loch, and his wife holidayed there in 1884, immediately convincing the government to purchase a vice-regal summer retreat there. When East India Company official Rolf Boldrewood visited Derriweit Heights, Charles Ryan's summer retreat at Mount Macedon, he described it in his *Old Melbourne Memories,* published in 1884, as the 'Simla of Victoria', evoking the elitism of the Raj.

Perhaps nowhere in Australia was the aspiration represented by the Hill Station Garden more evident than among the picturesque villages of the Southern Highlands of New South Wales, which as early as 1820 was described by Governor Lachlan Macquarie as a 'fine, extensive pleasure ground'. There was Throsby Park, named by Macquarie in 1820 for the early settler and pastoralist Charles Throsby, and leased as a summer residence from 1865 to 1872 by the then Governor, the Earl of Belmore. Nearby Hillview was selected by the British Government in 1882 as the country house for the incumbent Governor, Lord Loftus.[19] Grand estates were created in the English landscape manner, with stately cold-climate trees, thousands of spring bulbs and a rhododendron dell. Exotic conifers, introduced from America in the mid nineteenth century, with their evocation of

the wild and picturesque, became status symbols, so that the unique vernacular of the place was quickly replaced with a northern hemisphere footprint. The gardens of the Southern Highlands, including those Winifred West created at Frensham, epitomised, intentionally or not, the paradigm of transferred vision.

Literary and Dramatic Society and the Music Club. Students who chose to be in the gardening club were each given a small square of ground to maintain; some grew vegetables, some flowers.

West's achievements at Frensham were celebrated in 1934 with the release of *The Frensham Book,* a collection of one hundred photographs of the school by the renowned photographer Harold Cazneaux. West wrote in the introduction that the book:

IS INTENDED AS A REMINDER OF PLEASANT PLACES AND HAPPY DAYS FOR THOSE WHO HAVE LIVED AT FRENSHAM ... THERE ARE NO PICTURES OF CLASSROOMS, BUT BOWLS OF FLOWERS AND WIND IN THE TREES GIVE JUST AS VITAL AN IMPRESSION OF THE SCHOOL AND WILL BRING BACK FLASHING MOMENTS OF DELIGHT.[20]

In the Frensham garden, therefore, quiet, restful, uncluttered space is arranged in counterpoint to the small, private, secluded space and an exciting wilderness, planned for escape and for inspiration. To West these different areas, each with a unique personality and assuming a different mood at varying times of the day or with the changing seasons, were the exemplification of beauty. She made her fondness for these areas and the importance she placed upon them clear when she told the community on 1 June 1918, 'We want the beauty of the House, Garden and The Holt to be the outward and visible sign of the inward and spiritual grace of Frensham'.[21] West used the metaphor of the garden to outline her philosophy of education, in which leadership and selflessness were paramount. That education should be like a tree growing from a seed to maturity, putting forth living branches, was fundamental to her thinking.

left: The pretty spring garden at Sturt craft centre

centre: Hedges of may (*Spiraea* spp.) flower in September

right: A quiet corner for sitting in the Frensham gardens

The dependence upon the garden to provide lessons to live by is further exemplified by the choice of the iris as the school emblem. West chose the iris as Frensham's emblem as it will thrive, growing strong and beautiful, in any condition; the school's colours are the green and purple of the iris and the brown of the earth. It is likely, however, that West also chose the iris because she had loved it in the English gardens with which she was familiar, those that flourished near her home village in Surrey and throughout the comfortable nearby counties of Berkshire, Hampshire, Sussex and Kent.[22]

An iris picked from the garden is the only prize awarded at Frensham School. This is the greatest accolade a student can receive, and, after it is presented, an iris is embroidered on the blazer pocket. In her discussion of this prize Cynthia Parker reveals something of the school's philosophy:

THE AWARD IS NOT GIVEN TO A GIRL WHO IS SELFISH IN THE USE OF HER TALENT. LOVE AND SERVICE MUST BE OF AN EQUALLY HIGH STANDARD WITH THE PERFORMANCE. AN IRIS MIGHT BE AWARDED FOR EXCELLENCE IN LATIN, OR FOR SPORT, OR MUSIC, OR FOR BEING WARDROBE MISTRESS IN THE DRAMA DEPARTMENT.[23]

Linked with her use of the garden as a metaphor for her philosophies was the notion of the garden as a site of good, of reclaimed Eden, a site for the ideals of Romanticism, for the personification of Paradise. And women have always been part of this metaphor. The garden belongs to the female persona, the female ideal, and the garden is where men place women. Eden is also, however, a symbol of woman's fall from grace; Eve tempted Adam there, resulting in the expulsion of both from a state of grace. The Garden

of Eden became the embodiment of a woman's disempowerment, a gendered space in which she is entrapped.

But the garden is also a place where a troubled soul can return to a perfect state, or at least to a place of possible redemption. The creation of a garden provides salvation and hope for both man and woman; it is a place where the seasons will go full circle, where winter will be followed by renewal in spring. Even for those for whom the understanding of these concepts is fleeting, or whose sentiments toward the garden are not based on biblical teachings, the garden represents Paradise, Utopia, Arcadia.

West, with her education steeped in both Christian doctrine and in the ideals of Romanticism, explored these concepts in the Frensham gardens. Eden—the perfect garden—represents a state of good for which West encouraged her students to strive through living virtuously, and serving the community in love. Idealised womanhood was most often placed there. Although Frensham is a non-denominational school, Christian ethics and principles underline its teaching and activities of the school.

The secret garden at Frensham

While West espoused independence for all women, her school, whether she intended it or not, negotiated a clearly defined sphere for women; for many, Frensham was an imperial metaphor that spoke a language of gendered stereotypes. Privileged women at this time were still expected to devote themselves to their family, their community and their garden. Some who sent their daughters to Frensham—graziers made wealthy from their wool clip—expected them to receive an education that continued to create colonial stereotypes. In 1930 West told the assembled audience:

MANY PARENTS SEND THEIR GIRLS TO SCHOOL SO THAT THEY MAY LEARN ACCOMPLISHMENTS—'ORNAMENTAL KNOWLEDGE'—AND MAY BECOME SOCIAL SUCCESSES, AND THOUGH EACH YEAR FEWER PEOPLE TAKE THIS NARROW VIEW, THERE ARE STILL TOO MANY WHO DO ... THESE PEOPLE ARE GRIEVOUSLY WRONG.[24]

But while girls educated at Frensham School personified womanhood, and in an era and an environment in which the role of women was interpreted narrowly, West crossed gender boundaries. She did not confine her teaching to the role that had been prescribed for women, whatever the parents of her students expected. West tapped into the beginning of a

The wisteria-covered pergola at the Sturt craft centre

movement that allowed, encouraged even, women to step outside the bounded space of the garden, a movement that refused to accept the notion of separate spheres, the concept that advocated the separation of work places from home places, of male spaces from those occupied by females. Her engagement with changing expectations can be traced through her regular addresses to the school community. 'We cannot be good citizens if we confine our work to our own family and our personal friends,' she advised on 1 September 1923.[25] And in 1930:

A MAN'S LIFE IS MORE THAN HIS BUSINESS AND A WOMAN'S LIFE IS MORE THAN HER SOCIAL ACTIVITIES. WE ARE HUMAN BEINGS BEFORE WE ARE DOCTORS, LAWYERS, ARCHITECTS—AND WE ARE HUMAN BEINGS BEFORE WE ARE MEN AND WOMEN.[26]

The success of Frensham must be attributed to Winifred West and the values she instigated and bequeathed as an extraordinary legacy. Many who knew her comment on her determination to improve the education of women. They applaud her ability to convince businessmen, family and friends alike that her ideas were not wildly impractical but eminently sane and correct. Her cousin, George Sturt, wrote to her on 21 June 1915, 'At the new purchase of a house I rejoice—not without wonder at your confidence that you can get the needful money, I don't think anyone in Farnham would lend me £300 without security!' One of her former students recollects:

I THINK THE FIRST IMPRESSION MISS WEST MADE ON MY YOUTHFUL MIND WAS ONE OF COLOUR, VITALITY & ENERGY. I DON'T THINK I HAD MET MANY ENGLISH PEOPLE THEN & THE RICHNESS OF HER SPEAKING VOICE IMPRESSED ME ... ALSO SHE USED TO DISCUSS WITH US MATTERS CONNECTED WITH THE SCHOOL ...[27]

Other students write of the joy of being taught by someone of West's talent. Integrity and service to others were seminal beliefs that formed the core of the education she prescribed for Frensham.

In the gardens at Frensham

West was highly successful in conveying her ideas, on gardens and on life, to her students. Visiting the gardens of Frensham alumni reveals that she influenced generations of gardening women: the gardens of past students, with their wide lawns, cool-climate shade trees and sturdy pergolas covered in wisteria and roses, can be found, cherished and nurtured, in a variety of climates throughout Australia, both in the cities and on country properties. Some of these women are well known, but most are not. Ann Hawker, a former student, travelled 34 000 kilometres throughout Australia in 1990 to track down old girls and to photograph and record their gardens. She wanted to address the influence of living and learning in such beautiful surroundings. 'The thrill that life can be lived in lovely surroundings made a deep and lasting impression,' she wrote of her days at Frensham in her book, *Echoes of Dreamland*:

WALKING BENEATH WISTERIA TO BREAKFAST, LUNCH AND DINNER; THE SMELL OF LILAC ENTERING AND LEAVING THE HOUSE; THE SCENT OF ROSES WAFTING THROUGH THE FICTIONAL LIBRARY; AN AROMA OF CYPRESS IN THE GROVE ... WRITING LETTERS ON SUNDAYS BENEATH TRAILING WILLOWS ON THE ISLAND OR BESIDE THE WEEPING ELM ON THE ENORMOUS FRONT LAWN ... HOW LUCKY ONE IS TO HAVE BEEN OFFERED AN EDUCATION IN SUCH SURROUNDINGS.[28]

The gardens of former students living all over Australia are recorded in *Echoes of Dreamland*. These women are garden photographers, writers and designers, doctors, diplomats, accountants and housewives. Among the best known is Beatrice Bligh, the subject of the next chapter and the creator of the much-lauded country garden, Pejar Park; she, in turn, has influenced hundreds of gardening women. But whether famous or not, there is a common thread of a love of the garden and an appreciation of its importance that runs through Frensham girls.

The most important contribution Winifred West made to the story of garden making in this country is the set of principles that she gave to her students, ideals that they applied in a variety of fields. West saw that women of the twentieth century were living within a world of conflicting aspirations and expectations, and empowered them to make choices. Her philosophy that the creative life is essential to wellbeing is exemplified in many gardens throughout New South Wales. Her teachings found a voice in the creation of large and small, grand and modest gardens—but each seems to be the repository of the influences of the years spent at Frensham School.

Stating that change was necessary for her school to grow and prosper, Winifred West retired as headmistress on the school's twenty-fifth birthday, 17 July 1938. She was fifty-seven years old. That was by no means the end of her considerable influence at Frensham, however. She continued to live in a cottage in the grounds and the following year established Sturt, adjacent to the main school, as a craft centre for spinning, weaving, woodwork and pottery, and as a place where her philosophy of education for all might be extended.[29]

In June 1953 Winifred West was awarded an MBE in the Queen's Coronation Honours in recognition of her outstanding contribution to education. Her investiture was performed by the Queen.

Two weeks before she died, on 26 September 1971, aged eighty-nine, West was still gardening, digging with a full-sized spade, transplanting and reshaping, and planning future gardens. Although she was born at the end of the nineteenth century, in England, West's influence on the aspirations of Australian women, and on their garden making, continues into the twenty-first century. Her prediction that while her girls might not have always noticed gardens while they were at school, they would find them essential to their adult lives, has proved true.

I WAS NEVER LONELY

If there is a Heaven on earth it is here, it is here.

UNKNOWN *An inscription Beatrice Bligh found while researching the gardens of ancient Persia*

Beatrice Bligh 1916–1973

BEATRICE BLIGH WAS BORN TO THE LAND and was born to garden. The daughter of Gladys and Jim Gordon, her childhood was spent at Werriwa, the family property at Bungendore on New South Wales' Southern Tablelands north-east of Canberra. This is cold and wild granite country, some would say desolate, but it has its own grandeur, a certain magnetism in its bald, treeless plains and dun-coloured hills. Nearby, at Braidwood, was Manar, the beautiful and mysterious garden of her father's childhood. Established when the Gordons first arrived in the district from Scotland in the 1830s, it is a rambling garden of lilacs, hawthorns and honeysuckle, set within a cattle and sheep property. 'This large, romantic, natural place where I spent so many blissful, irresponsible days became my ideal,' wrote Beatrice Bligh in her first book, *Down to Earth,* published in 1968.[1]

Manar was one of three major influences in Beatrice's gardening life. The second was her education at Frensham School, in Mittagong. No one who was taught by the headmistress, Winifred West, escaped her influence, nor the importance of understanding and respecting the earth, its landscapes and the gardens that could be created upon it. The third influence was the garden writer and landscaper, Edna Walling. In turn—like Walling, West and Frensham School—Beatrice Bligh has influenced generations of Australian gardeners.

Grand gardens provided women like Beatrice Bligh with a profile and a position outside their marriage. Like the majority of women discussed in this book, Beatrice's garden demonstrated that some European settlers set out to replicate the eighteenth-century English landscape park, determined that the Australian landscape and conditions should present

no obstacle. Their gardens provided comfort during times of greatest loneliness. More than that, however, the domestication of her environment expressed Beatrice's strength of character, and her ability to stand undaunted in the face of any adversity.

~

Beatrice Bligh was born Rosemary Beatrice Gordon on 27 September 1916 at Edgecliff, a Sydney harbourside suburb. After an early childhood at Bungendore and Braidwood, where her parents grazed cattle, Beatrice became a boarder at Frensham from the age of twelve. She was a keen sportswoman—a tennis player, horsewoman, a brilliant skier—a botanical illustrator and a gifted pianist. After leaving school she spent a year at the Sydney Conservatorium of Music, achieving the demanding AMusA level. Beatrice then returned to Werriwa as money was too scarce to allow her to remain in Sydney. From Werriwa she would ride across the windswept plains and hills to another large property, Currandooley, to do bookwork.

Beatrice met Francis Leonard Bligh when he came to the district from Sydney to seek advice from her father about the purchase of land. He had been a close friend of a Gordon cousin at The Kings School and had finished his university education at Cambridge before deciding that it was from the land, rather than the family wine and spirits import–export business, that he wanted to earn his living. In an early display of her renowned determination, Beatrice, who had discovered that Leonard, like herself, was a member of the Ski Club of Australia, ensured that she booked into the Chalet at Charlotte Pass in the same weeks as Leonard was there.

left: Manar, the garden of her grandfather, was a major influence in Beatrice Bligh's garden making.

centre: Beatrice described Manar as 'large, romantic [and] natural'.

right: From the garden, into the landscape…Pejar Park today

Beatrice and Leonard married on 1 March 1941 at St Philip's, the stone church at Bungendore. She moved to Pejar Park, the 1600 hectares that Leonard's father had funded at Woodhouslee, 30 kilometres north-west of Goulburn, while her new husband embarked upon war service across the South Pacific and in Canada. At Pejar Park Beatrice found an unfenced property overrun by rabbits, where stock had been purchased on overdraft. Woodhouslee, at 800 metres above sea level on the Southern Tablelands, is open country, of granite soil that provides the perfect environment for the deadly tiger snake, and with only small parcels of the rich, red basalt soil so valued by gardeners. This is difficult gardening country. Summers can be tough, with temperatures reaching 32 °C, and with an annual rainfall of 700 millimetres. Most testing, however, are the severe winters, when the frosts that arrive in March can continue until December, and when winter temperatures can drop to -15 °C.

In addition to supervising the overseer, Arthur Yates, in the running of the property, Beatrice set about creating a garden around the bleak blue-stone cottage—which was devoid of electricity or heating, untouched from when it was built in the previous century. Her daughter, Lucinda Nicholson, born in 1948 (after Diana, in 1945) today recalls her mother's determination to cope in this hostile environment:

Dawn lights the house and garden: Pejar Park in the early spring.

SHE LIVED IN THE KITCHEN BY THIS BIG OPEN FIRE, WITH A GUN BY HER BED. FOR THE TIGER SNAKES, THE BUSHRANGERS, THE ESCAPED PRISONERS, THE SWAGGIES, WHO USED TO COME TO THE DOOR LOOKING FOR FOOD. AND KATH AND ARTHUR LIVED DOWN ON THE ROAD ... HALF A MILE AWAY. SHE WAS INCREDIBLY STRONG.[2]

When Leonard returned from the war, there were no rabbits, the property was fully fenced and the overdraft fully paid out, a testament to Beatrice's will, and to her skill in managing the land. In addition, there was a garden.

Irises, loved from Beatrice's Frensham School days, grow in generous swathes at Pejar Park.

Garden making provided Beatrice with companionship while Leonard was at war, and kept her so occupied that she 'felt neither lonely nor afraid'.[3] Her books tell of the creation of her garden, not of fences, sheep and mortgages. 'In spite of the inevitable vicissitudes of such a capricious climate,' she wrote, 'and the exigencies of life on a sheep station, I have found the making and maintenance of my garden a joy and a delight, a continuing interest and an absorbing occupation.'[4]

Those practised in observing the social meaning of gardens also reflect upon what the garden contributes to the lives of those involved in its creation and nurture. For Beatrice Bligh, the process of creating the garden—the planning, the designing of the structure and shape, and the selection of the plants and the research involved—provided an intellectual journey that ran parallel to the solace it offered. It must have been a saviour in those first years of her marriage when she was so alone. In later years, when the garden was fully laid out, she realised with some regret that the mental stimulation and the excitement of planning and creating new sections of the garden were over. And the garden was an even greater comfort toward the end of her life, when she was undergoing treatment for cancer. As she had learnt at Frensham—and as many, from writers to philosophers and psychologists have observed—it is not just plants that are being raised in the garden, it is the human spirit.

There was not much in the garden when Beatrice arrived at Pejar Park: on the east side was a dilapidated poultry house, a garden path lined with upturned beer bottles and two half-moon shaped beds filled with weeds. She responded to the challenge this presented by quickly setting about striking cuttings from gardens on nearby properties, taking off-shoots from quinces, cherries, poplars, hawthorns and elms and rescuing

from cattle layers of the pink-flowering rambling rose 'Dorothy Perkins' that was growing over a neighbour's fence. This was frontier country, but, undaunted by the limitations of soil and climate that she found there, perhaps partly because of her upbringing among hardy Scottish immigrants, Beatrice determined to dominate and feminise the land.

The lack of money that might be spared for the garden presented no obstacle to Beatrice's garden making. She would ride out from the property, pulling up suckers by the creek and stuffing them into the pommel of her saddle. 'I like to recollect,' she wrote in *Down to Earth*:

THE ORIGIN OF THE PLANTS I HAVE GATHERED MYSELF: THE QUINCES PULLED UP BY HAND FROM THE SOFT BANKS OF THE WOLLONDILLY RIVER IN WINTER, AND CARRIED HOME STUFFED INTO THE POMMEL OF MY SADDLE; THE FERN DUG OUT OF A ROCK CLEFT AT 7000 FEET ON MOUNT RAMSHEAD WITH MY SKI POLE AND BROUGHT DOWN THE MOUNTAIN ON SKIS; AND THE WATER HAWTHORN TAKEN FROM A WILD POOL IN THE PEJAR CREEK, WRAPPED IN PLASTIC, AND PUSHED UP A SLEEVE WHEN BOTH HANDS WERE NEEDED FOR THE REINS.[5]

She was adept at dividing plants and propagating cuttings; the skills taught by Winifred West, whom she described as a brilliant and dedicated gardener, were soon utilised in her own garden making. She had observed how West had created the gardens at Frensham:

AS A CHILD I NOTICED WHEN THE SCHOOL WAS ENLARGED AND THE GARDEN EXTENDED HOW PIECES OF *SPIRAEA GRACILIS* WERE DIVIDED UP AND USED AS A HEDGE TO SEPARATE SECTIONS INSTEAD OF A FENCE.[6]

The Blighs enjoyed a small, but close-knit circle of friends from the surrounding properties, people whose parents had been friends and who had attended The Kings School or Frensham together. Entertainment took the form of tennis parties, with friends staying on for afternoon tea or dinner. There were trips to Sydney for Beatrice to attend concerts and exhibitions. Gardening also provided women in remote districts like the Southern Tablelands with a common interest and a further bond of friendship.

There were several excellent gardens developing, in the English style, in the district. Close friends Janet and Geoffrey Ashton had inherited Markdale, at Binda, to the west; Jeanette and Jock Mackay were creating a wonderful garden, Mona, at Braidwood, to the east. Sheila and Hugh Hoskins owned Charlton, outside Goulburn, and Pamela Maple-Brown was gardening in the historic grounds of nearby Springfield. Beatrice had attended Frensham with most of these women.

The perfectly formed *Camellia* x *williamsii* 'E. G. Waterhouse' was named for Professor Waterhouse, who, at his home, Eryldene, did so much to promote a love of camellias in Australia.

Cuttings were supplied by these friends so that the gardens, Beatrice said, 'like my recipe book, gradually became and still are dotted with my friends' names'. She had learnt to garden in this way from Winifred West, and many of the plants at Pejar also came from the gardens at Frensham. A support system formed within this rural network as Beatrice and her friends inspired and assisted each other in the making of their gardens. Gardens were created like this not only on large country properties; 'slips' and plants were exchanged, along with general gossip, in the towns and in the cities as well, so that a vernacular front garden, in particular, was created by the repetition of certain plants in any suburb.

Beatrice wanted her garden to be natural, a little wild, with 'a sea of unstaked white shasta daisies, foaming onto the gravel paths', as she had loved at Manar. She recalled the magical and mysterious plantings at Manar with trees and shrubs meeting overhead:

... ALONG THE WINDING GRAVEL PATHS, MAKING THEM INTO DIM TUN-NELS OF GREEN, AND THERE SEEMED TO BE NO CLIPPED EDGES OR REAL FLOWER-BEDS; IT WAS NOT AN ATMOSPHERE OF ACTUAL NEGLECT, BUT ONE OF CASUAL OLD-WORLD CHARM.[7]

Cuttings came from the gardens of friends, including Mona, today under the care of Greg and Kerry Schneider.

She was also influenced in both her garden making and in her writing by the garden designer Edna Walling who was at the height of her success at the time, with thousands of followers through her books and articles in the Murdoch-run magazine *The Australian Home Beautiful*. Discussing the influences on her gardening styles, Beatrice wrote in *Down to Earth*, 'I always comfort myself with the words of Edna Walling. A garden should be just a little too big to keep the whole cultivated, then it has a chance to go a little wild in spots, and make some pictures for you.'[8]

In 1947 Edna Walling came to Markdale, the Ashton property some 50 kilometres west of Pejar Park, over a period of several months to create her third garden in New South Wales. Whether she came to Pejar Park on one of these visits is uncertain. Some think that Walling consulted at

Pejar—and left a simple pencil sketch on butter paper which has Walling hallmarks—for the garden. Sheila Hoskins is certain that Walling went to Pejar Park during one of her visits to Markdale, and gave Beatrice several ideas for the garden which were utilised. Others believe that Beatrice went to Markdale and spent a day there with Walling. Jock Mackay recalls Beatrice teaching him and his wife Jeanette a trick that Walling taught her: how to run out a hose to form a template for a garden bed or edge.

Whatever the truth, Beatrice Bligh's books reveal that the creation of Pejar Park was, in part, informed by Walling's love of English trees and shrubs, of languid stone walls and paths, of expanses of water and sweeping vistas. And, at Pejar, Beatrice created the same ethereal, tranquil quality that is felt in so many Walling gardens and which makes them so enjoyable, and so idiosyncratic.

Nineteenth-century settler culture understood space and place from a European, predominantly English, perspective. Mid twentieth-century colonisers like Beatrice and her friends, while at times acknowledging the importance, or even the beauty, of the Australian landscape, still assessed their surroundings in terms of how 'English' it could be rendered.

Beatrice was influenced by Edna Walling's love of English trees and shrubs, of languid stone walls and paths.

Beatrice and Leonard Bligh travelled to the United Kingdom and Europe every second year of their married life. Beatrice was very influenced by visits to the Savill gardens at Windsor and Wisley, home of the Royal Horticultural Society, and, in Europe, Holland's National Tulip Garden and the Generaliffe Gardens in Spain, although she thought the scale of these large public gardens somewhat impersonal. She was also moved by the work of the English landscape designer Lancelot 'Capability' Brown, and made several references in her second book *Cherish the Earth*—which she called 'my long history book'—to the influence he had on Australian gardens. She noted fine properties being 'set in spacious garden grounds based on the styles of the English landscape designers, Brown and Repton', and wrote approvingly of homestead gardens, where:

IN CAPABILITY BROWN FASHION, OAK TREES, ELMS AND POPLARS WERE SOMETIMES POSITIONED HALF A MILE FROM THE HOUSE TO IMPROVE THE OUTLOOK ...[9]

Leonard's sister lived in Buckinghamshire, a county where many of 'Capability' Brown's ambitious reconstructions remain extant. There is Blenheim Palace, the birthplace of Winston Churchill, re-landscaped by Brown in the 1760s to create sweeping vistas framed by natural-looking copses of trees and massive bodies of water, and the grand Cliveden, former home of the Astors, with its parklands and waterways. Stowe, where Brown was head gardener in 1741 and which many garden historians believe contains all the elements of eighteenth-century landscape perfection, is another of the nearby gardens that Beatrice probably visited. We can imagine that the layout and planting of these landscape parks and

wonderful gardens, with the various messages they relayed, must have resonated with the ideas for the garden Beatrice was creating 28 000 kilometres away.

Beatrice and Leonard would also have visited Sissinghurst, the Kent
garden created by Vita Sackville-West and her husband, the amateur architect and diplomat Harold Nicolson, from 1930. Together they created a
garden of themed 'rooms', walks and wild areas; Nicolson set out the
formal structure while Sackville-West was responsible for the exuberant
planting. The garden opened to the public in 1938, became widely known
and influential through her garden columns and remains today the
epitome of English good taste, and a mecca for Australian gardeners.
Sackville-West's first gardening column appeared in the *Evening Standard*
in 1924, and she continues to influence gardeners in Britain, the United
States and Australia, long after her death in 1962.

At Pejar Park Beatrice Bligh created a formal garden around the
house which gave way to sweeping lawns. These lawns afforded views
across the lake that formed a boundary to the sheep and cattle grazing in
the paddocks beyond. She interpreted the messages her favourite English
gardens conveyed, and displayed her domination of the Australian landscape by planting out, to the north-east of the house, a parkland of exotic
oak, golden and claret ash, elm and poplar, which coloured brilliantly in
autumn at the high altitude.

Beatrice had inherited, at Pejar Park, a drive that travelled through
what garden existed, in a straight line to the front door. In due course she
re-routed this, perhaps on Walling's advice, to swing around the house and
behind and through a stand of massive radiata pines.[10] Such an approach,
which meanders slowly and romantically around the perimeter of the

left: Beatrice travelled to England
to look at gardens. Here, in June,
the white garden at Sissinghurst,
where the climbing white rose
(*R. mulliganii*) is about to burst
into scented, pure white clusters.

centre: The 'Capability' Brown lake
at Harewood House

right: Sissinghurst Castle

property, prevents the visitor from viewing the entire garden immediately. The approach to the house and garden, Beatrice said, was what people noticed first, 'and first impressions remain'.

Lawn, seeded from Yates 'English Mixture', was then planted to roll down unimpeded to the tennis court and toward the views beyond. A large pergola, created from strong, cement columns and massive wooden cross beams, was erected to one side to support a cascade of rambling roses. This structure is a replica of the scaled-up pergola that the architect John Moore had designed for the garden at Sturt, adjacent to the main school at Frensham. Both are reminiscent of the unpretentious, workmanlike, honest pergolas that Edna Walling recommended for country gardens. The scale of the structure was in keeping with the overall landscape park feel of the garden.

Stone flagging or paving was always part of Beatrice Bligh's ideal for a garden—just as it was in Walling gardens—and the slate terrace at Pejar provides a smooth transition between the house and the garden. She loved

GARDEN FASHIONS

above: The garden at Yering, in Victoria's Yarra Valley, was originally created by Baron Ferdinand von Mueller, the first Director of Melbourne's Royal Botanic Gardens. He imported trees from Europe, and, in 1864, planted the rare Chilean wine palm (*Jubaea chilensis*), that is now classified by the National Trust.

right: At Claremont, in the Victorian city of Geelong, the glasshouse built in 1910, is still in use today, filled with slipper orchids, begonias and cyclamen.

Prior to World War I carpet bedding, or 'bedding out'—the mass planting of annuals—was popular in public and large private gardens. But the exodus of working men to the war, and the resulting shortage of labour, necessitated a change in how plants were used. After World War II, staff to help with gardens was further reduced. Many grand country gardens could not be maintained: plantings were simplified, complicated rose gardens removed and detailed perennial borders replaced with easy-care shrubberies or lawn.

Between the world wars several garden styles, derived from the late Gardenesque style of the Federation period, developed to complement the different styles of popular architecture: the Arts and Crafts style (1900–20), the California bungalow (1916–30s), the Georgian Revival (1920s–30s), the Spanish Mission style (to the 1950s) complemented by a garden of cordylines and palms, and the 'P & O style'

(1930s–50s). Front lawns and standard roses in brick-edged garden beds seemed to feature in all of these styles. Paths, curved or straight, were of concrete, flagstones or brick. Hedges of plumbago, privet and English box were favoured by some designers, while in the cities waist-high wooden or wire fences were also fashionable.[12] Shade houses, ferneries and bush houses continued to be popular, with publications providing plans for construction.[13]

Pergolas and lattice work featured in magazines. *Garden Gossip* noted, 'Pergolas instantly add a dignity and charm, and relieve the home grounds of that characteristic "flatness" which too often mars the beauty of an otherwise appealing setting'.[14] Magazines like *The Home* and *Art in Australia*, featuring articles by architects Hardy Wilson, Leslie Wilkinson, John Berry and Stacey Neave, were influential in shaping the taste of educated gardeners. Their use of wide stone steps,

stone walls and paths, with plants making themselves at home there. She wanted small creepers and matting plants such as thymes, alyssum, white-flowering pratias and convolvulus to grow between paving stones. Clipped, manicured edges were not part of her gardening vocabulary; at Pejar Park catmint, dianthus, ajuga, alyssum, cerastium, thrift, violas and 'baby's tears' (*Erigeron karvinskianus*) were allowed to crowd and soften the edges, just as she would have seen at Markdale. She planted hundreds of daffodils along the driveway and amongst the fruit trees, leaving them to naturalise into drifts of thousands.

Beatrice did not sketch out her plans on paper, allowing the garden to evolve over fifteen or twenty years, hoping that it would:

GAIN WITH AGE THAT PRICELESS AIR OF INEVITABILITY AND NONCHA-LANCE WHICH CAN ONLY EXIST IN MATURE GARDENS. THIS SUBTLE ASSET OFTEN ALLOWS A RATHER RELAXED AND NEGLECTED FEELING WITHOUT SEEMING TO HAVE ANY POSITIVE DETRIMENTAL EFFECT ON THE OVERALL APPEARANCE.[11]

up-scale garden gates, pavilions, pergolas and grand terraces, inspired by the Italian period popular in Great Britain—and seen in gardens like the Jekyll and Lutyens-designed Hester-combe—were probably, however, the preserve of the wealthy in Australia. These structures, popular in country gardens, are features that have contributed to their endurance.

Hydrangeas and violets were grown on the shady side of the house, while hybrid tea roses, carnations, gladioli and dahlias graced front gardens in beds cut into lawns of couch or buffalo. In Sydney a palm

tree (often *Phoenix canariensis*) or a standarised bougainvillea might have graced the front lawn. The Lombardy poplar (*Populus nigra* 'Italica') was used as avenue planting in cool-climate districts.[15] Annuals, particularly sweet peas, pansies, stock and snapdragons, continued to feature.

In the cities the most significant development in the early twentieth century was the birth of the Garden Suburb. Improved transportation, particularly the development of the railway, removed workers from over-crowded and at times unsanitary cities to the great Australian dream, 'the house on a quarter-acre block'. Brush box (*Lophostemon confertus*) was popular as a street tree, particularly in suburbs such as Sydney's Burwood and Haberfield, along with crepe myrtle and prunus.

Anglo-Saxons still made up the majority of immigrants. Working-class women, whose gardening had largely concentrated on growing vegetables,

were now starting to take pride in cultivating flower gardens. The invention of the Victa mower in 1952 made the Australian ideal of the carpet-like lawn even more achievable.

By the 1950s, in the cities front gardens had become smaller, often dominated by one feature tree—a magnolia or a fig—to provide shade and some privacy from the street. There might also be a display bed filled with pansies and ranunculus with an edging of white alyssum.[16] Front gardens were still for show; the 'backyard', once the site of the washing line,[17] the outdoor lavatory, the chook house, the wood heap, the copper, the orchard and vegetable garden, had developed into a place of leisure, where Sundays were spent with family and friends gathered around the barbecue.

As in most things, Beatrice Bligh had very firm opinions on questions of taste in garden matters. She warned against 'ugly <u>boundaries</u>, <u>entrances</u>, bad layout (<u>planning</u>) overabundance and over-colourful flowerbeds … & general lack of <u>simplicity </u>in design.'[18] Like Walling, Beatrice criticised contrived Victorian 'bedding out' of gaudy annuals, preferring the blowsy plantings of pastel colours in English perennial borders. Cannas, with their bright colours and upright form, were a pet hate. Too many features or garden ornaments and fountains that were too ambitious for their setting were all pretensions that she advised against. In this she invoked all the major influences in her life: her upbringing in the Manar garden, her Frensham education under English-born Winifred West, her experience of the best English landscape gardens and the writings of the English-born Edna Walling that advocated scale and simplicity. For Beatrice a good garden was not necessarily a result of a lot of money. 'Don't automatically assume,' she wrote in *Down to Earth*:

THAT THE BEST AUSTRALIAN GARDENS ARE NECESSARILY A PREROGA-TIVE OF THOSE WHO CAN SPEND WHAT THEY WISH … A GEM OF A GARDEN OFTEN EXISTS OUT IN THE BUSH, WHERE THE SIMPLE

Beatrice adored peonies, with their voluptuous, blowsy form. Here, 'Etienne de France'

PLANTING IS GENEROUSLY SPACED AND THE PERFECT LAWNS AND ARTISTIC DESIGN ARE IN COMPLETE HARMONY WITH THE NATURAL LANDSCAPE.[19]

Beatrice was not, in fact, commenting on designing in harmony with natural surroundings. She was making a statement about class and aesthetic—that good taste does not rely upon funds available. In fact it is quite possible that she believed that taste and style were inversely proportionate to the money that could be devoted to the garden. Likewise, with Beatrice's family background set firmly on rural traditions and with ties to Australia's oldest pastoral and political dynasties, class could not be bought. Restraint in garden making, both in design and use of colour, is the result of background, a subtle class determiner, notions that find voice in both gardening and popular literature.

The Persian lilac (*Syringa* x *persica*), photographed at Manar, the romantic garden that so influenced Beatrice Bligh

These various subtle social performances were part of the scaffolding to social success that both colonial and post-colonial women employed. Well-known gardener, the late Lady (Joan) Law-Smith who gardened at the acclaimed Bolobek at Mount Macedon in Victoria, commented on the use of colour both as identifying a female aesthetic and as an indicator of class. She remarked that, at Bolobek, the male, working-class gardener liked lots of brightly coloured flowers while she preferred a predominance of white.[20] Sissinghurst's famous white garden continues to be emulated by gardeners throughout the Western world, including Australia, where it has become considered a leitmotif for good taste, style, restraint and all things British.

The aesthetic for gardeners of Beatrice Bligh's background, then, stipulated that whites, creams and pastel colours, profusion and gentle chaos, was called for in the well-bred garden. Bright colours were to be banished. Beatrice wrote to the Goulburn Council criticising its decision to paint each seat in the local Belmore Park a different colour.[21]

Beatrice liked the drive to meander, preventing the entire property from being seen immediately. Here, the long drive at Gostwyck is lined with elm trees, planted over a century ago by A. A. (Abbey) Dangar.

For Beatrice and her contemporaries there was a sense, whether conscious or not, whether stated or not, that the garden underlined their place in society, the way in which a garden was laid out and planted indicated breeding and background.

The social hierarchy that existed at this time was further underlined by the garden. A good garden gave you a place in society and good taste was exemplified by an English-style garden. Well-known and applauded gardens such as Mona, Markdale, Emu Creek at Walcha, nearby Gostwyck, and other competitors in the *Sydney Morning Herald* Garden Competition—which Pejar Park won in 1965—also planted English trees and opulent, wide borders of pastel perennials.

The gardens Beatrice admired in Australia included the lavish Milton Park, near Bowral on the Southern Highlands, built for the Hordern family, which she called an outstanding example of the grand style, and where roses were trained in vase patterns on the tennis court enclosure. Ponds were shaded by Japanese maples and the massive copper beech was already renowned. Invergowrie, also on the Southern Highlands, built in the English manner, with northern hemisphere, autumn-colouring trees, with bluebell woods and rhododendron dells, by the Danish landscaper Paul Sorensen for the Hoskins industrialist family, was also admired. Their owners shared a familiar vocabulary with Beatrice Bligh.

Deep borders hugged the house at Pejar Park, just as in the English gardens that Beatrice had visited and just as Walling's writing had advised. Her garden beds were filled with heavily perfumed November lilies, with valerian which happily self seeded, with delphiniums and foxgloves. There were soft grey senecios, lavenders and stachys. Groundcovers of the blue-flowering vinca, of violets and forget-me-nots were essential in creating a low-maintenance garden.

Beatrice loved climbers covering any upright surface, a habit observed during tours of English and European gardens, and one that when used in the very different Australian conditions annoyed Leonard, who had the job of removing them from drainpipes and roof tiles, and coping with the spiders and possums who availed themselves of the easy access into the roof. A high wall was built on the northern side of the house, dividing the front garden from the back. 'Beurre Bosc' and 'William' fruiting pears were espaliered there on wires, in the manner Beatrice had seen in Switzerland and in English country gardens. 'I was inspired to copy the superb esp-alier work I had seen on the houses in Switzer-land and Austria where not even a division between win-dows would be space wasted, and it was all a fas-cinating experiment,' she wrote in *Down to Earth*. She loved the brilliant new green of the hawthorn hedges emerging from their bare winter bones throughout the English countryside when she

Beatrice loved climbers: here, jasmine jostles with clematis.

was there in April 1959. She loved the thornless, white, cream or golden yellow Banksia rose, wisteria and clematis. 'We have so much English in our makeup,' she wrote in the manuscript for a third book that she was preparing. Although, according to her daughter, she was no admirer of Australian native plants within the 'garden proper' she saw that there was a place for plants from South Africa, with its similar climate:

SO MANY PARTS OF SOUTH AFRICA REMINDED ME OF AUSTRALIA THAT I CANNOT HELP THINKING THAT THEIR BEAUTIFUL PALE GREEN THORN TREE WOULD BE EFFECTIVE HERE ... ITS BRILLIANT NEW GREEN WAS A REFRESHING CONTRAST TO THE BEIGE SURROUNDINGS.[22]

Perhaps the most important feature of the garden at Pejar Park, however, was the large lake that Beatrice created just beyond the park. Water was pivotal to the aesthetic of this garden, as it was to other country gardens. In all farming areas throughout Australia, prosperity is determined by water. Bores are sunk, if viable, where rainfall is inadequate, dams are built, creating miracles; hearts break when the salt-water table rises, killing trees, and destroying gardens and pastures. Orchards are planted on slopes to garner any run-off in what Beatrice called 'the unending search for the management of water'. Without water, as Henry Lawson noted, even geraniums struggle. Without water there are no cooling streams to look down upon, no pools for reflection, no fountains to create the peaceful sounds of water falling over stone or metal surfaces. Water for reticulation had, from the mid twentieth century, fostered the development of the sward of green lawn, quickly becoming an essential part of any good garden, whether in the suburbs of the city, or in the country. With water, rich borders of soft and thirsty flowers become more than just a dream, gleaned from impracticable glossy garden books; vegetable gardens can become productive, fruit will be sweet.

The lake at Pejar Park—Beatrice discreetly referred to it as a pond— was a large kidney-shaped body of water that created a natural transition

from the formal garden to the landscape beyond. Only two-thirds extended into the garden proper, so that the stock could drink at the other side. She planted the edges with swathes of water iris and arum lilies, with bulrushes, spring blossom trees and weeping willows. 'I visualised a peaceful pool where I could watch the wild ducks cruising in perfect formation or continually upending themselves in search of treasure in the water below,' she wrote.[23]

Beatrice did not write of a love of the native plants of Australia nor those indigenous to the Southern Tablelands. While eucalypts were used strategically in the paddocks, to bring the garden into the landscape, there were no Australian trees in the garden proper. It appears that the Australian landscape in the background was simply part of the garden picture she was creating—as she had seen in large English gardens—not incorporated because she considered it beautiful.

Lucinda Nicholson does not remember her mother loving the surrounding bush:

IT WAS OFTEN VERY DROUGHT STRICKEN AND HORRIBLE ... THOUGH SHE DEFINITELY CREATED WINDOWS TO WHERE THE SHEEP GRAZED ... BUT THEY WERE MERE WINDOWS. SHE USED THAT WORD. SHE LIKED THE SHEEP TO COME TO DRINK AT THE OTHER SIDE OF THE DAM ... BUT SHE

left and right: Pejar Park today, photographed in spring

previous pages: Beatrice loved the high country of the Snowy Mountains.

left: Many a country garden has been happy to allow the tough periwinkle *Vinca major* to make itself at home.

centre: *Malus floribunda*, the first of the crabapples to flower in spring

right: Beatrice loved the natural forms of roses like the Cherokee rose (*R. laevigata*), naturalised in North America after arriving from China in the late eighteenth century.

SPENT HER WHOLE LIFE TRYING TO SCREEN THE SHEARING SHED FROM THE HOUSE. THERE WAS A HUGE EFFORT TO SCREEN THE SHEARING SHED. THERE WAS THE DAM, THEN THERE WERE THOSE HAWTHORNS BEHIND, THEN THE CONIFERS ... SHE WAS CREATING A STAGE. SHE DIDN'T WANT JUST THIS OASIS AND THEN THE DRY BARREN LAND. THERE HAD TO BE A GRADING AS YOU WENT OUT INTO THE HILLS.[24]

However, Beatrice's love of the Australian Alps does indicate that she admired the Australian landscape—provided it was kept in its place, outside the garden gate.

Beatrice Bligh was among the earliest generation of women for whom there were choices in life—even though she remained a product of her background and education. Leonard was consulted about the garden, but the ideas and decisions belonged to Beatrice and Lucinda recalls the garden dominating her mother's life.[25] Each year she would instigate the enhancement of another area: one year a new pergola would be built, the next more paving. Unlike women of one or two generations before her, Bligh never employed a full-time gardener. Demographics had changed after World War II, when labour became short and young people left rural areas to find work in the cities, demanding higher wages. As well, according to those who remember her, Beatrice prided herself in being able to work physically in the garden—although this did not mean that she was beyond hijacking any young jackaroo who happened to be on the station to help

her with the weeding.[26] Her twin sons, Hugh, who now runs Pejar Park, and Michael, remember their mother working like a man. At Braidwood Jock Mackay recalls, 'They never had a gardener; we never had a gardener. It wasn't just economics. If you do it yourself you do it your way.'

That Beatrice Bligh had great energy is personified by the garden she created. Her attitude to hard work, diligence and perseverance is also expressed in the title page inscription to *Down to Earth*. She quotes Rudyard Kipling:

... SUCH GARDENS ARE NOT MADE BY SINGING: 'OH, HOW BEAUTIFUL!' AND SITTING IN THE SHADE ...

Life in the country, while privileged in the good years of high wool and beef prices, could also be extremely difficult and often frightening. Popular literature, Australian history, women's diaries and oral history describe a litany of trials that city women might never have imagined. There were plagues of grasshoppers to contend with, and flies; there were possums and parrots that ruined orchards and precious rose gardens, rabbits to ring-bark young trees, and wombats to dig huge holes under trees and in the centre of carefully nurtured lawns. The threat of bushfire was ever present in summer; the country was either in a state of drought or ravaged by floods. There were man-made tribulations too: Beatrice told of a jackaroo who spilled kerosene at regular intervals across the lawn on his way to poison the tennis-court weeds.

Of the vicissitudes in the life of a country gardener, she wrote:

I CAN REMEMBER SWARMS OF GRASSHOPPERS DESCENDING ON US SEEM-
INGLY OVERNIGHT; THE ONLY SPRAY THAT KILLED THEM WAS A SHEEP-
DIP, BUT AFTER SPRAYING THERE SEEMED TO BE JUST AS MANY AS
BEFORE, REMOVING ALL THE LEAVES OF WHOLE TREES OVERNIGHT.
THERE WAS ANOTHER OCCASION WHEN I WENT AWAY FOR THE
WEEKEND, AND TWO HUNDRED SHEEP SPENT A DAY AND TWO NIGHTS
IN MY GARDEN ... THE MOB OF STATION HORSES HAVE BEEN LET IN BY
THE CHILDREN'S CUNNING PONY ON COUNTLESS OCCASIONS, AND
THEIR HOOVES SINK SIX OR EIGHT INCHES IN TO THE SOFT LAWNS.[27]

Beatrice Bligh country,
the Southern Tablelands
of New South Wales

Like Walling and West, Beatrice Bligh influenced gardeners throughout New South Wales; as well as her books, her lectures throughout the state are part of her legacy. Her two books, *Down to Earth,* which was followed by *Cherish the Earth,* published posthumously in 1973, are loved by generations of gardeners. Beatrice's books enjoyed nothing like the audience of Edna Walling's, however. She wrote from the heart, but for gardeners like herself, who were familiar with the design ideals she described—or at least were interested. She was not writing for the new wave of 'home gardeners' with small city gardens, for whom gardening had also become a hobby. She was not writing for the waves of migrant gardeners, to whom every square of a small front and back garden was to be put to fruit and vegetable production.

Beatrice had written much of the text for a third book, a gardening manual, in a light-hearted, chatty style, when she died on 18 January 1973 at Goulburn.[28] She had left detailed instructions for her funeral service at Canberra, where she was cremated, and for her memorial service at St Philip's, Bungendore. She was fifty-six years old.

Toward the end of her life, as her gardening style matured, and no doubt influenced by her earlier love of the high country, and her mentor, Edna Walling, Beatrice professed to being captured by the Australian landscape. She came to appreciate that the surroundings, the Australian bush, could be aesthetically incorporated into the reconstructed landscape, that of the garden. 'We should be careful to cherish any native trees which may exist and avoid surrounding them with exotics which might interfere with their individual dignity, and perhaps obstruct the natural outlook,' she wrote in the manuscript for her third book, and in contrast to her earlier thoughts and ideas.[29] She planned to start each chapter with a verse from Dorothea McKellar's poem 'My Country':

> I love a sunburnt country,
> a land of sweeping plains,
> Of ragged mountain ranges,
> Of droughts and flooding rains,
> I love her far horizons,
> I love her jewel-sea,
> Her beauty and her terror—
> The wide brown land for me![30]

Beatrice Bligh left no diaries and only a few letters to and from her survive, but her two published books show that the garden provided the focus to her life. She has inspired a generation of gardeners, just as the words of her mentors influenced the creation of Pejar Park.

As a girl, Beatrice would ride across the hills and plains

BOOK THREE

TOWARDS AN AUSTRALIAN STYLE
1945–2000

Prologue

Gravetye Manor: once home to William Robinson,
often called the father of English, natural, gardening.
Today it is a wonderful country house hotel.

When we think of English gardens today we imagine green lawns and voluptuous flowering borders, created within a comparatively homogenous climate and from a relatively consistent palette of plant material. We imagine soft colours and forgiving, misted light. French gardens rely upon structure and formality, on severely clipped hedges and parterres which may house a mass of seasonal flowers. Italian gardens pay tribute to the clear light, the climate and the landscape in which they are set, and rely upon a restricted index of evergreen conifers, stone and water for their character.

But what makes an Australian garden? In this country, the quality of the light distinguishes the landscape absolutely from gardens of the northern hemisphere. This is most clearly demonstrated by observing it through the photographer's lens. In Australia, the light is so severe that the only time to photograph gardens is in the 'magic hours' just after dawn and before sunset. At any other time of the day the harsh light will bleach all detail from a photograph.

Native flowers are brightly coloured to counteract this light. The native wisteria (*Hardenbergia violacea*) is a brilliant blue and *Kennedia* (commonly called the running postman), that Georgiana Molloy admired, is a bright red. But Australia's indigenous flora is most often depicted in literature or art as washed with muted colours, with olive or yellow-greens, and with grey or silver foliage.

It takes a mature eye to appreciate the subtle beauty of the twisted snow gum (*Eucalyptus pauciflora*), its silver trunk bent against the sleety winds of the high plains of the Snowy Mountains. The charcoal black, confronting strength of the furrowed trunks of the mugga ironbark (*Eucalyptus sideroxylon* 'Rosea'), so loved by Kath Carr, is not immediately evident to those used to learning about gardens from coffee-table books written for northern hemisphere

conditions. It takes time to appreciate that Australian trees do change with the seasons, as the Sydney blue gum (*Eucalyptus saligna*) strips its bark each summer, in great, seeping, sticky leather straps to reveal a smooth, renewed trunk splashed vibrantly with ochres, pinks and greens. It's only with familiarity that we can appreciate the scent of eucalypt oil that hovers over the gum forest, and bask in its warmth—rather than wince when confronted with its heat.

While it is not surprising that Australian gardeners have long abhorred, or at best ignored, indigenous flora—after all, many middle-aged female gardeners were raised on a literary diet of May Gibbs' 'gumnut baby' books and their terrifying tormentors, the Banksia Men—quiet contemplation among the pastel pinks, blues, yellows and creams of alpine meadows, or in the acacia woodlands, or forests of eucalypts, reveals numerous beauties.

There are many aspects of the Australian bush, however, that suggest it is tough and uncompromising. The ground from which native grasses, paper daisies and wattles spring is often comprised of granite: it is hard, ridden with boulders and stones. It reflects the heat, throwing up a shimmering, bloated haze, fat with the scent of eucalyptus. The eucalypt, the mint bush and the tea tree are perfectly adapted to survive the unforgiving climate. Leaves are small, narrow and brittle, nature's adaptations to the brutal environment of infertile soils and meagre rainfall. An inexperienced eye might see this vegetation only as drab, lifeless and unchanging, and, perhaps worst of all, supremely untidy. It is not surprising that the earliest European settlers gazed upon this Australian landscape with horror, little able and often unwilling to see its subtleties. It is easy to understand why they longed for the lush, mid to deep green of the deciduous trees and soft cover of the northern hemisphere, fed by high rainfall, cool temperatures and a short growing season.

Bougainvillea flowers at
Anna Creek Station

Australia is a continent of extraordinary diversity. Its size and the enormous variations in its soil, topography and rainfall, dictate that no one style of garden will suit each corner of the country. The eastern seaboard, where some 80 per cent of the population of 20 million live, within 50 kilometres of the coastline, is separated from 'out west' or 'the bush' by the Great Dividing Range, known colloquially as the 'Great Divide' or 'the Divide'. This mountain range runs from the northernmost point of tropical Queensland, with its rainfall of up to 4000 millimetres each year, to Melbourne, the capital city of Victoria in the south, a city now into its fourth year of water restrictions. Gardens in Queensland, which should be cut back and fertilised fortnightly to counteract the rapid rate of vegetative growth and nutrient depletion due to the high rainfall, contrast with those in Victoria. They are vastly different from those created at, for instance, Ivanhoe, in the far west of New South Wales, where rainfall is 125 millimetres in a good year and which rely on drought-tolerant species such as emu bush (*Eremophila* spp.), native to the arid regions of inland Australia, saltbush and succulents that require little or no water. But gardens in some outback regions, created in town or on country properties watered by the irrigation schemes of the great Murray, Darling and Goulburn rivers, can indulge in a diverse range of plants, from tropical palms to cold-climate bulbs.

The size of stations, or pastoral 'runs', also varies greatly in Australia, dependent upon the availability of water. On the eastern side of the Divide, where much of the soil is volcanic and land can sustain many head of cattle or sheep per hectare, properties may be commercially viable at just a few hundred hectares. West of the Divide, where soils can be fragile and rainfall scarce, properties are vast, large enough to be marked on maps. A few hours' drive from the

The Australian outback: here,
the Breakaways, near Coober Pedy

Giant pigface, *Carpobrotus acinaciformis*

South Australian opal mining town of Coober Pedy, Anna Creek Station, the world's largest cattle station, is 24 000 square kilometres of salt pan, lakes, rivulets and saltbush in the South Australian desert, and sustains just one head of cattle per square kilometre. You can fly for more than two hours and not leave Anna Creek Station air space.

Days can reach 50 °C in summer at Anna Creek Station, although winter nights can be freezing and spring brings frosts. But they garden there. The tough, carpet-forming silver convolvulus (*C. althaeoides*) and the white-flowered bush convolvulus or morning glory (*C. cneorum*) are favourites. The bright red bougainvillea 'Mrs Butt' does well along with *B. glabra* 'Magnifica' with its purple flowers. The ground-covering pigface (*Carpobrotus* spp.) which needs no water at all, flowers in hot colours in November, and the native emu bush, grevilleas, potato vine and the native wisteria all form the matrix to this garden. The indigenous paperbarks (*Melaleuca* spp.) and the Flinders wattle (*Acacia iteaphylla*) grow side by side with the endemic coolibah (*Eucalyptus microtheca*). The white cedar (*Melia azedarach*) and the pepper tree (*Schinus areira*) love the dry conditions, as do oleanders, the rhododendron of the desert. Yellow-flowering lantana covers the ground along with *Plumbago* 'Royal Cape'.

There are no soft, water-loving, English species in this garden, for the brutality of the climate forced other choices, but the layout of the garden and the arrangement of plants bow to those of the English gardens displayed in the myriad glossy gardening books sent by British publishers to subsidiary offices in Australia. Despite the diversity of the continent, the gardens created in Australia over the past two centuries have been largely derivative of, and have mimicked, an Anglo-Saxon heritage.

A BRIDGE BETWEEN TWO WORLDS

Would that I could gather your houses into my hand, and like a sower scatter them in forests and meadow.

Would the valleys were your streets and the green paths your alleys, that you might seek one another through vineyards, and come with the fragrance of the earth in your garments.

KAHLIL GIBRAN The Prophet, 1923[1]

Edna Walling 1895–1973

In 1952 Australia's most celebrated female garden designer, Edna Walling, wrote in her fourth book, *Country Roads: The Australian Roadside*:

THOUGH THERE IS NO BRILLIANT FOLIAGE COLORATION IN AUTUMN, NO EXCITING BURST OF BUD IN SPRING, NO EXQUISITE TRACERY OF THE BRANCHES IN WINTER, AND NONE OF THE 'GREEN THOUGHT IN A GREEN SHADE' IN SUMMER ABOUT THE AUSTRALIAN LANDSCAPE, THE THOUGHT OF ANY JOURNEY TO A PLACE WHERE THE TREES AND NATURAL GROUND COVER ARE STILL UNSPOILT IS THRILLING TO ME. NOTHING CAN EQUAL THE EXHILARATING JOY OF THOSE EXQUISITE PIECES OF LANDSCAPE IN WHICH THE PLANT GROUPS ARE STILL HAPPILY JOINED TOGETHER.[2]

An accolade for Australian indigenous plants, indeed—but this was the mature Walling speaking, in the thirtieth year of her career, and these words represented a paradigm shift for the designer. The year before, 1951, she had planned her first 'native garden' and the Western District pastoralists were less than impressed. The landscape gardens for which Walling was, by this time, renowned, employed sweeping drystone walls, expansive bodies of water and magnificent vistas, and were replete with collections of plants from the northern hemisphere. These gardens carried clear messages of success and power, of good taste and refinement—and of British power over its ex-colonies. A garden of Australian plants was just not going to convey the desired information.

Edna Walling's design career can be divided into two distinct periods. Her early gardens demonstrate a love for the English plants of her childhood and the influence of the design partnership of Edwin Lutyens and Gertrude Jekyll, whose gardens in turn paid homage to the discipline,

structure and formality of the Italian Renaissance. With maturity Walling became captivated by Australia; by its light, its water masses, the arrangement of its indigenous flora, by the natural landscape. Walling's two design periods could be considered metaphors for the social changes taking place in Australia: the exchange of the constraints of Empire for a post-colonial appreciation of Australian nationhood.

If Una Falkiner was gardening with visions of Empire firmly in sight, if Winifred West was creating gardens within an Australian setting that, nevertheless, spoke of her English heritage, and Beatrice Bligh was inspired by the landscape gardens of England, Edna Walling provided the turning point towards an appreciation of the use of Australian native plants within the garden boundary. Walling bridged the old and the new: she promoted a move away from gardens that sought to replicate those of England to gardens that described an emerging Australian vernacular. Her work exemplified the maturing of Australian garden design into a style that was comfortable within the unique landscape in which it rested. And Walling showed women that they could cross the accepted gender boundaries of the time and demand a career outside marriage.

Edna Margaret Walling was born in Yorkshire, England, on 4 December 1895. The younger daughter of William and Margaret Walling, she spent most of her childhood in the small village of Bickleigh, on the southern edge of Dartmoor, in Devon, and attended the 'best school in Plymouth' before a business disaster forced her father to transfer her to the local convent. She was more interested in nature and drawing, however, than in

left: The Devon moors, in England, over which Walling walked as a child

centre: The Grampians, in Victoria's Western District, a place that Edna Walling loved as an adult

right: The grass trees (*Xanthorrhoea* spp.) of the Grampians

lessons. In an unpublished article Walling wrote that her father had hoped for a boy and brought her up as such, showing her how to use tools and teaching her woodwork, a skill that she would later put to full use. A devout Christian Scientist, he would also stride out with her across the moors, teaching her to observe nature in all its forms. From these walks she developed her lasting 'intense love of low-growing plants, of mauves and soft greens, of mossy boulders and gritty pathways and closely nibbled turf'. She wrote that this was, 'the type of garden I love best'.[3]

The Walling family travelled to New Zealand when Edna was sixteen, before arriving in Melbourne three years later. There, in 1916, her mother convinced her to enrol at the School of Horticulture at Burnley in Melbourne (now Burnley College, University of Melbourne), at a time when gardening was still considered mainly a job for men. After what Walling depicts as two somewhat desultory and austere years where she found the study uninspiring, she emerged from Burnley with horticultural qualifications. She was later to write of that time '… so began two years of insubordination, fittingly brought to a close with an illuminated certificate which magnificently refrained from telling the world all that I did not know!'

In about 1919, while on holiday and peering over garden fences, she saw a large, curving stone wall supporting a semi-circular terrace and, as she describes it:

Edna Walling was likely to have been influenced by the natural plantings in Gertrude Jekyll gardens. Here, the meadow garden of The Manor House at Upton Grey

I WAS FASCINATED. I STOOD THERE DRINKING IT IN ... THAT WALL CAUGHT MY IMAGINATION. I SHALL BUILD WALLS. FROM THEN ON, GARDENS FOR ME BECAME A CHANCE TO CARRY OUT THE ARCHITECTURAL DESIGNS GOING AROUND IN MY HEAD ...[4]

This was a crucial moment for Walling; soon after, she persuaded an architect friend 'to let me design the garden for one of his houses. So one of his clients was persuaded to let me design his garden. I aimed to unite the house and garden.'[5] In less than a decade after graduating from Burnley her work as a garden designer was being lauded in the press.

Walling was an early environmentalist, influenced by her camping expeditions into the Australian bush. She wrote regularly to newspapers against urban development that she felt was inappropriate. In 1921, at twenty-five years of age, she purchased 1.5 hectares of land at Mooroolbark, now a suburb on the eastern outskirts of Melbourne and in the foothills of the Dandenong Ranges. There she built her first house, Sonning, from packing cases.[6] The next year she borrowed heavily to purchase an adjoining 8.2 hectares so that she could control what was built upon the landscape around her.

Walling also wrote on gardening and design for magazines and newspapers over a period of four decades. Her first garden column appeared in *The Home* in 1924; in 1925 her work appeared in *The Australian Woman's Mirror* and *The Australian Home Builder*. From that year she also wrote monthly for *The Australian Home Beautiful*, owned by the Herald and Weekly Times, run by Keith Murdoch, and later for Murdoch's *Adelaide News*, becoming a household name. In 1943 her first book, *Gardens in Australia*, was published and went into several editions. This was followed by *Cottage and Garden in Australia* in 1947 and *A Gardener's Log* the following year. *Country Roads: The Australian Roadside* was published in 1952. As well as giving her readers advice on the walls, paths and water features that were essential to her designs, she stressed that simplicity was crucial to a successful garden. Her writing made her a household name, and influenced even those who could not afford to commission her.

During her career, which spanned more than fifty years, Walling designed some 350 gardens around Australia, from Hobart and South Australia to Queensland, for some of the country's leading figures. The majority of her gardens were in Victoria in the affluent eastern suburbs of Melbourne and the 'hill station' properties at Mount Macedon and the Dandenong Ranges, as well as in the Western District, the centre of the state's pastoral elite. In South Australia she created gardens for successful city clients and in New South Wales grand country gardens for some of the leading grazing families, particularly on the Southern Tablelands.

Edna Walling was most productive in her garden design work at a time when women were starting to demand greater agency in their lives. After the Great War women were starting to expect that academic and professional qualifications would result in employment outside the accepted, unpaid, role of homemaker. The 1930s, the years of the Great Depression, were also a time when the proliferation of newspapers and magazines, along with radio, brought information—including about gardening—to a larger audience. But those who could commission Edna Walling expected her to create a garden that underlined their social position and the power that set them apart from most of the population.

A natural track leads into The Barn

The Walling gardens discussed in this chapter are mostly large country gardens, created for the wives of successful pastoralists. There are several reasons for this. First, Walling's gardens were not for those without substantial means, those who had the money to implement her bold designs and the leisure to develop and maintain them. Second, it is largely the country gardens that have survived, gracing properties inherited through generations, not bought as investments and sold for capital gain. Most of the gardens Walling designed in the city, mainly in Melbourne, have been sacrificed to the developer's bulldozer.

Walling's early gardens reflect her English heritage, and in turn mirror the aspirations of Anglo-Saxon Australians in the first half of the twentieth century. The gardens she created at Mooroolbark were examples of the English vision that pervaded most aspects of Australian life at this time. Walling had purchased the land at £50 an acre; she then subdivided and sold it at £100 an acre. She named it Bickleigh Vale, after the English village in which she was raised, and called it her 'Devonshire village'[7]. She retained control over the style of houses built 'to conform to English lines'[8] and the creation of English-style cottage gardens of foxgloves, hollyhocks and the Westmoreland thyme.

Apart from her own home, Sonning, Walling also built—or super-vised the building of—the other cottages in the group, including Downderry for her mother, Mistover, Lynton Lee and Good-a-Meavy, later named The Barn.[9] In each case she designed their gardens and provided the plants, 'to assure the future success of this adventure in the landscape development of a village'. She did not envisage that Bickleigh Vale would be a carefully planned garden suburb, however. 'Rather will it develop along haphazard lines that are more likely to produce a picturesque result,' she wrote in June 1934 in *The Australian Home Beautiful*, where the plan for the subdivision had been published four years earlier.

Downderry, at Bickleigh Vale, today

The cottages and their gardens, while English in design and planting, were to sit lightly on the canvas that was their Australian sur-roundings. In 'An Adventure in Rural Development' in *The Australian Handbook* in 1939, Walling wrote of the realisation of her dream for a development that would be peaceful, with buildings in keeping with their surroundings:

THERE IS A LITTLE VILLAGE OF NINE COTTAGES CALLED BICKLEIGH VALE ... EIGHTEEN ACRES [8 HECTARES] OF ROLLING FIELDS MADE A PEACEFUL SETTING FOR 'SONNING' AND WHEN THIS LAND WAS PUT UP

FOR SALE MY HEART SAGGED WITH THOUGHTS OF POULTRY FARMS, AND, EVEN WORSE, WEEK-END SHACKS AND NOISY OCCUPANTS ... AND SO IT WAS DECIDED THAT IF BUILT UPON IT MUST BE, I WOULD DO THE BUILDING. AND NOW THE LITTLE COTTAGES NESTLE INTO A LAND-SCAPE SET ABOUT WITH LOVELY-FOLIAGED TREES AND HEDGES OF FLOWERING SHRUBS BETWEEN, WITH QUIET PEOPLE HAPPILY WORKING IN THEIR GARDENS.

Walling advocated simplicity in all elements of design, so that nothing detracted from the integrity of the setting. The buildings were to be simple, of rock, timber and wooden shingles. 'The very simplest construction,' she later wrote in *Cottage and Garden*:

IS ALWAYS THE BEST. AS IN SO MANY OTHER THINGS IT IS BETTER TO STICK TO SIMPLICITY IN ORDER TO ESCAPE THAT 'NOVEL' EFFECT THAT SO SOON PALLS AND STAMPS A THING AS ORDINARY.[10]

Like so many colonial properties, the name of Walling's first home—after the picturesque village of Sonning on the River Thames in Berkshire, just outside London—reflected her English heritage. '"Sonning"', she wrote:

IS NOT, PERHAPS, A VERY APPROPRIATE NAME TO HAVE CHOSEN FOR THIS LITTLE HOME IN THE AUSTRALIAN COUNTRYSIDE, BUT IT WAS INEVITABLE. AT THE AGE OF SEVEN I WAS ROWED ON THE RIVER THAMES FROM READING ... TO THE LITTLE HAMLET OF SONNING, AND WAS SO ENTHRALLED THAT I MADE A VOW THAT WHEN I OWNED MY OWN LITTLE COTTAGE I WOULD CALL IT SONNING; SO DEEPLY DID THE SOFT-SOUNDING NAME BECOME ENGRAVED ON MY MIND ... HAD IT BEEN IN ALASKA OR THE SAHARA IT WOULD STILL HAVE BEEN 'SONNING' ... NO ATTEMPT HAS BEEN MADE TO COPY THE STYLE OF THE COTTAGES I SAW THERE: RATHER I TRIED TO BUILD SOMETHING THAT LOOKED HAPPIEST AND LEAST OBTRUSIVE IN THE SETTING IN WHICH IT HAS BEEN PLACED.[11]

There is much conjecture among those interested in garden design and history in Australia over the major influences upon Edna Walling's design career. The evidence reveals that in many ways Walling was a conflicted character. Her comments on her time at Burnley, which she portrays as uninspiring and somewhat uninformative, contradict the school's recollections of her performance. Examination records for 1917 indicate that Walling was one of the brightest in her class, with her instructors commenting that she was 'a very fine student, making excellent progress' and 'alert and hard-working'.[12]

The daffodil walk at Mawarra

Perhaps Walling felt that her talent was innate, and her ability to draw and design was a special gift. Later, she was to write to her favourite and most trusted stonemason, Eric Hammond (1898–1992), appealing to him not to divulge any of her design and construction secrets to other landscapers:

AS YOU KNOW ANY DESIGNING ABILITY I MAY HAVE IS NOT THE RESULT OF ANY UNIVERSITY COURSE OR ANY OTHER TUITION BUT IS PURELY A GIFT FROM ABOVE, AND APART FROM BEING MY BREAD AND BUTTER I AM ETERNALLY GRATEFUL FOR IT, AND FEEL THAT I MUST GUARD IT AGAINST ANY DUPLICATION.[13]

Walling's English upbringing certainly influenced the gardens she designed in the first part of her career. And Gertrude Jekyll, the English artist and garden designer popular in England at the time and available to an Australian audience through her many publications, was just one of several influences. (In 1936, when a devastating fire burnt 'Sonning the First', as Walling referred to it, to the ground along with all its contents, signed

GERTRUDE JEKYLL

Gertrude Jekyll (1843–1932) was already an acknowledged artist and craftswoman when deteriorating eyesight and a consultation with an eye specialist in 1891 resulted in her turning to gardening and garden design. By the time she died Jekyll had published a dozen books, the first of which, *Wood and Garden*, was released in 1899. Next came *Home and Garden* in 1900, then *Lilies for English Gardens* in 1901; *Wall and Water Gardens* was released the same year, *Roses for English Gardens* in 1902. *Old West Surrey* was published in 1904, *Flower Decoration for the House* in 1907, *Colour in the Flower Garden* and *Children and Gardens* in 1908 and *Gardens for Small Country Houses,* with Lawrence Weaver, in 1912. She also contributed almost a thousand articles to magazines including *Country Life, Gardening Illustrated* and *The Garden*—the creation of her friend, William Robinson (1838–1935), an advocate of an informal, natural or wild style—and widely available to gardeners in the colonies.

copies of Jekyll's books were lost.) The 1920s, when Jekyll was at her most active and was most celebrated as a garden designer, were the years when Edna Walling's ideas were being formulated.

The evidence presented through Walling's watercolour garden plans suggests that she was impressed by the structure of the Lutyens–Jekyll gardens, rather than simply by Jekyll's famed concentration on detailed colour borders of perennials—although, in 1929, Walling acknowledged Jekyll as 'one of the greatest writers on colour in the garden'. But Walling writes of her frustration with clients who sought to distract her from the big picture—from her walls, water, voids and expanses.

For comparisons between the structural aspects of Jekyll's designs and that of Walling we need look no further than The Deanery, an arrangement of rills, pools and stone steps, designed by Jekyll and Lutyens in 1901 at the English village of Sonning that Walling had loved as a child, and Mawarra in the Dandenong Ranges, designed by Walling from 1932 (when the property was called The Grove) and described by her as 'a symphony in steps and trees'. Each plan shows the designer's use of formal axis and structure, of flights of steps, both linear and semi-circular, of extensive use of stone, of geometric bodies of water and expert treatment of sloping land with terraces bound by walls of local stone. Jekyll used a mix of formal Italianate terracing with blowsy plantings of catmint, poppies, lavenders, rosemaries, gypsophila, campanulas, alyssum and tumbling clematis, all plants used by Walling in the earlier phase of her career.

Walling's design work also pays considerable tribute to the philosophies of landscape designer Geoffrey Jellicoe, who, with his colleague Jock Shepherd, published *Italian Gardens of the Renaissance* in 1925. A passage from this used by Walling to introduce her article 'The Design of the Garden', almost twenty years later, speaks clearly of the importance she placed upon structure in garden design:

PANDORA NEVER LOOSED A LIVELIER SPIRIT THAN THE ONE FOR EVER PARTING FANCY FROM DESIGN. IN THOSE RARE MOMENTS WHEN THE DEMON SLEEPS IS BORN A WORK THAT STANDS FOR ALL TIME. SO CAME INTO BEING THE FINEST OF THE ITALIAN GARDENS, WHERE, IN A WORLD OF BEAUTIFUL THOUGHTS, FANCY AND DESIGN ROAMED UNDIVIDED.[14]

Walling had first expressed this idea years earlier. 'There is little doubt that as we advance in the designing of our garden in Australia, we shall derive more and more inspiration from the old gardens of Italy,' she wrote in *The Australian Home Beautiful* in December 1933. 'The chief elements of the Italian Garden—stone, water and trees—are most appropriate to the conditions governing the construction of gardens in Australia.' [15]

Walling was also influenced by the work of the American writer Lewis Mumford (1895–1990), who wrote the first major dissertations of the modern era on the built environment, and that of the pre-eminent American landscaper of the nineteenth century, Frederick Law Olmsted (1822–1903), the 'Father of American Landscape Architecture'. Walling described Olmsted as 'one of the world's greatest landscape architects' and he was a clear influence in her later campaign to preserve the natural beauty of roadside plantings.[16] Towards the end of her life, the work of the American environmentalist and biologist Rachel Carson, with her warnings of the dangers of pesticides to the food chain articulated in her book *Silent Spring*, became more relevant to Walling as her views on conservation crystallised.

While Walling's work was, at least in part, derivative of that of the leading northern hemisphere designers of the nineteenth and early twentieth centuries, her greatest achievement was in providing a wide group of women with a means by which to assume power through the garden—either through following a career in design, or by creating their own gardens. Walling began her career at a time when both gender and class boundaries were clearly defined. As we

A chance meeting in May 1889 with the twenty-year-old architect Edwin Lutyens, when Jekyll was forty-six, resulted in a collaboration that left a legacy of gardens of exuberant plantings constrained within the formality of a structure borrowed from the Italian Renaissance, and observed during her travels on the Continent. While Jekyll is often remembered for her colour borders, she was as influenced by the chief elements of the Italian Garden—stone, water and evergreen trees—as by the decorative properties of plant material.

Walling, while fifty-three years Jekyll's junior, envied this creative partnership which resulted in house and garden being considered as a design whole, writing in 'Planning the Garden to Suit the House' in *The Australian Home Beautiful* in 1925 of the need for collaboration between garden designer and architect.

Nowhere is the collaboration between Gertrude Jekyll and Edwin Lutyens better demonstrated than at Hestercombe, the Somerset garden created from 1904. It was Jekyll's employment of water and stone, influenced by the structure and scale of the gardens of the Italian Renaissance, that most informed Edna Walling's approach to garden making.

Those three essentials of good gardens, water, stone and evergreens, were employed by Walling at Mawarra. Here, the stone work that was such an important part of the garden

have seen, in the early decades of the twentieth century middle and upper-class women married and created gardens as an acceptable creative outlet, not as a source of income. Decorative gardening was still a pursuit of the moneyed elite; those less wealthy were more likely to keep vegetable gardens. In the early twentieth century Australian leaders in the landscape design world were men like William Guilfoyle (1840–1912), most notable as the second director of Melbourne's Royal Botanic Gardens as well as for his work on many of Victoria's botanic gardens in country towns. Physical work in the garden was mostly carried out by labouring men; few women were involved in gardening in any professional way and those who wrote for publication used pen-names. The Victorian botanist and artist Jean Galbraith wrote a monthly column for *The Garden Lover* under the pseudonym 'Correa', the garden designer Emily Gibson wrote for the *Argus* as 'Culturalist', 'Wilma' wrote for *Everylady's Journal* and 'Trefoil' for the militant suffragist paper *The Sphere*. Even Walling, at the beginning of her career, adopted the pseudonym 'Barbery', although probably because she wanted to write for competing titles rather than any concern about the acceptance of women in paid employment.[17]

Walling, with a small group of women, crossed a number of these gender boundaries. Until she, with her colleagues, virtually stormed the gates of Burnley, women were allowed to attend two days per week but did not graduate with qualifications. Olive Mellor (1891–1978) became the first full-time female student at Burnley in 1914, and the first woman to graduate from the full Certificate of Competence course. By 1916, when Edna Walling enrolled, full-time classes for women students were an accomplished fact. 'Their rig-out,' wrote 'Wilma', 'is not un-like the bus girl's, with which we have become familiar—breeches, leggings and a tunic.'[18]

Walling's dress, particularly early in her career, set her apart from other women of the day and must have caused some interest, even disapproval. She was given to wearing a shirt, tie, jacket and jodhpurs—she had fourteen pairs—highly unconventional at a time when women wore breeches only for riding and, for that, were only just out of long skirts and side saddle. This manner of dress suggests that Walling and her colleagues were asserting their equality with men, and demanding to be given equal consideration at a time and in an environment where some male clients still considered that the professional world of landscape design was not for women.[19]

Walling set out her views on these issues early in her career, in a 1925 article for *The Australian Woman's Mirror* titled 'Garden Designing by Women'. 'Fortunately the women of to-day are showing a decided tendency not to take so readily the advice of the unimaginative male person with a predilection for palms and standard roses,' she wrote dismissively. Nevertheless, by the 1920s there was a lively debate taking place in newspapers and women's journals over whether women should be allowed to practise horticulture as a profession. The years after World War I saw cultural and social values upturned in Australia and, although women were expected to return to unpaid domestic work after the war, the barriers to women entering previously male-dominated fields were now less rigid.[20] 'Wilma' noted also that the Great War had provided new opportunities for women:

IT MEANT TIME AND PATIENCE BEFORE THEY WERE ALLOWED TO ENTER INTO COMPETITION WITH MEN, WHO LAUGHED AT THEIR PRETENSIONS AND ENDEAVOURED TO SHUT THEM OUT. THE LAUGH IS NOW WITH THE WOMEN, FOR THEY HAVE NOT ONLY MADE GOOD AT THE JOB, BUT MANY WOMEN PREFER THE GIRL GARDENER. NOT ONLY IS SHE MORE RELIABLE, BUT QUITE EFFICIENT, IS MORE DEPENDABLE, AND, THEY SAY, SHE GETS THROUGH THE WORK QUICKER.

As well as a new environment that accepted, however regretfully, that women would remain part of the workforce, it is possible that gardening, even when conducted as a profession by some women, was more acceptable than many other jobs as it was a natural extension of domestication, a 'feminine profession'. 'Wilma', in a 1927 article for *Everylady's Journal*, noted that the female aesthetic was particularly suited to gardening: 'Colour sense helps women to make a more artistic garden than a man, though in the early days a man generally did the rough work'. In addition, gardens were treated by women as intensely personal spaces, places where hopes and dreams could be invested. These spaces, and most particularly the plants within them, were also the recipients of their nurturing skills.

Snow gum (*Eucalyptus pauciflora*), in the Snowy Mountains that Walling loved.

Conversely, it is interesting to conjecture that, while the changing political climate and attitudes to women in careers may have allowed more women to enter this previously male area, Walling's somewhat dispassionate, even masculine approach to her designs was crucial in ensuring that she was the most successful of the handful of designing women who were emerging at this time.[21] Walling was a designer, not a plantswoman. She was unemotional about plants and employed that most important of design rules: plant many of just a few species. For Walling, unmarried and without children, gardening was not about the feminisation, the domestication, of space, as it had been for pioneer settler women in the previous century. Walling was not nurturing a space to create a familiar place for herself; she was not nest-building. She imposed her will upon nature with a ruthless, professional vision, as an artist creating a work upon a canvas. She was rearranging spaces into more pleasing forms within the context of space and scale, upon which she placed such importance. 'There's no sentiment about my job,' she declared, 'though some gardens do develop into such pets that one hates to part with them; but when a contract is finished, it means good-bye to that particular garden, and, like the builder, one passes on to the next work to hand'.[22] And of plants and planting she wrote, 'Often I have longed for a collaborator to whom I could hand over this side of the garden making while I go on with more building'.[23] Even her development of house and garden 'packages' at Mooroolbark had been undertaken in a business-like manner, essentially to prevent the encroachment of development she considered unattractive. 'Wilma' described Walling's professional attitude:

ASKED WHAT DIRECTED HER ENERGY IN THIS SPECIALISED WORK, SHE SHRUGGED SLIGHTLY AND ANSWERED WITH A MASCULINE DIRECTNESS, CHARACTERISTIC OF HER ATTITUDE TOWARD LIFE IN GENERAL: 'I DON'T KNOW, IT JUST CAME MY WAY, AND IT FASCINATED ME.' ONE COULDN'T PICTURE HER SOMEHOW IN ANY OTHER JOB. HER BREEZY PERSONALITY IS FRANKLY BOYISH AND DECIDEDLY UNIQUE. IT SUGGESTS WIDE SPACES AND LONG TRAMPS IN THE OPEN. PARLOUR DIVERSIONS, LITTLE FEMININE TRICKS AND WILES WOULD FIND NO PLACE IN HER LIFE, SO CROWDED WITH PRACTICAL INTERESTS.[24]

Walling's somewhat detached approach to the gardens she designed set her apart from her clients. Her clients wanted gardens to domesticate and familiarise the broad, and—given the vicissitudes of the Australian climate—often unsympathetic, landscape in which they found themselves. A beautiful garden was a way in which the wealthy underlined their position in society. For the wives, the garden provided a window into their lives, reflecting, they hoped, their idyllic situation. To Walling, however, the garden was none of these things, but rather a professional commission.

Paths wind naturally through Edna Walling gardens.

The earliest Walling plan that survives is the 1920 'Proposed Treatment of Garden on the Property of L. Heath, Esq.' in Toorak. This was followed by designs for many other gardens in Toorak and nearby suburbs, for sections of the Melbourne Zoological Gardens and for Victorian country properties. By the late 1920s, Walling's success was becoming recognised. 'The College heads are very proud of Miss Edna Walling, whose ability they seasoned with scientific lore,' wrote 'Wilma' in *Everylady's Journal*:

AS AN EXPERT DESIGNER, AND ONE WHO IS RATHER A GENIUS AT HER JOB, MELBOURNE IS BEGINNING TO VALUE HER, FOR IN THE LAST SIX YEARS SHE HAS GIVEN US A NUMBER OF LOVELY SUBURBAN GARDENS, EXPRESSIONS OF PASTORAL DELIGHT, AND MOREOVER, A FIT SETTING TO THE HOMES THEY MATERIALLY ASSIST TO BEAUTIFY.[25]

Walling undertook commissions for many prominent Australians. They included the internationally renowned soprano Dame Nellie Melba, Alice Paterson, the wife of 'Banjo' Paterson, and the newspaper magnates Keith Murdoch and Sir Frank Packer.

Wairere, near Mansfield in Victoria's high country, designed in 1925 for Major and Mrs Foster Rutledge and thought to be her first country

Wairere, in the Victorian high country, is thought to be Walling's first country garden.

garden, demonstrated the young Walling's lack of experience as well as her enthusiasm. Her vision for the 1.5 hectare garden resulted in a wide front lawn encircled by a gravel carriage-drive lined with formal herbaceous borders and a languid drystone wall separating the flower garden from the lawns and parkland. Other features were up-scale pergolas and extensive trellises covered with rambling *wichuriana* roses mixed with wisteria, a hazelnut walk underplanted with bulbs and a sunken rose garden. There were sheltered garden seats and secret corners, and a large vegetable and fruit garden. It was a romantic—that is, English—but high-maintenance garden, as the owners realised when their gardener left in 1940 to join the army.

Another of Walling's earliest commissions was for Mrs Keith Murdoch, now Dame Elisabeth, who was nineteen and just married. Walling, who was writing for *The Australian Home Beautiful,* was engaged in 1929 to design the garden at the Murdoch property, Cruden Farm, on the Mornington Peninsula, south of Melbourne.

While it is today a beautiful garden, its design demonstrates that at this early stage in her career, Walling was not infallible. The curving sweep of the drive was in place when Elisabeth Murdoch arrived as a young bride. The lemon-scented eucalypts (*Corymbia citriodora*) with their ghostly, smooth grey trunks, were chosen by Dame Elisabeth after the garden had been designed. She had loved them as a child, at home in Toorak, an exclusive Melbourne suburb, and had wanted them planted close to give the effect of an avenue. At Cruden Farm Walling installed two small-scale walled gardens reminiscent of landscape gardens in the English countryside and the cottage gardens of the villages. One, which housed perennial flower borders, also featured fruit trees espaliered on the walls; the other garden was for roses. Both soon proved unsuitable, the spaces too small, creating an overheated micro-climate. Cruden Farm demonstrates that the young designer was still learning the behaviour of the plant material she was using, was still experimenting with scale and space, and was still to understand what would thrive in the difficult Australian climate. Perhaps she assumed that her client, the wife of one of Melbourne's most prominent citizens, would want a garden that emulated those of England.

Walling's affection for the pretty, flowering shrubs of the northern hemisphere is demonstrated in much of her writing. In 1933 she told her readers about the plants she loved—the crabapples, the flowering plums and hawthorns, hedges of white, pink and red-flowering japonica, the autumn-colouring silver birch and poplars; all plants of her English heritage:

ALL THE DEEP ROSE COLORED FLOWERING APPLES ARE SIMILAR IN HABIT, MALUS ALDENHAMENSIS, M. ELEYII, M. NIEDSWETZKYANA AND M. FLORIBUNDA PURPUREA, AND WITH MALUS SPECTABILIS AT EACH CORNER THE EFFECT SHOULD BE VERY CHARMING IN SPRING AND AUTUMN. SPECTABILIS HAS DELICATE PINK FLOWERS AND IS MORE UPRIGHT GROWING THAN THE DARKER FLOWERED VARIETIES; THE YELLOW FRUIT IN AUTUMN CONTRASTING WITH THE DEEP RED FRUIT OF THE OTHER VARIETIES, THE PALE PINK FLOWERS AGAINST THE DEEP ROSE FLOWERS AND THE CONTRAST OF FORM IN WINTER WILL ALL HELP TO ACCENTUATE THE CORNERS.[26]

The scented viburnums found a place in many Walling gardens. Here, *Viburnum* x *carlcephalum*

She was still designing and planting according to visions of England when quoted in a 1939 interview:

WITH A TYPICALLY ENGLISH HOUSE ENGLISH TREES SHOULD BE EMPLOYED IN THE LANDSCAPE SCHEME. I KNOW OF ONE GARDEN SURROUNDING SUCH A HOME WHERE THE MAIN LANDSCAPE FEATURE WAS A GROUP OF THREE LOVELY POPLARS. NEW OWNERS HAD THESE UPROOTED IN FAVOUR OF AUSTRALIAN TREES, AND THE WHOLE EFFECT WAS LOST. NOT THAT I DO NOT LOVE THE GUMS IN LARGE AUSTRALIAN GARDENS.[27]

Seven years later she felt the same way. In *Gardens in Australia—Their Design and Care,* she wrote of one of her signature plantings, a copse of purple-leaved birch (*Betula pendula* 'Purpurea') set against a plain wall:

THE PURPLE-LEAFED FORM OF THE SILVER BIRCH DOES NOT SEEM TO ENJOY MUCH FAVOUR, POSSIBLY DUE TO THE FACT THAT IT IS A LITTLE THIN IN HABIT. HOWEVER THERE ARE POSITIONS IN WHICH IT IS QUITE GOOD. SOMETIMES TREES ARE NEEDED MORE FOR SOFTENING WALLS THAN TO PROVIDE DENSE SHADE. AGAINST A WHITE PLASTERED WALL THE TRACERY OF THE BLACKISH BRANCHES, WHICH CHARACTERIZES THIS TREE IN WINTER, MAKES AN EXQUISITE PICTURE.[28]

A study of Edna Walling's work cannot avoid pointing out some contradictions in her career. Tension was created by her appreciation of the Australian bush from the earliest days of her career while, nevertheless, constructing gardens influenced by her childhood in the English country-side. But even in her 'English phase' Walling was never a box-hedges-and-spaded-edges designer. She hated lawns too manicured, edges too trimmed. Of thymes, phlox, veronica and other creeping plants, she wrote,

'They … will form a much prettier edge than that meticulous curve or the perfect straight line'.[29] And she dictated that the most pleasing setting for a house was with grass rolling up to the building.[30]

She described her admiration for relaxed and spontaneous plantings of Chinese forget-me-nots, columbines and sweet william, all jostling for position in a garden. 'Really, for gate-crashing, commend me to foxgloves,' she wrote. While she was influenced by the formal lines and strong bones of Italian gardens, she liked her plants to grow seemingly naturally and in happy profusion. She outlined her garden philosophy in one early article, published in March 1929 in *Australian Home Beautiful* where, in sentiments reflected in the words of Beatrice Bligh, she admonished against 'those dreadful examples of "formal" gardens that are generally made up of beds and borders painfully suggestive of the pastrycook's art'.[31] In another article she advised her readers to be bold in the design, scale and planting of their gardens:

HOWEVER, WHEN, OR IF, YOU SUCCEED IN PERSUADING YOURSELF TO TAKE A BOLD COURSE, BE SURE THAT IT IS BOLD, AND DON'T SUCCUMB TO THE TEMPTATION TO REDUCE THE BREADTH OF THE BORDERS WHERE THEY ARE TO EXTEND INTO THE LAWN. IF YOU DO YOU WILL HAVE NEITHER ONE THING NOR THE OTHER.[32]

Eric Hammond was Edna Walling's favoured stonemason. His work is seen here at Markdale.

Like Beatrice—and Kath Carr, another gardener whom she inspired—Walling had definite ideas on colour. She loathed garish or bright colours, disliked red, recommending swathes of gentle pinks, blues and lilac, with white to light up corners or to reflect in the moonlight.[33] In her first article, written with Katharine Ballantyne for *Woman's World*, 1 September 1924, it is clear that Walling considered too-bright colours vulgar, a sin of over-enthusiasm more likely to be committed by men:

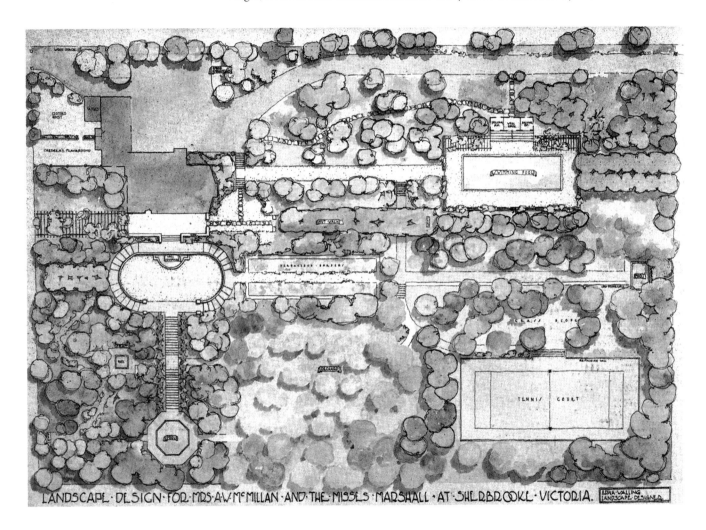

LANDSCAPE · DESIGN · FOR · MRS · A·W·MCMILLAN · AND · THE · MISSES · MARSHALL · AT · SHERBROOKE · VICTORIA.

Edna Walling's
watercolour plan of
the gardens at Mawarra
Courtesy of Mr Jess Exiner

THERE ARE ALSO SOME LAMENTABLE RESULTS WHERE MAN, THE OSTEN-TATIOUS, HAS ROOTED UP EVERYTHING ON THE LANDSCAPE, AND CREATED SUCH BELLIGERENT EFFECTS AS MOST CAREFULLY-TRAINED AND CIVILISED STANDARD ROSES AGAINST A BACKGROUND OF GRIM ROCK. OF COURSE THERE IS NO MORE HOPE OF TEAM WORK UNDER SUCH CIRCUMSTANCES THAN THERE IS BETWEEN RED GERANIUMS AND PURPLE IRISES.

She wanted her plantings, even of exotics, to be as natural, as wild as possible. Walling's words on the subject remain relevant today. In *Gardens in Australia—Their Design and Care*, she instructed:

THE GARDEN MAKER SOON BECOMES KEENLY OBSERVANT AND BY CULTIVATING A WATCHFUL EYE LEARNS MUCH THAT CANNOT BE FOUND IN BOOKS. RETURNING FROM THE COUNTRY YOU WILL REMEMBER HOW THOSE TREES WERE CLOSELY CLUSTERED.[34]

Among the reasons that Walling is so celebrated is the large repository of words that she left. The exquisite watercolour plans that she executed for clients in the 1920s and 1930s is another reason she is considered so skilled. These are works of art in themselves; the bones that would be laid down in the finished garden are strongly articulated on paper, but as ethereal in their delicate colouring as the finished product is light upon the landscape. Walling sketched the design first in 6B pencil on cartridge paper and then in Windsor and Newton watercolours—the very best—on Watman's hand-made paper, her elegant lettering executed in Indian ink with a mapping pen and a fine nib. It is due in part to the fact that she used materials of such fine quality that the plans survive so many decades later.

Walling's talent also lay in selecting gifted contractors, people she trusted to implement her designs faithfully. Among the best known were her master landscape contractor, Eric Hammond, who worked with her throughout her career, and her other preferred garden builder, Ellis Stones (1896–1975), who credited Walling with starting him on his design career. Both Hammond and Stones were gifted with a talent that Walling called 'the art of stonework', and which she believed was instinctive. By the late 1940s she rarely executed the detailed watercolour plans, instead sketching out quickly a pencil plan on a piece of butter or brown paper.[35] Glen Wilson was another with whom Walling liked to work, knowing that he would implement her design wishes from just such a simple sketch.[36]

Old man banksia, *B. serrata*

GLEN WILSON

Glen Wilson (1927–), one of the few students that Walling took on and the only male student, worked with the designer in the 1950s. He recalls that Walling met some resentment from male clients. Wilson, a retired landscape architect, teacher and author, met Walling in 1955, was given private tutorials for a fee over a period of a year, and invited to work with her on some of her jobs. In his book *Landscaping with Australian Plants*, Wilson writes of the restful nature imparted by Australian native plants and credits Dulcie and Ben Schubert of Schuberts' Nursery as the 'main source of my inspiration' for his love of native plants. 'Through Schubert's connection with the late Miss Edna Walling,' he writes, 'I had the good fortune to enjoy a period of study with that great lady. I saw the same soft restfulness in Miss Walling's plantings, and under her encouragement and experience advanced further.'

The Markdale homestead, today owned by Mary and Geoffrey Ashton, looks out upon the Australian landscape.

In order to appreciate Walling's design focus, an examination of the crucial features of her work is necessary. Great gardens are those in which space and scale are integral to the design, those that display the right balance of mass and void. As Edna Walling gained experience, these concepts became central to her designs. Stone walls which add strength to the garden design and become its bones in winter were crucial; her sweeping walls with their wonderful languid curves, now a Walling signature, endure, more than half a century later. The walls in the gardens Walling designed were both practical and decorative. They were designed to delineate levels, retain bodies of soil and to restrict movement of stock without intruding upon the vista. They were not walls that had to 'pay their way', created to clear rocky paddocks and mark out boundaries, as were those built by Scottish immigrants across country Victoria. Walling's walls resulted in the viewer's eye being led across expanses of lawn into the distant landscape which was framed by trees carefully placed in the garden. A wall created with local stone also connected the garden to the landscape in which it rested and served to provide a local vernacular. Unlike many of her clients Walling was not greatly interested in planting details, except in so far as they filled out the spaces. In that way

the planting masses, rather than the individual plants, were integral to the scale of the garden.

One of the best examples of Walling's design philosophy of the importance of space and scale is Markdale, at Binda near Crookwell on the Southern Tablelands of New South Wales. Markdale is a 5 hectare garden set within a working sheep and cattle property of several thousand hectares, designed for Mrs Geoffrey (Janet) Ashton Snr between 1947 and 1949. Part of the success of the garden lies in the re-routing of the drive to the south side of the house to allow a wide sweep of lawn to flow, uninterrupted, down to a classic Walling stone wall, in which *Erigeron* and *Centranthus* have been allowed to self seed.

Around the house raised beds contain snow-in-summer (*Cerastium tomentosum*), its grey leaves matching perfectly with the pale blue-green of the painted wooden shutters. While Walling would have applauded the plants volunteering themselves across the path, in a letter to her friend, the architect Mervyn Davis, in June 1965, Walling complained that her client, Janet Ashton, often wanted to divert her from her bigger picture and 'liked to have me messing around the house telling her what to plant in some border or other!!'[37]

above: The languid walls at Markdale, built by Eric Hammond, provide structure and scale—and a perfect spot for sitting.

following pages: Walling felt the most important aspect of her plan for the garden at Markdale was the lake, over which the homestead looks.

Stone walls at Ardgartan: walls made from local materials ensure that Walling gardens endure, more than half a century after they were built.

Walling's understanding of space is apparent also at Ardgartan, a half-hectare garden she designed in 1935 on a grazing property near Hamilton in the Western District of Victoria.[38] There, as at Markdale, her use of hard surfaces to create structure has resulted in a distinctive garden that survives half a century later. The large-scale walls, built simply by local tradesmen in local stone, have proved most successful in this garden. The strong features idiosyncratic to her gardens—sweeping walls, large-scale paving, wide expanses of lawn, beautiful northern hemisphere trees, now mature, and the planting by a restraining hand—are clearly evident.

While scale, and the balance between planted space and peaceful void were crucial to Walling's designs, she also insisted on using simple, natural materials. In 1939, in a regular 'Letter to Garden Lovers' in *Australian Home Beautiful,* she expanded upon this philosophy. 'It is only a matter of a restraining hand and the most careful introduction of some very large weathered boulders, and we shall have a piece of restful landscape that should prove of much joy to the owners,' she wrote. Of walls she wrote in the introduction to *Cottage and Garden in Australia*:

CLEARLY WHEN WE EMPLOY LOCAL MATERIALS WE ACHIEVE A FAR
BETTER RESULT. LOW WALLS ADD GREATLY TO THE PLEASURE OF OUT-
OF-DOOR LIVING. FOR CASUAL SEATING THEY ARE MOST USEFUL—ONE
ALWAYS LIKES TO PERCH IN UNEXPECTED PLACES ABOUT THE GARDEN,
RARELY IN THE SPOTS WHERE SEATS HAVE BEEN CAREFULLY PROVIDED.
HERE, TOO, WE ARE GLAD TO REST THE TEA TRAY.[39]

Walling was captured by the landscape as she matured as a designer.
In the early part of her career, her 'English stage', she designed almost
exclusively with the exotic plants that spoke of her childhood. She had
even written, after leaving Burnley, that of the many things she disliked
about the college, the greatest was working on the Australian border, which
she 'positively hated'. But as her design eye developed and as she read more
of the work of a range of designers and environmentalists, Walling also
became more confident in her appreciation of the matt Australian colours
in dull yellows, olives and sages, and the forms of the landscape, which she
increasingly referred to as 'nature's gardens'.[40] Her earlier dislike of the
native plants in the borders at Burnley probably reflected a more widespread, public, misunderstanding of the design and cultural needs of
native flora. Inappropriate use of Australian native plants and poor understanding of their maintenance requirements were problems then that
result still in their lack of widespread appeal to gardeners in the twenty-
first century. In the late 1940s Walling wrote the manuscript for *On the
Trail of Australian Wildflowers*, outlining her views on the environment,
conservation and the beauty of indigenous plants, but could not find a
publisher. It would appear that, while the leading thinkers in horticulture
were beginning to understand and appreciate native plants, the public
was not yet ready for them. The book was published posthumously in 1984
and reveals that the Australian landscape resonated with her more deeply
as she matured, and increasingly influenced her work as she gained in
experience.[41]

In the gardens Walling designed in the second half of her career she
sought to touch the landscape with a lighter hand. 'Man has a duty,' she
wrote, 'to leave behind him as small account of his activities as possible'.[42]
She had already told her readers of the importance of treating the landscape carefully. In *Cottage and Garden in Australia* she wrote:

FITTING THE COTTAGE ON THE LANDSCAPE HARMONIOUSLY, AS WELL
AS TO THE REQUIREMENTS OF THE INMATES, SHOULD DIRECT THE
PLANNING. EVERY ADVANTAGE WILL BE TAKEN OF THE LANDSCAPE
FEATURES OF THE SITE.[43]

By the late 1940s Walling was deeply engaged with Australian landscapes. Among her favourite places was the New South Wales high country around remote Mount Kosciuszko, at 2228 metres Australia's highest peak. There, in late summer, carpets of snow daisies, billy buttons and other alpine plants form shimmering meadows of delicate colour among the bare, imposing peaks and brutal granite outcrops. She described the grandeur and the spiritualism of the high plains in *On the Trail of Australian Wildflowers*:

HERE AT CHARLOTTE PASS IN THE LEE OF THE WIND-SWEPT TREES, AMONGST ENORMOUS GRANITE BOULDERS AND SPREADING DENSE SHRUBS OF DWARF MINT BUSH WE MADE OUR CAMP AND SLEPT THERE FOR TWO NIGHTS.[44]

Her increasing reverence for the countryside as the best teacher of garden design is evident. It's where you go, 'if you want to see gardens,' she wrote in *On the Trail of Australian Wildflowers*:

HOW PLEASANT A LIGHT IS THROWN UPON THE SUBJECT OF MAKING NEW GAR-DENS FROM A STUDY OF THESE WE HAVE BEEN LOOKING AT IN THE MOUNTAINS AND OTHER WILD PLACES. HOW IMPORTANT TOPOGRAPHY IS. HOW VITAL EVERY BOULDER PROVIDING A SHELTERED POCKET, OR HOLDING BACK SOME STEEP BANK ... THE GROUND MAY BE COVERED WITH A MAT OF FOLIAGE OF SOME CREEPING PLANT SUCH AS THE FAN-FLOWER, OR CREEPING PRATIA, AND AS IF THE PLEASANT GREEN OF THEIR LEAVES WAS NOT ENOUGH OUT COME MINIATURE MAUVE OR WHITE FANS, AND MYRIADS OF WHITE AND BLUE STARS.[45]

Walling was an early conservationist. She worked tirelessly against inappropriate development projects—such as the building of a restaurant and viewing platform atop Mount Dandenong—gathering hundreds of signatures for any one of her causes. And as her appreciation of the beauty of what grew naturally increased, Walling became even more energetic in her efforts to preserve the landscape. In *Country Roads: The Australian Roadside* she highlighted the importance of preserving natural plantings along our country roads and made suggestions for highway planting. The work—which only enjoyed a small print run—was a picture book revealing her love of the individual characteristics of a myriad species of eucalypt.

In a lament for her adopted country and in frustration at the mismanagement of bureaucracy, Walling continued:

POOR AUSTRALIA! WE HAVE NOT YET GIVEN UP THE NATIONAL SPORT OF BURNING OFF BEFORE WE TAKE ON THIS GENTLE ART OF BULLDOZING! IN SOME PLACES WHAT SCANT HERBAGE IS LEFT ON THE ROADSIDE IS SCRAPED UP WITH THE TOP-SOIL AND USED TO BUILD UP THE HIGHWAYS![46]

Walling's experience and reputation as a garden designer and her increasing love for the natural beauty of Australia collided in 1951, in the creation of Naringal, at Skipton in the Western District of Victoria, a run that had been taken up by the Rowe family in 1841. The garden, for Mr and Mrs William Rowe, is generally considered to be the first Walling designed

left: The granite outcrops house wildflowers that burst into bloom in summer.

centre: Carpets of wildflowers at Mount Kosciuszko

right: The delicate blooms of the high country that Walling loved

using Australian flora, and represents a turning point in her career. The owners were somewhat unimpressed with Walling's shift in vision, however.

The graziers and city businessmen for whom she largely designed envisaged owning gardens created within an imperial framework and her gardens became, and remain, symbols of establishment and success. Edna Walling may not have been commenting upon class or aspiration in her designs—although she had very definite and particular tastes—but those who commissioned her expected a garden that would underline their position. That meant a garden that spoke of the English landscape tradition, where generations of ownership had resulted in broad lawns, graceful lakes, elegant perennial borders and sweeping vistas framed by mature, deciduous trees. Even her close colleague Eric Hammond questioned her move away from European plants. Glen Wilson recalls, 'One day, Eric Hammond said to me, "Back when Edna used to do her good work, before she went native …".'

And a somewhat plaintive plea, in *On the Trail of Australian Wildflowers*, seems to indicate that Walling knew that she was before her time:

IT IS REASONABLE TO EXPECT THAT NATURE'S GARDENS SHOULD RECEIVE AS MUCH RESPECT AS ONE THAT HAS BEEN ARTIFICIALLY PLANTED. THEY HAVE A SUBTLE BEAUTY NEVER TO BE ACHIEVED BY MAN AND THEREFORE A CERTAIN REVERENCE SEEMS DUE TO THEM.[47]

When Walling arrived at Naringal she found a typically Victorian garden, where a massive lawn surrounding the house was edged with flower beds. As she had done so successfully at Markdale, she moved the entrance. A simple driveway now approaches the homestead, winding, without fuss, through the trees. From the house end of the drive a stone wall unfolds in a beautiful and dramatic gesture that is typically Walling. She wanted the area below the wall to be planted exclusively with Australian native plants, but the owners' wish for a lawn housing northern hemisphere trees won.

Such tension, between a determination to cling to the status markers of English superiority and a growing desire to celebrate Australian nationhood, mirrored the social changes taking place in Australia, changes brought about by such factors as further immigration and education for women. Such tension is shadowed also by the growing awareness of the dangers of the wholesale use of pesticides. Those sensitive to environmental issues remained an educated minority, however, and it would be several decades—and in an environment of global warming and drought—before Walling's ideas on the use and preservation of Australian flora would gain more widespread currency.

Changes in philosophy and any awareness of environmental concerns are perhaps most clearly articulated by changing attitudes to the use of water. Large bodies of water for purely decorative purposes are one of the most dramatic signs of Australian wealth and position. In a country where drought is a constant reality, only the privileged could afford to lay out expanses of water for aesthetic purposes rather than conserving it solely for the survival of stock. Water was seminal to Walling's designs. In her country gardens in particular, water was essential in providing the garden with both a feeling of serenity and a sense of openness: 'The gleam of water gives to any country garden the qualities of tranquility and coolness,' she wrote.[48] All the gardens she created contained water, but until the lake she created at Markdale—which Walling considered to be one of her most interesting and successful commissions—her water features were mostly formal, again reflecting the influence of her readings on the formal gardens of Italy as well as the of the design partnership of Jekyll and Lutyens. They were small rectangular or octagonal, stone-edged pools at gardens such as Mawarra in the Dandenongs, or Durrol at Mount Macedon.

At Markdale the expanse of water on which the homestead looks down demonstrates Walling's growing confidence in her ability to incorporate features from 'nature's gardens' into her designs. Walling's growing mastery of natural forms when designing a body of water was evident in

The delicate, pale pink blooms of the crabapple *Malus ioensis* 'Plena' appear from downy, apple-green foliage.

another New South Wales country garden. She took on a commission for the Osbornes at their property, Bundarbo, near the New South Wales town of Coolac, in the 1950s, and wrote to Mrs Osborne about a planned swimming pool:

I RATHER HOPE THAT IT WILL BE A DAM NOT A CEMENT LINED POOL. THE DAMMED BACK WATER WILL FORM ITS OWN NATURAL LINE WHICH IS ALWAYS MORE PLEASING THAN A PLANNED ONE, INCIDENTALLY THERE IS NOT THE BOTHER OF KEEPING IT CLEAN ... THE EARTH LAKE AT MARKDALE IS PROVING QUITE SATISFACTORY FOR SWIMMING AND 'BOATING' AND FISHING.[49]

Walling is well remembered by her clients for her determination and eccentricities; she first demonstrated her strong personality when building Sonning at twenty-five years of age.[50] Along with her determined nature came her irritation when clients changed her plans or quibbled over costs. Sometimes her clients would balk at her charges; many, while appreciating Walling's ideas, would not commit funds for the hard elements, such as the massive stone walls that Walling considered essential and on which she would accept no compromise.[51] She would rail against owners who would argue at the cost of plants after having previously overspent on what she considered tasteless hard surfaces. She rarely charged anything but a modest fee, nevertheless occasionally enduring disappointing arguments with clients over money. Glen Wilson recalls that

Bickleigh Vale Road at Mooroolbark wends its way quietly through woodland…

when a well-known Western District pastoralist would not pay him the £1 per hour that Walling stipulated, Walling told the garden owner, 'Oh you can go hop it. If you won't pay Glen what he's worth then forget it.'[52]

In 1967, disheartened by the march of council-approved development and by her failure to prevent commercial projects that she felt degraded the landscape around her home at Mooroolbark, and as Melbourne's suburbs spread ever closer, Walling retired to Buderim, in the Queensland hinterland. From her new home, Bendles, she was, if anything, even more outspoken for the cause of conservation, fighting for the recognition of the integrity of natural landscaping along Australian roadsides.

'It seems to me a bad sad world—or rather era, with so much disregard of beauty rampant,' she wrote to her friend Daphne Pearson in August 1969. She bemoaned the building of large houses on small blocks of land that 'so often look horribly like cardboard cabins'.[53] She despaired that her neighbours were 'more interested in Hibiscus & Azaleas & Poinsettias than stone walls!'

A simple, rustic sign pegged to a tree trunk: Badger's Wood

Three years before she died Walling was still writing, asking Australian gardeners to look around them at the natural beauty of the landscape. 'When you are fortunate enough to inherit natural country for the setting of your home, leave as small an amount of yourself as possible and you will have less regrets,' she wrote in 'Just a Gentle Hint', published in her local paper in May 1970. 'Fussing up a country driveway with stone edges and superfluous guttering destroys the restfulness of the scene.'[54]

But with refusals from publishers for reprints of her books, Walling became less relevant to garden design until a new interest in her work emerged in the 1990s. She never married and, after a series of minor strokes, she died at Buderim on 8 August 1973, aged seventy-eight.

Edna Walling provided a bridge between old and new Australia, between Empire and nationalism. Although some of her clients demanded gardens that were British in their inspiration, there was a slowly growing empathy for Australian plants, symbolic of a developing appreciation of the Australian landscape. Walling's life and career also epitomised changing possibilities for women and an environment that gave women the right to choose both career and marriage. Her legacy survives through the word and deed of devotees like Glen Wilson, Ellis Stones, Gordon and Gwen Ford and Kath Carr who, travelling throughout New South Wales, encouraged women to plant 'Edna gardens'.

A NATURAL, BORN OF NECESSITY

South of my days' circle, part of my blood's country,
rises that tableland, high delicate outline
of bony slopes wincing under the winter,
low trees blue-leaved and olive, outcropping granite—
clean, lean, hungry country. The creek's leaf-silenced,
willow-choked, the slope a tangle of medlar and crabapple
branching over and under, blotched with a green lichen;
and the old cottage lurches in for shelter.

JUDITH WRIGHT *1946*

Kath Carr 1909–1999

IF EDNA WALLING PROVIDED A BRIDGE between an English style of gardening and a unique Australian style, Kath Carr, little known except to a devoted group of women whose gardens she designed, represents the vision of what an Australian garden could be. Her work marked the 'Australianising' of the garden, the placing of the constructed, created garden within the natural, Australian, landscape. Carr, of all the gardening women discussed here, recognised most that a garden already existed when the colonists arrived at Port Jackson in 1788.

While Kath Carr was a disciple of Walling, worked with her over a period of twenty years in the 1940s and 1950s and visited her often, even after Walling moved to Queensland, her work was by no means derivative of that of her predecessor. Carr, like Walling, knew the importance of balancing space and scale, and looked to the natural landscape as the best of teachers. Water, also, was paramount in her designs and she talked about it as a whimsical, magical phenomenon.

Carr's sensibilities reached beyond the garden into every aspect of her clients' houses. She advised clients on how to best use the rooms in their houses to attract the most light, on how to place ornaments in the house so that they invoked a sense of nature having moved indoors. She even suggested how books should be arranged in a bookshelf so that the colour of the bindings formed the most natural progression of tones and hues. But in all things she dictated restraint, constantly teaching her

Boorowa Flats, near Galong on the New South Wales south-west slopes and plains

clients, 'What you take out is more important than what you put in.' She believed that skill in garden design and in the creation of things of beauty came from having a light touch.

Kath Carr is a vital part of the story of garden design in Australia, but her modesty and reticence mean that she is not widely known, except by the garden owners who commissioned her work. One of the difficulties encountered in reconstructing her life is the fact that, like many women, she left no archive. Unlike Edna Walling, Carr had no legacy of books, magazine articles, drawings or plans. Unlike many women, however, who felt their experiences were unworthy of being recorded or who were too busy to write, Carr kept meticulous records of her garden visits. But her notebooks, in which she recorded each visit, her ideas and the plants she recommended for the client, have been lost. The notebooks and letters, correspondence from Walling and signed copies of Walling's books, sketches and other papers she read, received or treasured—'boxes and boxes', according to a relative—were thrown away when Carr was moved to a retirement home in 1998. In this way, Carr joins countless other women whose lives were not considered worthy of preservation. This has made the job of reconstructing and analysing her life and work difficult, and it has been necessary to draw largely upon the memories of family, friends and clients.

Kath Carr loved the fine, soft leaves of the honey myrtle (*Melaleuca incana*) with its cream-to-yellow flower spikes.

~

Born in the Sydney suburb of Haberfield on 14 September 1909, Kath Baldick grew up at 69 The Boulevarde, Strathfield, a wide, tree-lined avenue in a suburb of large estates with colonial gardens laid out around carriage circles. The Strathfield house that Kath shared with her parents and two younger brothers, Allen and Kenric, was a large Federation construction of stucco, brick and wooden fretwork on sandstone foundations. It was set in three blocks of land, with a tennis court and gardens tended by a full-time gardener. Kath's aesthetic was shaped by the artistic family in which she grew up. Her father was a grain broker, but her mother, Hazel, was a gifted pianist and an artist—a china painter, a potter, a woodworker and an embroiderer—whose father, Kenric Bennett, was a well-known ornithologist. Hazel's upbringing, in the far west of New South Wales, the dry country around Ivanhoe, some 700 kilometres due west of

Sydney, was in a scientific and enlightened family, and must have had a profound influence on Kath.

It seems likely that an early love of the bush was engendered in Kath by her mother's stories of her own life on the land, and Hazel named the family home at Strathfield 'Moolah', after a property near Ivanhoe her parents had been given as a wedding present.

Kath attended Meriden Anglican School for Girls in Strathfield until leaving school at the fifteen. Her artistic talent and early love of plants were displayed in the detailed botanical illustrations of flowers in her school botany book.[1] Unfortunately, these early school records, like her letters and garden notebooks, have been lost, making it difficult to know for certain why Kath—who, her brother remembers, excelled at school, receiving many prizes—left at that early age. However, this was not uncommon among young women in Australia in the 1920s; perhaps her mother encouraged her to further her artistic talents preparing herself for marriage, rather than to strive for a vocation. Like many privileged young women of the period Kath spent the years between school and marriage as a 'home girl', playing cards and tennis, attending tea parties and sailing on Sydney harbour.[2]

On a visit to her mother's childhood home, Yandemah, a property between Hillston and Ivanhoe, Kath met Bob Carr, who was managing for his uncle the neighbouring Moolbong, a property that had once been in

The garden at Emu Flat

Kath's great-grandmother's family. Bob was the eldest of several sons of a large, well known—but not well-to-do—farming family who had once owned properties in the district. Despite Bob not owning land, he and Kath married at St Philip's Anglican Church, Church Hill, on the corner of Grosvenor and Jamison streets in the centre of Sydney, in 1937.

Kath's appreciation of Australia's native flora was perhaps born of necessity. After her marriage she settled at Moolbong, where the rainfall is 250 millimetres in a good year, the soil a sandy loam, and summer temperatures reach over 40 °C for days at a time. Kath was forced to select native plants that could survive the tough conditions and she enclosed the garden with tall saltbush to keep out the dust. It is easy to imagine that despite the hardships imposed by the climate and although a city girl, Kath soon fell under the spell of a landscape that her mother had loved, one uncluttered by the symbols of modern city life—telephone poles and wires, small claustrophobic gardens, automobiles interrupting the line of sight and fences constructed to hide neighbouring properties. Apart from gardening, she occupied her time with entertaining in great style, enjoying the services of an excellent Chinese cook. In 1947, after Moolbong was sold, Kath and Bob moved to Hidden Brook, their own 480 hectare property at Binalong, on the south-west slopes and plains of New South Wales, a successful farming and grazing region, today about five hours' drive south west of Sydney, just beyond Yass.

If a fence were essential, Kath Carr advised against strong horizontal lines, which would cut across the horizon. Here, the fence at Emu Flat is of vertical palings.

We can only speculate about when Kath became interested in the work of Edna Walling, but by the time she designed her first garden, in 1947, Kath was well versed in Walling's writings, and soon advised friends and clients to buy sets of Walling's books.[3] At some point after the move to Binalong Kath wrote to Edna Walling, and asked if she might travel to Victoria to work with her. At first Walling declined her request but—perhaps early evidence of Kath's charm and persuasiveness—eventually relented. It is impossible to be precise as to how much time Kath spent with Walling, but Kath's close friend and first client (Mrs) Ronnie Henderson remembers that Kath travelled frequently to Victoria to work with Walling and stayed with her at Sonning for varying lengths of time, over a period of a decade or more. Ronnie Henderson recalls:

SHE'D GO OFF SEVERAL TIMES A YEAR—FOR THREE WEEKS OR MORE. SHE USED TO GO JUST FOR A FEW DAYS SOMETIMES, AND SHE'D HAVE QUITE A LONG TIME WITH EDNA AT VARIOUS TIMES. THEY'D BE DOING A GARDEN SOMEWHERE ... SHE STAYED WITH EDNA ... SHE AND EDNA WERE REALLY, TERRIBLY CLOSE FRIENDS.[4]

The post-war years were difficult for those on the land. The Carrs were no exception and Kath, with no formal education in horticulture but with the invaluable time spent in the company of Walling, launched into garden design to supplement the family income. Travelling from Hidden Brook, she created a body of work reminiscent of that of Walling, but nevertheless original.

Kath Carr designed gardens for money, but she charged so modestly that it is difficult to imagine that the fees provided much more than pocket money. In her first letter to Victorian client Susie Sutherland, in 1968, Carr outlined her charges:

MY FEE IS $30.00 PLUS TRAVELLING-AWAY-FROM-HOME-CHARGE, WHICH WHEN POSSIBLE, IS SHARED—BUT SHOULD I VISIT YOU AT PRESENT I WOULD NEED THREE DAYS AWAY AND I WOULD HAVE TO ADD $20.00 WHICH YOU WOULD POS-SIBLY FEEL WAS TOO MUCH.[5]

Her real motives were no doubt her love of designing, fed by her upbringing, and the enjoyment she gained from putting her artistic talents to good use. And, like many other gardening women, both amateur and professional, she also enjoyed the companionship and friendship of like-minded people, and travelling the countryside that she had come to love. She had no children; the gardens were her family. Just as botanising had provided solace and inspiration for Georgiana Molloy, in the early nineteenth century in the south of Western Australia, as gardening was Beatrice Bligh's companion on the Southern Tablelands of New South

A rustic pergola at Emu Flat

Wales during lonely war years, garden design provided Kath with the excitement and satisfaction of an intellectual passion. While she charged modestly, however, she was professional in her approach to her work. She would never stay with clients, even when those clients became close friends. She liked to sleep overnight in a nearby motel, where in the evening, she could quietly write up notes from the day in the work book that she always carried with her.

Kath Carr first saw Edna Walling's work at Mawarra, in the Dandenong Ranges, in about 1948. This first encounter would change her life and affect dozens of gardening women throughout New South Wales. Walling considered Mawarra to be among her finest gardens. She had commenced work on the property in 1932, but a disagreement with the original owners, probably over the expense being incurred, had caused her to walk off the job. Her favourite stonemason, Eric Hammond, was retained to complete the work. Later, when she read that the garden had been sold, Walling contacted the new owners and a lifelong friendship began. The precise date of Carr's meeting with Walling is unclear, but it was during those later years that Carr visited the garden with the designer.[6] Susie Sutherland recalls that Carr 'trailed around behind' Walling, rather than actually working with her. Carr told Susie, 'I was her shadow around gardens like that'.[7]

Carr, like Walling in the later period of her career, admonished against anything that was not as nature would have intended, repeatedly advising, 'bring the landscape into your garden picture', 'observe how nature paints her garden pictures', and 'don't gild the lily'.[8] Carr also knew when to leave the landscape alone and when to augment nature with her designer's pencil. Walling must have been impressed with Carr's ability and appreciated her skill and restraint. In a note to Mervyn Davis and Daphne Pearson in the late 1960s, Walling wrote of Carr that 'this student has done remarkably well with the little she learnt from me'.[9] She had written earlier, in 1941, in *Australian Home Beautiful*, 'How desperately we need gardeners trained in an appreciation of landscape effects; trained to know when to leave well alone'.

When Walling was no longer accepting commissions she commended the skills of Kath Carr to Susie Sutherland. On 31 August 1968 she wrote, from her home, Bendles, at Buderim:

One of Kath Carr's favourite plants, the coastal tea tree (*Leptospermum laevigatum*)

I VERY MUCH REGRET THAT I AM NOW TOO FAR AWAY TO COME TO SEE YOUR GARDEN—IT SOUNDS JUST THE SORT OF PLACE I WOULD HAVE LOVED! PERHAPS KATH CARR, WHO HAS THE SAME IDEAS, WOULD DO IT FOR YOU ... SHE GOES TO VICTORIA QUITE A BIT SO I HOPE SHE WILL FIT YOU IN—YOU'LL LIKE HER I FEEL SURE. I KNOW SHE IS MOSTLY ENGAGED ON SOME WORK IN NSW AT PRESENT SO MAY NOT BE ABLE TO COME FOR A WHILE; BUT I DON'T KNOW ANYONE ELSE WHO IS LIKELY TO SUIT YOU SO WELL.[10]

The friendship between Walling and Carr continued until Walling's death in 1973; Carr also stayed with Walling after Walling moved to Buderim. Several for whom Carr designed remember the close friendship between the two women and remarked on the physical likeness between them. Even their handwriting was similar.[11]

Apart from her notebook, Kath was not a prolific writer, nor a record-keeper of her ideas. 'I believe it was all in her eye,' commented one of her clients, Rhonda Daly:

SHE JUST PERCEIVED IT. SHE NEVER WROTE ABOUT IT, SHE NEVER DREW IT. SHE SAW IT AND SHE KNEW WHAT HAD TO HAPPEN. KATH WAS VISUAL. SHE DIDN'T WANT TO WRITE IT DOWN; SHE DIDN'T WANT TO DRAW PLANS, SO SHE WAS ON THE SPOT. WHAT SHE SAW SHE SUGGESTED.

Carr had an enormous influence on garden making on the south-west slopes and plains of New South Wales in particular, an area that includes towns like Young, Galong, Binalong and Harden. It is an area of rich black soils, good rainfall and rolling, open pastures. There are tall, spreading eucalypts still standing in the paddocks, unlike in areas on the edge of the Southern Tablelands, where tree clearing has caused the water table to rise, resulting in devastating salinity problems. The land around Binalong is reminiscent of the quintessential Australian landscape depicted by painters like Arthur Streeton and Tom Roberts, who saluted the aestivating golden grasses, the shimmering, limpid blue light of summer and the shady mass of quivering gum leaves on the twisted trunks of the eucalypts, images that spoke eloquently of an Australian sense of space.

A cool, quiet corner at Goonawarra, Ross and Gail Flanery's garden

Carr created more than fifty gardens, over a period of more than forty years; in addition, her style was much copied in the district. Most of her commissions were for gardens on substantial rural properties near her home, although a few were large Sydney gardens, in Canberra or in the Southern Highlands of New South Wales, more traditionally the venue for the creation of 'Hill Station' gardens for successful city merchants. Some were located in country Victoria. Jean Holt recalls that Carr was in great demand:

LOTS OF PEOPLE WANTED HER TO COME TO THEIR GARDENS. SHE WAS VERY BUSY AND SHE WAS EXTREMELY SELECTIVE. I HAD TO PERSUADE HER TO COME TO MY GARDEN. BUT ONCE YOU GOT TO KNOW HER AND SHE BECAME A FRIEND, SHE COULDN'T DO ENOUGH FOR YOU.[12]

No other designers worked in the area, according to Ross Flanery, for whom Carr consulted over the garden at his Galong property, a design originally commissioned from Carr by his parents:

THERE WOULD BE NO OTHER LANDSCAPER IN THE LAST TWENTY OR THIRTY YEARS THAT'S HAD THE EFFECT ON THE GARDENS IN THIS AREA THAT SHE HAD. IT'S JUST THE ONE COMMON THREAD THROUGH MOST OF THE COUNTRY GARDENS HERE ... ANYONE WHO'S HAD A DESIGNER, IT SEEMS TO HAVE BEEN KATH CARR.[13]

left: The entrance to Goonawarra

centre: Relaxed, exuberant plantings frame the meandering drive at Goonawarra.

right: The pergola at Goonawarra is covered in wisteria each spring.

following pages: The lake at Goonawarra: large bodies of water were central to Kath Carr's design aesthetic.

While all her gardens possessed the same ethereal quality, that was their only common characteristic: each was unique to its owners, and its situation. According to Gail Flanery, 'She never copied from one to the other. She sought an atmosphere.' And Rhonda Daly adds:

SHE WOULD PUT THINGS IN THAT WERE UNIQUE TO EACH GARDEN. IF SHE SAW ONE PERSON HAD AN APRICOT IN THE GARDEN, SHE'D PUT AN APRICOT AT THE MAILBOX. AND SHE GAVE ME THE SILVER PEARS BECAUSE I HAD THE BIG PEAR TREE. SHE DID SOMETHING UNIQUE IN EACH GARDEN.

Carr's first garden commission—although she did not charge a fee—was Emu Flat, for Ronnie Henderson, in 1947, just after she and Bob had moved to Binalong and before she had met Walling. Carr created a garden of sweeping lawns, stone walls and vistas. The next garden, Bobbara, was created for Mfanwey Friend. After working on these two gardens Carr was convinced by her friends to consult professionally.

Carr designed a town garden in the 1950s for Dr and Mrs Geoff Holt in Young; in 1958 she designed Kikobel for Bin and Ken Ross at nearby Holbrook. In the 1960s she returned to Galong to further advise Ross and Gail Flanery on their garden, Goonawarra, designed in the early 1950s for Ross's mother; she designed Boorowa Flats for John and Kerry-Anne Flanery, also at Galong, and Bimbadeen, a garden at Binalong for Miriam and Ken Skene. In the late 1960s Carr was called in to help renovate Kildrummie, a well-known Walling garden near Holbrook. She designed Seaton Vale through the 1970s for Susie Sutherland at Yarck in Victoria and, in the 1980s, Milgadara for Rhonda and Bill Daly. In Canberra, town gardens featuring rock walls supporting plantings of alpine species were designed for Helen Hufton, who knew Carr at Binalong, and for the Holts, who had moved there in the late 1970s. During the 1990s she was still constantly travelling, visiting these gardens to advise on tiny details that would make a difference to the subtle character that was crucial to her designs.

Not all the gardens Kath Carr created remain. She did not always employ the range of strong structural features that contributed so much to the Walling designs. Carr designed with such restraint and with such a light touch that if the property changed hands and the new owner did not appreciate her philosophy, the garden could be quickly spoiled or dismantled. The elements that make large-scale English gardens easy to photograph—their formal, hedged parterres, box-edged, decorative vegetable gardens and resplendent perennial borders—are the very aspects that are absent in Carr's designs, rendering their spirit difficult to capture on film. For these same reasons the whimsical quality of her gardens can be swept away with the stroke of a heavy hand.

Ducks in the garden
at Goonawarra

Kath Carr knew that it was an intangible set of successful factors that contributed to landscape, and to sublime beauty. She was acutely aware that the landscape was a changing dynamic and that it could never be possessed, neither completely by the imagination, nor in actuality. Its ephemeral nature, its constant character but its always-changing face, was a quality essential to a successful garden. The word she used for this ethereal quality was 'dreamy'.

When Susie Sutherland wrote to Carr explaining that Walling, who had designed her parents' garden, had recommended Carr for Sutherland's garden, Carr wrote to accept, adding that she regretted 'that Edna cannot help you with your garden—I feel there is just nobody who can create the subtle, understated atmosphere that she imparts upon a garden!'[14]

Rhonda Daly recalls Carr's work:

SHE ALWAYS THOUGHT YOU'D SUCCEEDED IF, WHEN PEOPLE LEFT YOUR GARDEN THEY COULDN'T ARTICULATE JUST WHAT IT WAS THAT MADE IT SUCCESSFUL—WHAT IT WAS THAT MADE IT TRANQUIL. IT WAS JUST THE WHOLE EFFECT.[15]

Tranquillity was an essential characteristic of a Carr garden, but is a feature that is probably most difficult to create. An uncluttered landscape, without pretension, created with due respect to its location and created slowly, layer upon layer, one element after another, was one key to the gardens she

created. In this way, the mind and spirit was not overwhelmed and con-fused, but could remain quiet and peaceful.

The garden Carr created at Hidden Brook—one of those subse-quently destroyed—was, according to those who visited it, supremely peaceful. The house had a wide terrace shaded by a loggia overlooking the Cubbramurra Creek that ran through the property. It is likely that it was replete with the plants Carr loved, those that she instructed her clients to use in their gardens. The peppermints, *Eucalyptus nichollii*, which she liked to coppice, would have provided a shimmering, misty quality; *Westringia fruiticosa*, the native rosemary with its glaucous leaves, would have been there, along with the eriostemons, native mint bush (*Prostanthera violacea*) and the tea trees (*Leptospermum scoparium* and *L. sandersii*). There would have been *Melaleuca incana*, *M. styphelioides* and *M. armillaris*, with their fine, soft foliage, and *Ceanothus impressus* and *C. edwardsii*, with the clouds of dreamy blue blossom that she loved. The evergreens she recommended were *Pyracantha yunnanensis*, *Cotoneaster franchetti* and *C. pannosus*, and the flowering *Crataegus tanacetifolia*. She allowed snow-in-summer, armeria, arabis, alyssum and soft pink dianthus to make themselves at home in rock walls or stone paths, just as Edna Walling had advised. Swathes of blue-flowering catmint were regulars in her gardens. For the birds she planted *Grevillea* 'Poorinda Queen', *G. sericea* and *G. jenkinsii*.

The drive wanders past the lake and through the shrubberies at Goonawarra.

Carr loathed citrus trees for their unsubtle, glossy leaves; she hated the strappy-leaved agapanthus, often a saviour in the tough Australian climate. She despised the two species of dietes, with their spiky, unsympathetic fronds. And she empathised with Walling in her disdain of formal training at horticultural colleges. She rejected anything unnatural and was appalled by the widespread and fashionable use of English box hedges in country gardens, blaming the fashion for them on horticultural colleges.

She advised against stark, white-painted garden furniture, signs or fences, against garish embellishments such as ornate, shop-bought garden lamps. She would provide the name of a local blacksmith and instruct clients to have simple, 'workmanlike' lamps made; fences were also to be simple, painted a dark brown or stained black. Most clients heeded her instructions resulting in the creation of the restrained, un-fussy, tranquil gardens that can only be achieved through years of careful selection and placement of plants.

The opening words of Walling's *A Gardener's Log*, one of the books Carr encouraged her clients to read, encapsulate the feeling that Carr was seeking for her gardens:

Winding paths and natural plantings are signatures of the gardens designed by Kath Carr.

WALKING AROUND THE GARDEN THIS MORNING I CAME UPON A MOST
BEAUTIFUL FLOWERING SHRUB WITH SMALL SOFTLY-GREY FOLIAGE OF
GRACEFUL AND RATHER OPEN FORM AND EXQUISITE CLUSTERS OF
WHITE FLOWERS, SILKY BUDS CROWDING AROUND THEM AWAITING
THEIR TURN TO BLOOM. THE EFFECT ON THE TIPS OF THE BRANCHES
WAS A SYMPHONY OF GREY-GREEN AND WHITE ... THERE IS NOTHING
LOVELIER![16]

Miriam Skene, who, with her husband Ken, lived at Hidden Brook for
three years after Kath and Bob Carr
retired to Sydney in 1964, remembers
the beauty of the garden, and that it
was the landscape that inspired Carr.
She recalls that Carr was not moved
by English garden styles. 'Everything
was natural, [influenced by] the
Australian landscape. Kath never had
an English period like Walling.'[17] Her
favourites were planted at Hidden
Brook: the prostrate rosemary 'Blue
Lagoon' and Walling's beloved Westmoreland thyme, massing by the

Weeping branches at Boorowa
Flats. Kath Carr encouraged
branches to weep—'Ballerina
arms,' she would say…

front door. Paths snaked through the plantings. In words that recall those
that Carr used when consulting with clients Skene remembers, 'Trees were
holding hands, with ballerina arms'.

All Carr's clients were instructed to keep a book in which to record
her advice. Jean Holt's much-used blue notebook records Carr's 'Rules' and
explains her aesthetic of restraint:

WALDEC 'POTTERY BLUE' ON IRON GATES; CUT NICHOLLI APPROX
9 FEET FROM THE GROUND AND AFTER 2 OR 3 YEARS ANOTHER 2 FEET
FROM THE TOP; ALL EYESORES PLANTED OUT; FOLIAGE MISTY AS POS-
SIBLE; AS MUCH GREY FOLIAGE AS POSSIBLE; ALL HARD CORNERS
PLANTED OUT WITH EVERGREEN SHRUBS; USE TREES AND SHRUBS WITH
CROOKED STEMS AND PICTURESQUE SHAPES.

Among the most important of all Kath's dictums followed: 'everything to
be related'.

For Kath Carr, a 'well-cultivated sense of place' was essential to any
successful landscape treatment. She appreciated the unique spirit idiosyncratic to each garden she worked on, and touched the landscape with the

lightest of hands. And for Carr, the garden, as part of the landscape, did not represent a bounded entity.

The gardens Carr designed were not simply a socially acceptable vehicle for her creative talents. While the garden no doubt nurtured Carr, maintaining a 'good garden' was not synonymous with 'successful woman-hood' for her; it was not merely another 'polite accomplishment'. For Carr it did not exemplify good housekeeping, ultra domesticity or ultra gentility, as it did for Louisa Anne Meredith and Una Falkiner.

At Boorowa Flats, iris jostle with swathes of daisies and forget-me-nots.

Nor were Carr's landscapes intended to represent a rediscovered Eden, a place for female redemption. For her good gardening was not an exemplification of moral restitution. Garden design liberated women like Walling and Carr despite the fact that for them a choice between home and career was unnecessary. Neither had children nor sought, through their gardens, to fit with any acceptable mould prescribed for middle-class women.

But for Carr, the garden was a space to be claimed for her women clients, where they could take positions. She would use her considerable charm to achieve her vision, her ideas of a perfect landscape, devoid of the uglier symbols of civilisation. A central theme was her desire to ensure that no ugly marks were left to spoil the landscape. Whether it was a neighbour's domestic detritus cluttering the entrance to a garden, or fences, poles or blocks of unsightly pine trees interrupting the view, Carr felt no compunction about negotiating their removal.

Judith Friend—whose mother-in-law, Mfanwey, was one of Carr's earliest gardening companions—recalls that nothing daunted her:

KATH WOULD WANT THE MEN TO DO THE WORK AND THE MEN WOULD BE PERHAPS RELUCTANT. SHE WOULD SAY, 'WELL, GET THE COUNCIL TO MOVE THOSE TREES, AND WE'LL MOVE THAT DAM'. SHE HAD A TREMENDOUS EYE FOR DETAIL, AS WELL AS THE BROADER LANDSCAPING OF THE GARDEN. NOTHING DAUNTED HER; SHE WAS GREAT FUN AND HAD TERRIFIC IDEAS. KATH WAS VERY OUTGOING ... [18]

Jean Holt also remembers Carr as having great charm. 'She had a very disarming way with her,' she recalls:

SHE COULD GET PEOPLE ON SIDE VERY QUICKLY. I DIDN'T THINK MY
HUSBAND WOULD BE PREPARED TO GO ALONG WITH EVERYTHING KATH
SAID. SHE ALWAYS GOT THE MEN ON SIDE SO WELL ... WHEN SHE GOT
THE ELECTRICITY PUT THROUGH TO HIDDEN BROOK, SHE GOT THE
ELECTRICIANS TO PUT THE POLES BEHIND A TREE ... ALL THE WAY ...
SHE COULD CHARM ANY MAN ... ALL THE HUSBANDS. SHE MADE THEM
FEEL THAT IT WAS THEIR IDEA.

Carr was a perfectionist, with an exacting eye for the details that would
each contribute to the purity of the scene she was creating. Jean tells
another story, of Carr going to a country garden a little further west and
managing to convince the men to re-hang all the gates into the paddocks,
even though they had only been hung the previous week.[19] Miriam Skene
remembers Carr's energy: 'She would dart here and there and would balance herself on a rock to capture the picture. She never wanted to come in
and have a cup of tea.'

　　Carr, like Walling in the latter part of her career, was a strong advocate of native Australian flora. She rejected the concept, still in existence if
not prevalent in Australia, that the station garden should imitate the grand
estates of England. In a land where country properties, and even modest
'weekenders', are named after the grand English estates re-worked by the
great eighteenth-century landscapers—we have Panshanger, Valleyfield,
Studley and even Chatsworth—Carr's gardens were designed to be in harmony with their surroundings, to sit quietly, in peace with the landscape.
She eschewed any pretence, taking her references from the environment.

The house and the
shearing sheds at
Milgadara look upon
a vast body of water.

Ronnie Henderson recalls that Carr's vision was broad: 'Not cottage-y. She was big. She looked out into the paddock and she'd say, "that tree has to go". But she was never pretentious.' Carr dictated that the house must always be simple, low and unostentatious. 'She said you shouldn't look up to the house,' remembers Rhonda Daly. 'She would lower the house into the background.' Similarly, Carr advocated simplicity. Country house signs were to be just a name burnt into a plank and painted with creosote, ideally attached to a heavy slab fence.

Many writers, including Jill Ker Conway in her autobiography *The Road From Coorain,* the story of her childhood near Ivanhoe, where Carr started her married life, observe that as late as the post-war years, Australians, including rural Australians, were informed by images of the British landscape:

IT TOOK A VISIT TO ENGLAND FOR ME TO UNDERSTAND HOW THE AUSTRALIAN LAND-SCAPE ACTUALLY FORMED THE GROUND OF MY CONSCIOUSNESS, SHAPED WHAT I SAW, AND INFLUENCED THE WAY A SCENE WAS ORGANIZED IN MY MENTAL IMAGERY ... MY LANDSCAPE WAS SPARER, MORE BRILLIANT IN COLOR, STRONGER IN ITS CONTRASTS, MAJESTIC IN ITS SCALE, AND BATHED IN SHIMMERING LIGHT.[20]

above: Sweeping lawns at Seaton Vale

opposite: At Seaton Vale, a gate leads, tantalisingly, through a copse of silver birch.

Even though Carr's plant lists included some northern hemisphere species, she never attempted to reconstruct an English Arcadia: her gardens were celebrations of the Australian landscape. She understood the futility of trying to tame and control the Australian bush and sought to garden within it, not confront it with a garden solely of thirsty exotics and derived from a British imagination. At Goonawarra, Ross Flanery recalls Carr's respect for the landscape:

SHE WAS TRYING TO REPLICATE NATURE. ABSOLUTELY. IN LAND FORMS, PLANTINGS. SHE WAS TRYING TO REPLICATE THE BETTER PARTS OF THE NATURAL BUSHLAND, WITH THE SAME SHADES AND COLOURS AND CLUMPS OF TREES AND FORMS. SHE ALWAYS SAID THAT NATURE DOESN'T DESIGN ANY STRAIGHT LINES. IT WAS HER STRONGEST POINT.[21]

Observing how nature designs, Carr advised her clients not to read gardening books. In a letter to Susie Sutherland, Carr suggested, 'Just stick to Edna's and you won't go wrong'.[22] The exotics she employed, such as crabapples, were usually planted close to the homestead. She used their tone and colour, foliage texture and mass, to attract the line of sight toward vistas and connect the garden to its surroundings. Carr loved silver pears teamed with the paperbark, *Melaleuca styphelioides*. Another favourite was *Eriocephalus africanus*, the African cotton bush, that Walling called 'the quiet one'. She would plant the Mudgee wattle (*Acacia spectabilis*), with its fine foliage, next to almonds, which provided depth. Carr used grey, fine foliage to create a sense of distance; she advised that broad foliage brings a vista closer.

The garden that Carr created for Rhonda and Bill Daly, Milgadara, settled against the Black Range near the town of Young, was completely at home in its Australian setting. Perhaps Carr's most important advice to Rhonda Daly was to 'look for vistas'. Her intention was to incorporate into the garden the grandeur of the landscape. She talked of framing the view by planting trees on either side of the garden picture, rather than surrounding the property, or creating a tunnel effect. 'You don't want to be hemmed in,' she advised.[23]

On her first visit to Milgadara, Carr observed it from the outside, sitting for some time at the front gate and then driving slowly in toward the house. Rhonda remembers, 'She would sit in the car outside and look in. You'd start painting the picture from the front gate. Often a lot of work had to be done before you got into the garden: you'd work from outside, in toward the house.'

Carr's philosophy was to create mystery by bringing the visitor right around the perimeter of the garden, to catch enticing glimpses of the house before entering the 'garden proper'. Her first task was always to determine what to take out, particularly any plants that hid the view.

Rhonda explains the process by which Carr would work with a new client:

A LOT OF HER EARLY VISITS WERE SPENT DISCUSSING WHAT YOU'D
TAKE OUT, RATHER THAN WHAT YOU'D PLANT. THE FIRST THING SHE
WOULD DO IS WALK AROUND THE GARDEN AND GET THE FEEL OF THE
GARDEN. THEN YOU WOULD GO INTO THE HOUSE, TO DECIDE ON YOUR
PLANTING, ENSURING THAT YOU WEREN'T BLOCKING THE VIEWS FROM
THE WINDOWS. SHE WOULD TELL YOU WHAT VISTAS TO FRAME.

At Hidden Brook, Carr installed massive picture windows to capture the views of the garden and the creek. And, after she moved from Hidden Brook in 1962, she created Myoori, at Wentworth Falls in the Blue Mountains, west of Sydney, where she built a huge terrace of Western Australian jarrah to afford beautiful views down the Jamieson Valley.

Telephone lines were 'removed' and poles obscured with planting; fence posts were 'painted out' in the colour of the surrounding landscape. She loved 'scrub gum green', a Taubman's colour. Rhonda Daly remembers, 'And if you had to paint your roof, she would look at what was in the background, and paint the roof a similar colour'. Walling's words in *Cottage and Garden in Australia*, 'That the cottage will rest upon the landscape in sweet and quiet accord instead of being a dull bruise that never departs must be the unconscious wish of all,' clearly resonated with Carr.[24]

And Walling's admonition in her books to observe how nature places trees also found a sympathetic audience with Carr, who would explain, 'Nature doesn't place trees in straight lines, she puts them in clumps, and doesn't mix the species too much'.[25] The gardens that she designed were integral with the landscape. The garden perimeter was to be planted with whatever was indigenous, thus bringing the landscape into

left: Fields of canola flower near Milgadara

centre and right: Milgadara shed and landscape

following pages: Shearing sheds at Milgadara

the garden while the pretty, deciduous trees would be painted at the front of the garden picture, closer to the house.

'She would recommend plants in threes. There would be two here, and then, one, over there. You'd always "throw" one away,' explains Rhonda Daly, who insists that Carr designed instinctively. 'She just knew it. She didn't read it. She was a natural.' At Seaton Vale, Susie Sutherland's garden in the foothills of Victoria's Strathbogie Ranges, part of the Great Dividing Range, Carr also advised her client to blend the garden with the landscape. Mahogany gums (*Eucalyptus botryoides*) cluster naturally around the front gate which opens to a long winding drive that almost circles the property. As you cross the cattle grid set into the drive you notice a copse of autumn-colouring poplars. Carr advised Susie to place another in the paddock close by, as if it had seeded there naturally.

Closer to the house, on the front lawn, are apples and pears. Carr added more, further down in the garden, to extend it into the landscape. She would repeat plantings already in a garden. 'If you had silver pears or almonds, she would repeat them,' explains Rhonda Daly. Carr's notes from her first visit to Milgadara, on 9 March 1982, state, 'Setting beautiful—natural. Pottery hut—shingles—espalier pear on end. Must have definite connection between hut and house—meaning, connect outbuildings to house. Repetition of plants leading across.'[26]

Galvanised iron star posts, used in country properties for fencing, marked where trees would be placed. They would be left, sometimes for weeks or months, perhaps moved a little, observed over several days, and then moved again, to ensure the trees would be planted in just the right spot, framing, not blocking, views, and appearing to have been planted by the hand of nature.

left: The homestead at Milgadara nestles in the garden.

centre: Kath Carr's beloved ironbarks *Eucalyptus sideroxylon* 'Rosea' provide shade at Milgadara.

right: Mustering time at Milgadara

Carr's aesthetic was finely tuned to the balance required between shapes, scale and space. She abhorred straight lines. Rock walls, built in what she called 'big lazy Ss', were to have rounded tops because that's how nature would have created them. Her 1968 notes for the nearby garden Boorowa Flats, owned by John and Kerry-Anne Flanery, state, 'Driveway to approach house diagonally instead of straight. Poplars each side of ramp (2 & 3).'

Bin (Winifred) Ross remembers clearly Carr's advice on creating a drive during her first visit to Kikobel, the Ross property at Holbrook, in 1958:

HER THING WAS JUST TO GET IN THE 'UTE' AND SWOOP AROUND. 'THAT'S HOW YOU MAKE A DRIVE,' SHE'D SAY. 'YOU DON'T MAKE A BEE-LINE FROM THE GATE TO THE HOUSE.' AND THE NUMBER OF PEOPLE WHO CAME HERE AND SAID 'OH, HOW PEACEFUL.' TRADESMEN ALSO.[27]

Carr's drive at Hidden Brook was, according to Miriam Skene, simple and rustic, winding across rough grass and through plantings to the house. She preferred natural grass over manicured lawn, and liked to see the wheel tracks of cars indented in the grass. At Young, where Jean Holt's garden was sited on a corner block, the first thing Carr stipulated was that the front gate had to be moved around the corner, so that guests would wend their way to the front door instead of moving directly, in a straight line. 'She didn't want you to walk straight down the front path and see everything at once,' remembers Jean. A deodar (*Cedrus deodara*) planted on the foot-path, anchored the entire scene.

Carr was insistent that swimming-pool fences must not include a strong horizontal line along the top, which would arrest, or 'stop', the eye

and cut short the view. Upright palings were to be used, which, she instructed, would blend into the background more easily. Ronnie Henderson, at Binalong, recalls:

ONCE KATH WENT DOWN TO EDNA WALLING'S FOR SEVERAL WEEKS. WHEN SHE CAME BACK BOB, KATH'S HUSBAND, HAD PUT A FENCE UP—RIGHT IN THE MIDDLE OF THE VIEW TO THE HILL. KATH SAID 'BOB, THAT FENCE ... IT WILL HAVE TO GO, DARLING.' DARLING BOB, THE NEXT DAY, HE AND THE MEN TOOK IT DOWN, AND EVERYONE IN THE VILLAGE SAID, 'OH THAT BOB CARR.'[28]

The black, furrowed bark of Kath Carr's beloved pink-flowered mugga ironbark (*Eucalyptus sideroxylon* 'Rosea')

At Boorowa Flats mature ironbarks (*Eucalyptus sideroxylon* 'Rosea'), with their black furrowed bark and glaucous, weeping foliage, form the frame for the 'garden picture' and the uncluttered sweep of lawn takes the eye out to the country beyond. Groupings of crabapples—*Malus* 'Gorgeous', *M. purpurea* and *M. spectabilis*—are planted closer to the house. They not only give continuous blossom throughout spring but replicate Carr's advice to 'plant for horizontal lines, which are much more pleasing than vertical. Look for ballerina arms.' She would weigh down the arms of such small trees with string and a stone to gently encourage the branches to fall the way she wanted. Underplantings are of Carr's beloved small-leaved may (*Spiraea thunbergii*), of *Westringia fruticosa* and *Ajuga reptans* as well as pale pink verbena, English lavender and iris, a palette of plants perhaps learned from her time with Walling. When planting bulbs Carr showed her clients how to pick the shadow line of the tree and then plant within the shadows, again as if nature had placed them there.

Carr knew the importance of designing features of the correct scale. Grand sweeps of stone walls and expanses of grass would impart the atmosphere she sought in her gardens. Judith Friend recalls Carr's vision:

IT WAS DIFFICULT TO GET SOME OF THE THINGS DONE BECAUSE KATH DIDN'T DO ANYTHING ON A MINOR SCALE ... SHE REALLY BUILT A BEAUTIFUL GARDEN AT BOBBARA ... SANDSTONE WALLS AND AN ORCHARD OF ALMOND TREES AND A HIDDEN ROSE GARDEN, ALTHOUGH SHE WAS NOT WILD ABOUT ROSES.[29]

While Carr loved blue, she never coveted the pretty arrangements of English perennial borders. Ross Flanery remembers:

SHE WASN'T A PERSON FOR MUCH COLOUR IN THE
GARDEN. SHE WOULD TOLERATE AUTUMN COLOURS,
BUT SHE CERTAINLY WASN'T ONE FOR COLOURED
FLOWERS IN THE SPRING. CRABAPPLES AND SO ON
WERE FINE, BUT THAT WAS ABOUT IT. SHE WOULD
NEVER SUGGEST ANY OTHERS. SHE CONCENTRATED
ENTIRELY ON DIFFERENT SHADES OF GREEN AND
GREY. SHE WAS BUILDING UP A TAPESTRY OF
LEAVES.[30]

Water was an essential part of Carr's garden
designs. Indeed, water plays a crucial role in the lives of
any Australian who lives outside cities, where a tap can
be turned on without thinking of water as a limited
resource. (Prolonged drought in the early years of this
millennium has resulted in increasingly rigorous water
restrictions, however. Now even city dwellers have
become conscious of water as a diminishing com-
modity.) In country Australia the dependence upon
water—usually the lack of it, but occasionally its
excess—controls almost every outcome, from the success of the pastoral economy to the beauty—the possi-
bility, even—of the garden. Water, and its availability,
also directs the imagination and contributes enor-
mously to the 'poetics'—the ephemeral, almost intangible and indefinable qualities that combine in any
space to make it pleasing—of the landscape in country
Australia.

The garden of Jill Ker Conway's childhood was
one of 'struggling geraniums' when it did not rain. But
after rain it became full of colour and life. Her experience of the difference rain makes is one that is regularly
repeated throughout rural Australia:

IN THE NEXT FEW WEEKS IT CONTINUED TO RAIN
MORE, SO THAT AN UNHEARD-OF EIGHT INCHES HAD
FALLEN WITHIN LESS THAN A MONTH. THE TRANS-
FORMATION OF THE COUNTRYSIDE WAS MAGICAL. AS
FAR AS THE EYE COULD SEE WILD FLOWERS EXPLODED
INTO BLOOM. EACH BREEZE WOULD WAFT THEIR
POLLEN ROUND THE HOUSE, MAKING IT SEEM AS
THOUGH WE LIVED IN AN ENORMOUS GARDEN.[31]

Water birds have returned to the wetlands
at Banrock Station, in the heart of South
Australia's Riverland region, as a result of a
decade-long programme of rejuvenation.

LIFE-BRINGING WATER

Water—or the lack of it—is a theme
running through all aspects of Australian
country life, and represents most vividly
the image we have of ourselves and the
land in which we live. Many writers have
used water, or its absence, in their work to
evoke the image of a recalcitrant country.
Water is seminal in the lives of gardening
women (and men) as, through two centuries, they have sought to recreate an
English Arcadia. Gardening women today
talk of the need for water, the hardships
encountered in garden making where economics make the purchase of water impossible, the difference piping and irrigation
have made to their gardens and their sense
of wellbeing. The provision of water—
either by ponds or fountains, dams or
lakes, or by irrigation—in the gardens discussed throughout this book forms an integral part of the story of garden history.
Throughout Australia's (European) settled
history, the availability of water has been
crucial in the creation of a garden. 'The
arrival of the water wrought miracles,' said
Jill Ker Conway, describing the difference
the sinking of a bore made to life of the
country woman.[32]

Kath Carr's preference for native plantings stemmed firstly from her years in the bush and her love of the subtle beauty of their colours, textures and shapes. But she was also sensitive to rural Australia's dependence upon water. She did not need to be reminded that water shaped outcomes, limited possibilities and imprinted a personality on a country community.

Landscapers know that water is essential to the success of their designs. For Edna Walling, water was a central element of each design. 'The best thing I did there was to deal with the erosion in the paddocks,' she wrote of her work at Markdale:

'WHY NOT DAM IT BACK & HAVE A LAKE' I SEZ! & IN CONSEQUENCE THIS SHEET OF WATER IS THE PRINCIPAL FEATURE OF THEIR LANDSCAPE SEEN OVER & BEYOND MY LOW STONE WALL THAT ENDS THE DRIVE ... WE PUSHED THE DRIVE AROUND IN NO TIME WITH A [BULLDOZER?] TO THE OTHER SIDE OF THE HOUSE. I LIKE TO THINK THAT THOSE THINGS MADE IT WORTHWHILE TO PAY ME ...[33]

Cement toadstools
became birdbaths

The use of water was also central to Carr's gardens, particularly if you could look down upon it from the homestead. She invested water with living, spiritual qualities and would call the water expanses she designed for clients, often on a massive scale, 'Lord bird sanctuary'.

Carr wanted to create a bird sanctuary at the Sutherland garden, Seaton Vale, in a natural depression that forms several hundred metres down from the house, along the willow-lined creek that runs through the property. That part of her vision has not yet been implemented, but there is a smaller pool, nearer and below the house, against a backdrop of those beautiful blue-shimmering ranges. It is set beyond the close-mown grass of the front lawn, beyond the ha-ha, so that the brolgas created by the Adelaide sculptor Ces Norris appear to emerge from long grass to drink at the pool.[34] Carr would have placed the brolgas carefully, wanting them to appear as natural as possible. (Similarly, she placed a small brass bird on a hall table at Seaton Vale as if it had flown in from the garden through a nearby window.) And she loved blue-flowering iris planted near a pool, the water and the plants reflecting the blue expanse of a wide Australian sky.

Carr did not advocate the profligate use of water, its expenditure for a cosmetic or aesthetic end alone, nor did she advocate frivolous

accoutrements such as fountains. The dams, or expanses of water, she wanted in her gardens doubled as catchment areas from which stock could drink. The manner in which she incorporated water into her landscape plans, as well as her recommendations for water-sensible plantings, was emblematic of a still embryonic, but growing, environmental consciousness.

At Seaton Vale, Kath Carr wanted the brolga sculptures placed as if they were alighting on a billabong.

After half a century of creating gardens, mostly in country New South Wales and Victoria, Kath Carr died in Sydney on 17 September 1999 at the age of ninety. Almost until the last year, and while she was too ill to travel following a series of minor strokes, she was still talking of her dreams, and always on a grand scale. The light touch that Carr brought to her garden design, her admonishments to look to nature as the best teacher, and the simplicity of the garden hardware that she used, taught those who saw her work a deep appreciation for both the landscape and the environment.

Kath Carr leaves no archive, but her legacy remains in the dozens of gardens she designed, many of which are extant, in the notebooks she admonished each owner to keep, and in those owners' vivid recollections of her energy and enthusiasm for creating her 'garden pictures' in the Australian landscape that she honoured.

Conclusion

I may walk in the garden and gather
Lilies of mother-of-pearl.
I had a plan that would have saved the State
—But mine are the thoughts of a girl.

The Elder Statesmen sit on the mats,
And wrangle through half the day;
A hundred plans they have drafted and dropped
And mine was the only way.

A Woman's Lament, *China, 670 BC*

WITH SOME BITTERNESS the author of this poem wrote of her sense of separateness, her sense of disempowerment, and the lack of agency—not that she would have put it that way—she held in her life. Had she possessed a garden, she might have felt differently.

An awareness that gardens reveal much about a society has increased dramatically over the past decade. In Australia, the ways in which we read history, study its signposts, interpret its canvasses, have also changed. We now acknowledge the relevance of oral history, contemplate the implications of movements in society and its demographics, make sense of changes in fashion and in taste. And we study gardens.

Remembered Gardens explores the ways in which women have used gardening to improve their daily lives, express their aspirations, their hopes and, at times, their despair; how they have claimed a voice through

their gardens. The garden has been the means by which many women transplanted the desire to appear British—in background, sensibility and taste—and the contribution of women to the development of an 'Australian Garden' has been significant.

The gardens of the imagination for almost all the women in this book were English—for a variety of reasons. The lack of confidence felt by Australians in their own culture and identity has been highlighted by writers who have considered whether our history of convictism has contributed to our self-consciousness. The tension between native and exotic flora, between an 'Australian' cultivated garden and an exotic garden of imported, northern hemisphere species, can be seen in the gardens created by all the women discussed here.

Edna Walling eventually sought to show Australian gardeners a new way, a way to use native species appropriate to the Australian environment, the climate and the landscape. She spoke out against the degradation of the bush and sought to raise awareness of the impact of European settlement on fragile, ancient soils. Ahead of her time, she was optimistic that Australians would come to love the quiet beauty of a landscape of native flowers, shrubs and trees, once they took the time to understand its subtleties. While Walling's work was most often met with varying degrees of opposition, her disciple, Kath Carr, carried on the work she had started, with design ideas that were parallel to a growing national pride.

The women in this book, however—at least until Walling and Carr incorporated native species into their designs—sought to replicate England. Even those who were botanists and wrote elsewhere of their appreciation of indigenous plants, found it necessary, when writing for the gardening public, to extol the virtues of exotic plants.

left: Golden barrel cactus, *Echinocactus grusonii*

centre: The way to the future: in the former garden of landscaper Michael McCoy, exuberant but natural plantings reflect the more relaxed nature of the Australian countryside.

right: Acorn banksia (*B. hookeriana*), native to the sands north of Perth

'Colonial curtsying before the motherland', as writer Barry Oakley has put it, has only given way to a more general Australian nationalism over the past thirty years, prompted by the 'Whitlam years' of Labor government of the early 1970s. Then, with an upsurge in national pride encouraged by messages of mild xenophobia, along with the early mutterings of republicanism, the native garden was considered politically correct in horticultural circles, assisted by groups such as the Society for Growing Australian Plants.

Mass planting of indigenous species, with little regard for or understanding of their horticultural requirements, however, resulted in unpruned and untamed, struggling gardens that were not pleasing, nor appropriate. There were few nurseries with the sufficient relevant knowledge to assist clients. In the 1980s attempts to re-create the bush with native gardens gave way to plantings of golden diosma and dwarf nandina.

In the garden of horticulturalist Diana Snape, the prostrate *Banksia petiolaris* edges a winding brick path.

In the last few years, due largely to another protracted drought, debate over the sustainability of many accepted gardening practices has reappeared. Native plants are again receiving attention and garden writers are, somewhat tentatively, promoting their use. Many municipal councils require that indigenous, even endemic, species are included in landscape plans for new houses, or to obtain development approval for renovations.

Intersecting with the problems created by past mismanagement of the land is the increasing popularity of gardening, perhaps indicating a desire to recall an idyllic, pastoral past. The value of the nursery trade in Australia rose to $4 billion in 2002, ahead of the wine industry; every television and radio station presents at least one gardening show, and garden tourism is increasingly popular.

Australian history has been related as one about men, and the landscape has shouldered a male identity. However, garden making was a means by which women could implicate the land with a female persona. The women who feature in these pages feminised the landscape in the only way they understood—by planting upon it gardens created with borders of soft English perennials, and with broad-leaved northern hemisphere trees that provided not only shade, but also light and shadow play. They nurtured lawns of close-cut green grass and added water features to provide a peaceful, cool element.

As well as comprising an integral part of the process of the taming of the land and providing for women a means by which to gain agency in their lives, the garden could be, however, a place where they found them-selves marginalised. It comprised a 'safe' space in which they could be easily contained, bound there by the limits placed upon them by their gender. Excluded from positions of male power, from politics, economics, even from the literary world, and confined to 'interior spaces', women turned to their gardens.

For some women, the garden also represented a nostalgia for an idyllic past, for a slow-moving, pastoral, economy. The idea of reclaiming Eden—a state of perfection—was a metaphor ever present in the activity of garden making and a theme invoked by many writers. It implies for most—and for the women profiled here—the creation of a lush green space, devoid of imperfection—a redemptive place. Low green hills, cool valleys and richly woven borders voluptuous with softly coloured flowers are the pictures gardeners still carry most often in their imagination, images that are confirmed by the plethora of English gardening books that are visited annually on Australian bookshops, a deluge that shows no signs of abating.

A good garden conveys a sense of peace and restfulness to those who observe it. To achieve this, a delicate balance between appearing per-fectly maintained, and appearing maintenance-free, is required. One of the reasons a garden of native flora is often maligned is that it can appear untidy and is, therefore, abrasive; not restful. The gardens created by the women examined in this book reflected this concern.

A superb example of indigenous planting, here at Stokes Bay garden on South Australia's Kangaroo Island

So, what type of gardens are fashioned in Australia and what do they tell us about their makers? Over the past two centuries, garden style has depended upon a range of factors. The size, scale, structure, decoration and planting of gardens have relied on each owner's financial position and upon the social position to which he or she aspired. They have also depended upon his or her education and the amount of time and resources that could be allocated to the creation and maintenance of the garden.

The Australian garden appears in many different costumes. The large country garden relies upon evergreens, stone and water: its mature northern hemisphere trees frame an Australian landscape of eucalypts and grazing sheep, safely beyond the garden boundary. The minimalist city garden, created by the designer for time-poor professionals, concentrates on hedges of *Magnolia grandiflora* 'Little Gem', a versatile, small-growing cultivar of the bull bay magnolia, and one that has replaced *Murraya paniculata* (orange jasmine) as the celebrity plant of the decade. Rising property prices in the city have resulted in gardens becoming smaller, although emphasis has increasingly been placed upon outdoor living. Back gardens have become more structured, relying upon formal hedges, clipped orbs and obelisks of box, privet and *Lonicera nitida* (box honeysuckle), with iceberg roses and groundcovers of mondo grass. Citrus—today limes, cumquat and multi-grafts—planted in pots of varying levels of sophistication and quality, add style to courtyard gardens in city and country.

The beautiful paperbark *Melaleuca quinquenervia* occurs naturally in the Lachlan swamps in Sydney's Centennial Park.

The modern Australian garden also includes those that display forests of staked tomatoes and flamboyant dahlias proudly maintained by the immigrant from a Mediterranean country. And—perhaps the garden for the twenty-first century, with the constant reminder of drought and global warming—one that combines water-wise agaves and sempervivums with the odd *Grevillea* 'Robyn Gordon', a small salute to the appeal of bird-song. Mulching, unheard of before the 1970s, and a term that is still met with some bewilderment by British and European gardeners, has become an essential part of modern Australian gardens, where water restrictions have forced gardeners into 'good garden-keeping' practices.

But not all 'native' plants suit every garden. The broad-leaved paperbark, *Melaleuca quinquenervia*, while stunning in the Lachlan swamp in Sydney's Centennial Park where it occurs naturally, if planted in a garden in adjacent Randwick will soon cause problems through its water-seeking roots. The 'Silver Princess', *Eucalyptus caesia*, endemic to the sands of Western Australia, is just as exotic in an eastern state garden as the box hedge or iceberg rose, today so often ridiculed as emblematic of gardening's cultural cringe.

Some writers and garden designers are attempting to negotiate a middle ground, to allow nature into our gardens while admitting that garden making is, indeed, a manipulation of nature. Perhaps a mix of species—of native and 'sustainable exotics'—comprises part of any solution. The Australian Garden History Society was formed in 1980, by a group of historians, writers and architects, in an attempt to understand our garden history within the context of today's environmental pressures.

Philip and Robyn Style's Adelaide garden. In the cities, back gardens have become more structured, relying upon formal hedges and clipped orbs and obelisks.

This book is, of course, an unfinished conversation. It cannot address every aspect of the development of gardens in Australia over two centuries. As garden styles change, and as people become increasingly mobile, gardens and their meaning will continue to be fluid. The question of what comprises the quintessential Australian garden remains largely unanswered. The Australian country garden remains derivative of its English heritage, but, either through coercion or education, attitudes are slowly changing. This book is a small contribution—through words and pictures—to our knowledge of women's gardening activities and aspirations, and the part they play in the story of the Australian garden. But there is a great deal more that can be said—the complete story is yet to be written.

Abbreviations

ADB	*Australian Dictionary of Biography*
AGHSJ	*Journal of the Australian Garden History Society*
BL	Battye Library, Perth
CRO (Carlisle)	Cumbria Records Office (Carlisle)
HRNSW	*Historical Records of New South Wales*
La Trobe	La Trobe Collection, State Library of Victoria
ML	Mitchell Library, State Library of New South Wales, Sydney
NL	National Library of Australia, Canberra
SLNSW	State Library of New South Wales, Sydney
SLV	State Library of Victoria, Melbourne
WAA	West Australian Archives
?	denotes a word that was obscured or difficult to decipher

INTRODUCTION

1 Coventry Patmore published his series, *The Angel in the House*, from 1854 to 1863, presenting himself and his wife as the ideal Victorian couple; they entertained Tennyson, Ruskin and Robert Browning, all influential writers for middle-class colonial women.

BOOK ONE

Prologue

1 Commissioner Bigge, in his *Report of the Commissioner of Inquiry (J. T. Bigge) into the State of the Colony of New South Wales*, noted that the women of the colony were usually married and were technically assigned to their husbands.

2 Tench, 'Complete Account of the Settlement at Port Jackson', p. 264.

3 Treasury (London) Records held in Public Records Office, London. Ref T 1/639 pp. 252–7. ML PRO3550.

4 Crittenden, *The Front Garden*.

5 Published in *The New South Wales Pocket Almanack and Colonial Remembrancer*.

6 As those who sought a better life in the colonies defended their hard-won position in the struggling new society, a class structure more pedantic than seen in the old country emerged. The freed convicts, the emancipists, felt keenly their alienation by the pure 'merinos', as those born free in the colony became known. The children of ticket-of-leave convicts were known as 'cornstalks', those who arrived as free citizens were 'sterling'. Free settlers were determined to set themselves apart from ex-convicts or the children of convicts.

7 Cited in Day, p. 57.

8 Howitt, p. 32.

Elizabeth Macarthur

1 Elizabeth Macarthur to her friend in England, Bridget Kingdon, 1 September 1795, ML MPA2908. (The copy of the letter is incorrectly dated 1798, according to King, *Elizabeth Macarthur and Her World*, pp. 8, 9.) Elizabeth was, of course, observing the results of Aboriginal land management.

2 Sir Thomas Mitchell papers, *Journal*, November 1831, ML A295, pt 3.

3 ibid.

4 Pike (gen. ed.), p. 153.

5 Hazel King (op. cit.) provides the details of Elizabeth Macarthur's early life.

6 Elizabeth Macarthur to Bridget Kingdon, 1 September 1795, ML MPA2908.

7 Elizabeth Macarthur to her mother, 18 March 1791, ML MPA2908.

8 Elizabeth Macarthur to her mother, 20 April 1790, ML MPA2908.

9 Elizabeth Macarthur to Bridget Kingdon, 7 March 1791, ML MPA2906.

10 Lang, *An Historical and Statistical Account of N.S.W.*, cited in Bligh, *Cherish the Earth*, p. 9.

11 Governor Phillip's geometrically arranged garden of vegetables and fruit trees was laid out neatly in front of his thatched house that overlooked Sydney Cove. Although the ground was pure sand, Captain Collins remarked:

> Some ground having been prepared near his Excellency's house on the east side, the plants from Rio de Janeiro and the Cape of Good Hope were safely brought on shore in a few days, and we soon had the satisfaction of seeing the grape, the fig, the orange, the pear and the apple—the delicious fruits of the Old taking root and establishing themselves in our New World. (Cited in Bligh, op. cit., p. 8.)

12 Crittenden, op. cit., pp. 17, 18.

13 In 1816 Elizabeth had written to her god-daughter Eliza Kingdon that:

> … This is a sort of mid-station visited by ships from many quarters of the Globe. At this time we have a vessel in the Harbour, from America, two from Bengal, one from Canton, one from the Cape, and one from Ceylon, one also from the Isle of France, several from Europe which are about to depart by way of Java, China or India. (ML MPA2908.)

14 Bligh, op. cit., p. 16.

15 Elizabeth Macarthur to Bridget Kingdon, September 1798, ML MPA2908.

16 Elizabeth Macarthur to Bridget Kingdon, 7 March 1791, ML MPA2906.

17 Elizabeth Macarthur to her mother, 18 March 1791, ML MP2908.

18 ML MPA2898; Reel CY832.

19 Elizabeth Macarthur to Bridget Kingdon, 7 March 1791, ML MP2906.

20 ML MPA2898; Reel CY832.

21 ML MPA2898; Reel CY832.

22 Elizabeth Macarthur to Bridget Kingdon, 1 September 1798, ML MPA2908.

23 ibid.

24 See King, p. 35, for a discussion of John Macarthur's land acquisition.

25 Her description of Elizabeth Farm in the spring of 1811 to John Piper, 13 November 1811, Piper papers, ML 256.

26 ML MPA2898.

27 Letterbooks, Library of Royal Botanic Gardens, Sydney.

28 Macleay papers, ML MSSA4300.

29 ML MPA2906.

30 By 1803 Governor Philip Gidley King could compile a 'List of Plants in the Colony of New South Wales which are not Indigenous, March 20th, 1803', which included, as well as those sent out by Banks, wallflower, columbine, rose campion, lupins, canna and larkspur.

31 Elizabeth Macarthur to Edward, 31 May 1828, from Parramatta, ML MPA2906.

32 ML MPA2906.

33 Elizabeth to Edward, 31 May 1828, ML MPA2906.

   Just the month before John had revealed his ambitions for his family when he wrote to Edward, 'we will transform you from a croaking half pay Major into a rich landed Esquire'. (8 April 1828, ML MPA2899.)

34 Elizabeth to Edward, 23 January 1834, ML MPA2906.

35 Elizabeth to Edward, 29 October 1848, ML MPA2907.

36 J. C. Loudon, *The Villa Gardener*, pp. 36, 37.

37 Cunningham, vol. 1, p. 87.

38 ML MPA2908. Louisa Anne Meredith also appreciated the local flora, while, nevertheless, comparing it unfavourably to that of home.

39 In 1838. Cited in Crittenden, op. cit., p. 14.

40 Day, p. 57.

41 The treasures found by the plant hunters of the early nineteenth century were quickly disseminated. A list of plants received by William Macarthur in 1817 includes olives, peaches, nectarines, plums, cherries, pears apples, crabapples, elderberry, China and moss roses, white and yellow jasmine, Portuguese laurel, rhododendron and peonies.

   By the 1850s William's nursery at Camden Park housed over 3000 plants;

he listed more than seventy varieties of roses and his orchid collection flourished in a complicated series of glasshouses. Echoing the pursuits of the leading families of Britain, William sponsored the expeditions of the explorer and naturalist Ludwig Leichhardt. (ML MPA2992.)

42 Elizabeth Macarthur to Edward, 1830, ML MPA2906.

43 Elizabeth Macarthur to Edward, 26 May 1832, from Woolloomooloo, ML MPA2906.

Georgiana Molloy

1 *Bible*, King James Version, Genesis 1:28.

2 Georgiana Molloy to Helen Story, 1 October 1833, BL 3278A/2. Georgiana was twenty-eight when she wrote this, three years after the death of the child. It is the first letter that survives of her discussing the tragedy.

3 The colony of Western Australia was known as the Swan River settlement for more than fifty years.

4 Hasluck, p. 3.

5 In her analysis of the Macleay family, *Taste and Science: The Macleay Women*, p. 37, Elizabeth Windschuttle discusses education in England for girls of middle and upper-class families.

6 BL MN 768 3278A/1.

7 In *The Native Born: The First White Australians*, p. 59, John Molony details that part of the attraction for the Swan River settlers was that the new colony was developing without convicts, and could be expected to attract a better class of emigrant.

8 *Journal and Proceedings of the Western Australian Historical Society Journal*, vol. I, part iv, p. 32.

   Lines, *An All Consuming Passion*, p. 76, also gives a very detailed list of what was brought on board.

9 Georgiana Molloy diary, BL ACC 4730A/17. Her diaries are contained in two collections, in the Battye Library and in the Cumbria Record Office in Carlisle.

10 Georgiana Molloy diary, Tuesday 20 October 1829, CRO (Carlisle) D/Ken/3 Bundle 28/2.

11 Georgiana Molloy diary, CRO (Carlisle) D/Ken/3 Bundle 28/2.

12 Interview with Stephen Daniels, University of Nottingham, 26 May 2000; see also Daniels, *Humphry Repton: Landscape Gardening and the Geography of Georgian England*.

13 Bussell papers, WAA139. Cited in Hasluck, op. cit., p. 45.

14 Georgiana Molloy diary, CRO (Carlisle) D/Ken/3 Bundle 28/3.

15 Georgiana Molloy diary, BL BLACC 4730A/17.

16 G. F. Moore, *Ten Years in Western Australia*, p. 150. Cited in Hasluck, p. 53.

17 Georgiana Molloy diary, BL BLACC 4730A/17.

18 ibid.

19 Stirling had been granted some 50 000 hectares, with priority of choice, even before he had left England. Other grants had been given to retired officers in England who sent out agents with a gang of workers to their land. By the end of 1829 some 250 000 hectares had been allotted.

20 Georgiana Molloy diary, CRO (Carlisle) D/Ken/3 Bundle 28/3.

21 ibid.

22 ibid.

23 Georgiana Molloy diary, CRO (Carlisle) Bundle 28/9. Georgiana is referring here to the grave of Elizabeth, her first-born child.

24 Georgiana Molloy to her sister Elizabeth, 7 November 1832, WAA501.

25 Georgiana Molloy to Helen Story, 8 December 1834, BL WAA501.

26 Georgiana Molloy to Margaret Dunlop, January 1833, BL A4732 1-2.

27 ibid.

28 Georgiana Molloy to her mother, 4 January 1835, CRO (Carlisle) D/Ken/3 Bundle 28/9.

29 Georgiana Molloy to Helen Story, 1 October 1833, BL3278A/2.

30 The *Hortus Siccus* dates to Renaissance times when botanical collecting and natural history reached a new importance and is the forerunner to the modern herbarium.

31 Georgiana Molloy to James Mangles, 25 January 1838, BL 479A/1-2.

32 ibid.

33 ibid.

34 ibid.

35 John Lindley to James Mangles, 1839, BL 479A/1-2.

36 Joseph Paxton to James Mangles, BL 479A/1-2.

37 Georgiana Molloy to Margaret Dunlop, 12 January 1833, BLA 4732 1-2.

38 ibid. Georgiana had not seen the Vasse River land at this stage.

39 Georgiana Molloy to James Mangles, 21 March 1837, WAA501.

Louisa Anne Meredith

1 Cited in Aitken & Looker (eds), p. 325.

2 Meredith, *Notes and Sketches of New South Wales*, p. 130. This was Louisa's first book published after her arrival in the colonies. And in the same publication, p. 142, she wrote:

> The trees called by the Colonists 'he-oak' and 'she-oak' (*Casuarina stricta* and *C. torulosa*) form a remarkable feature in Australian scenery … Perhaps none of all the novel trees in this Colony have so completely strange and un-English an aspect as these.

3 Meredith, *My Home in Tasmania*, vol. I, p. 57.

4 Vivienne Rae-Ellis' biography, *Louisa Anne Meredith: A Tigress in Exile*, discusses the family background.

5 Louisa Anne Twamley to George Meredith, 18 May 1833, cited in Rae-Ellis, p. 37.

6 Meredith, *Notes and Sketches*, p. 41.

7 ibid, p. 157.

8 ibid, p. 40.

9 ibid, pp. 40, 41.

10 ibid, pp. 37, 38, 39.

11 ibid, pp. 85, 86, 109

12 ibid, p. 90.

13 ibid, p. 124.

14 ibid, p. 60.

15 Tim Bonyhady and Bernard Smith are among those who have written of her appreciation for native flora.

16 Meredith, *Notes and Sketches*, p. 129.

17 ibid, p. 56.

18 ibid, pp. 109, 131.

19 ibid, pp. 140, 164.

20 ibid, p. 49. In thoughts that echoed those of Peter Cunningham, Louisa noted that the hostesses of Sydney preferred to serve food imported from Britain.

21 Meredith, *Notes and Sketches*, p. 49.

22 Meredith, *My Home in Tasmania*, pp. 25, 26.

23 ibid, p. 22.

24 ibid, p. 27.

25 Cunningham, pp. 239, 240.

26 Meredith, *Notes and Sketches*, p. 52.

27 Trollope, p. 109.

28 Phyl Frazer Simons' expression, in *Historic Tasmanian Gardens*, p. 8.

29 The Wardian case, first used in 1834, was a glass, sealed plant box that made the transport of plants much more successful.

30 Meredith, *My Home in Tasmania*, p. 28.

Although Trollope, p. 56, noted that 'Government House is, I believe, acknowledged to be the best belonging to any British colony'.

31 Meredith, *My Home in Tasmania*, pp. 66, 71–5, 82.

32 ibid, pp. 87–9.

33 ibid, p. 91.

34 ibid, p. 152.

35 ibid, pp. 153, 268.

36 ibid, pp. 94–6.

37 ibid, pp. 222, 239.

38 ibid, p. 57.

39 ibid, p. 51.

40 ibid, p. 55.

41 Meredith, *Notes and Sketches*, p. 157.

42 ibid, p. 157.

43 Meredith, *My Home in Tasmania*, p. 169.

44 Meredith, *Tasmanian Friends and Foes— Feathered, Furred, and Finned*, 1881.

45 Tanner, *Converting the Wilderness*, p. 36.

46 At Cambria she noted 'a pair of beautiful tame black swans' but 'I cannot in conscience pronounce them to be quite equal in majestic beauty to the white swan'. (Meredith, *Notes and Sketches*, p. 97.)

BOOK TWO

Prologue

1 ML MSS2009/2–22, newspaper cutting item 106.

Una Falkiner

1 Pike (gen. ed.), vol. 5, pp. 80, 81; Private papers, collection of Suzanne Falkiner, Una Falkiner's great-niece.

2 During her life, Una, a great beauty, was painted by Violet Teague and photographed by Harold Cazneaux, the leading society photographer of the day.

3 Una attended the National Gallery School, where she became friendly with Violet Teague. Her style was more influenced, according to the historian Suzanne Falkiner, her grand-niece, by her cousin, the acclaimed botanical illustrator Ellis Rowan, and by Ida Rentoul Outhwaite.

4 'Dizzy' (Ann) Carlyon grew up on Boonoke in the 1950s. Her father, Basil Clapham, was manager of all the Falkiner properties. She recalls the loneliness of women of Una Falkiner's class. 'Privileged wives were not at liberty to mix with the townsfolk and people of a different class,' she remembers. (Interview with Carlyon, 27 November 2002.)

5 Falkiner Archive, ML MSS 423 101.

6 ibid.

7 Colleen Morris, 'Up the Garden Path', in Morris et al. (eds), *Interwar Gardens*.

8 Cuffley, *Traditional Gardens in Australia*, p. 46; Tankard & Van Valkenburgh, p. 13.

9 Silas Clifford-Smith, 'Popular Period Plantings' in Morris et al. (eds), *Interwar Gardens*.

10 Marilyn Lake, 'Australian Frontier Feminism and the Marauding White Man' in Midgley, p. 123.

11 Falkiner, *Haddon Rig*, p. 86.

12 Photograph in Tim Hewat's *Golden Fleeces*, p. 176.

13 Otway was often absent. 'Otway … was extraordinarily active and mobile,' writes Hewat, p. 157:

> He hated to stay too long in any one place … He was particularly fond of good-looking women. He liked nothing better than to slip away from the homestead at Boonoke North without telling anyone, catch the train at Widgiewa siding and go up to Sydney for a few days drinking with his mates and chasing the girls.

14 Dutton Archive, NL, Series 43, Folder 5.

15 Dutton, *Out in the Open*, p. 23.

16 Una Falkiner diary, 1 January 1921, ML MSS 423/51.

17 Una Falkiner diary, 11 August 1922, ML MSS 423/51.

18 Hewat, p. 153.

19 Una Falkiner diary, 19 January 1939, ML MSS 423/51.

20 Suzanne Falkiner believes that as Una would have earned no money from this exercise it would have been acceptable to Otway; simply an artistic fling.

21 Holmes, *Spaces in Her Day*, pp. 158, 159.

22 Una Falkiner diaries, ML MSS 423/51

23 ibid.

24 Una Falkiner diary, 15 October 1940, ML MSS 423.

25 Boldrewood, introduction.

26 Falkiner Archive, ML MSS 423 101.

27 Una Falkiner diary, August–October 1942, ML MSS 423/80.

28 Suzanne Falkiner private papers.

> John was born on 6 July 1918. In 1923 Una had told her diary, in ominous words: 'If anything happened to my precious John I feel it is more than I could bear.'

29 Una Falkiner diary, October–December 1942, ML MSS 423 81.

Winifred West

1 From Winifred West, *Addresses and Talks*, p. 83. To mark each anniversary of Frensham's founding, West addressed the students, staff and parents, quoting from her readings, revealing her philosophies and detailing her hopes for the school and its community.

2 George Sturt's diaries reside at the British Museum. Extracts have been published in two volumes: E. D. Mackerness (ed.), *The Journals of George Sturt, 1820–1927*.

3 Interviews with Cynthia Parker, 15 April 2002; 9 March 2004.

4 Priscilla Kennedy collated the West archive that remained at Frensham in the 1970s and deposited it with the Mitchell Library. She believes, however, that some of West's papers were discarded by Phyllis Bryant, Frensham headmistress 1938–65.

5 West, *Addresses and Talks*, 1973.

6 For further information on West's childhood see Priscilla Kennedy's *Portrait of Winifred West*, pp. 4–7.

7 Cited in Kennedy, p. 9. The feel of Queen Anne's School (known as QAS), even in 2004, is very similar to that of Frensham School.

8 Alison McKinnon, 'Nowhere to Plant the Sole of the Foot?: Women, University Education and Subjectivity in the Early Twentieth Century', in Yates (ed.), *Feminism and Education*, pp. 22–38.

9 George Sturt diaries, op. cit., 8 May 1905, p. 469.

10 West's watercolours are held in the Mitchell Wing, SLNSW.

11 West, p. 39. Address given to the school community of parents, students and staff on 1 June 1931.

12 Winifred West, vol. 2, misc. papers 1910–1965, ML MSS 3367/1-5.

13 West, p. 3.

14 Noeline Kyle, in *Her Natural Destiny: The Education of Women in New South Wales*, p. 57, reports that in 1880 there were 531 private schools in NSW, 58 for girls only.

15 *Newcastle Morning Herald*, 1/10/1904, 18/5/1905, cited in Kyle, p. 55. Kyle, p. 34, reports that in 1900, 10 000 more boys than girls were enrolled in state elementary schools, a figure that had increased to 11 000 by 1915.

16 West, p. 6.

17 Winifred West, misc. papers 1910–1965, ML MSS 3367/1-5.

18 Kennedy, p. 81.

19 Cavanough et al.

20 Cazneaux, introduction.

21 West, p. 10.

22 Whether or not West was aware of the work of Jekyll, many in this area were created by the designer. Among several Jekyll gardens near the village of Frensham designed in the early twentieth century is The Manor House at the neighbouring village of Upton Grey.

23 Interview with Cynthia Parker, 15 April 2002.

24 West, p. 34.

25 ibid., p. 22.

26 ibid, p. 34.

27 Winifred West papers, ML MSS 3367.

28 Ann Hawker, *Echoes of Dreamland*, Macquarie Pastoral Press, Toowoomba, QLD, 1992.

29 Sturt was to be a place where boys and girls who had left the free, government-run Mittagong High School could come to further their skills. It opened on St Francis Day, 3 October 1941.

Beatrice Bligh

1 Beatrice Bligh, *Down to Earth*, p. 1.

2 Interview with Lucinda Nicholson, 12 March 2003.

3 Bligh, *Down to Earth*, p. 14.

4 ibid., p. xv.

5 ibid., p. 4.

6 ibid.

7 Bligh, *Down to Earth*, p. 1.

8 ibid., p. 20.

9 Bligh, *Cherish the Earth*, pp. 52, 91.

10 Sheila Hoskins insists that Walling advised Bligh to change the course of the drive, from arriving directly to the front door, to sweep around, through the trees, thus leaving an uninterrupted vista from the house, across the front lawn. (Interview with Hoskins, 2 June 2003.)

11 Bligh private papers.

12 For a more detailed discussion of the various styles popular in the inter-war years see Colleen Morris, 'Up the Garden Path', in Morris et al., *Interwar Gardens*, p. 8.

13 Cuffley, *Australian Houses of the 20s and 30s*, p. 157.

14 *Garden Gossip*, March 1929, cited in Matthew Devine, 'Built Elements of Interwar Gardens', in Morris et al. (eds), *Interwar Gardens*, p. 18.

15 Clifford-Smith, 'Popular Period Plantings' in Morris et al. (eds), *Interwar Gardens*, p. 21.

16 Friis & Stackhouse, *Australian House and Garden;* Morris et al. (eds), *Interwar Gardens*.

17 This was a string line propped up by a pole, Gilbert Toyne's rotary clothes line from the 1920s or, from 1945, the Hill's Hoist.

18 Unpublished manuscript. Bligh private papers.

19 Bligh, *Down to Earth*, p. xiv.

20 Law-Smith, *The Garden Within*.

21 Interview with Michael Bligh, 7 April 2001.

22 Michael Bligh private papers.

23 Bligh, *Down to Earth*, p. 6. Sheila Hoskins recalls that Walling advised Beatrice to move the garden fence out further, into the paddocks, so that the lake became part of the garden; while it is difficult to know how accurate the reminiscences of friends might be, Beatrice would certainly have observed with interest the progress of Walling's renowned lake at Markdale.

24 Interview with Lucinda Nicholson, 12 March 2003.

25 ibid.

26 Interview with Mary Ashton of Markdale, whose mother-in-law was Janet Ashton, 10 October 1998.

27 Bligh, *Down to Earth*, p. 21.

28 The author discovered this manuscript when given access to the Bligh family papers, private collection.

29 Beatrice Bligh, unpublished papers, private collection.

30 Dorothea McKellar, 'My Country', in Maggie Pinkney (ed.), *Classic Australian Verse*, The Five Mile Press, Melbourne, 2001, p. 3.

BOOK THREE
Edna Walling

1 Quoted by Edna Walling at the beginning of *Cottage and Garden in Australia*.

2 Walling, *Country Roads*, p. 13.

3 Unpublished article, 'My Mother and Father', Walling papers, La Trobe MS 13048 3727/2.

4 Walling papers, La Trobe MS 13048 3727/2.

5 ibid.

6 She noted that these packing cases were sent from her 'father's works'. It is likely that this was a business called Toledo Berkel, where William Walling was warehouse director.

7 *The Australian Home Beautiful*, 1 June 1934.

8 ibid.

9 These houses were simple in design and construction. Walling designed Good-a-Meavy (which was no doubt named after the Devon village of Meavy) in the style of a barn. The centre aisle allowed wagons to pass through, and there were lean-to buildings on either side. (Interview with Barbara Barnes, 7 September 1997.)

10 Walling, *Cottage and Garden in Australia*, p. 135.

11 Walling, *The Australian Handbook*.

12 Letter from then Burnley principal, E. B. Littlejohn to Peter Watts, 26 May 1977, Watts' private papers.

13 Edna Walling to Eric Hammond, February 1959, Walling papers, La Trobe MS 13048 3727/2.

14 Shepherd and Jellicoe, in *Italian Gardens of the Renaissance*. Walling's 'The Design of the Garden' appeared in *Australian Gardening of Today*, a collection of articles by the leading garden writers of the day, published by the *Sun News-Pictorial*, Melbourne. The book is undated but it is thought that it appeared in 1943.

15 According to Jellicoe in *The Landscape of Man*, p. 155, the Italian gardens that influenced English landscaping employed:

basically evergreens, stone and water—materials that were permanent rather than ephemeral. They included box parterres, clipped hedges, the dark cypress and groves of ilex; sculpture, stairways, pergolas and arbours; water in repose and in fountains. Flowers played little part.

16 Walling, *Country Roads*, p. 20.

17 Richard Clough, garden historian and former professor of landscape architecture, UNSW, discovered that Walling used this pseudonym by comparing writing styles and lettering in several rival publications.

18 *Everylady's Journal*, 1 January 1927.

19 Interview with Glen Wilson, 31 March 1998.

20 Fifty-eight thousand Australian men and boys were killed in World War I, and 156 000 were wounded or taken prisoner.

21 Such as Olive Mellor (1891–1978), the first woman to study full time at Burnley and the first instructress of horticulture there; Emily Gibson (1887–1974), horticultural journalist, lecturer and landscape designer and Margaret Hendry (1930–2001), landscape architect. (Aitken & Looker (eds).)

22 This comment appeared in the article by 'Wilma', 'A Career for Australian Girls', in *Everylady's Journal*, 1 January 1927.

23 Cited in *Friends of Geelong Botanic Garden Newsletter*, vol. 9, issue 4, December 1994. Article on Walling by Peter Fuggle, Burnley Horticultural College student.

24 Article by 'Wilma', 'A Career for Australian Girls', op. cit.

25 ibid.

26 Writing in *The Australian Home Beautiful*, May 1933.

27 Interview titled 'Acres of Loveliness: A Brief Interview with Miss Edna Walling. Australia's First Woman Garden Designer.' in *Woman's World*, September 1939, p. 526.

28 Walling, *Gardens in Australia—Their Design and Care*, p. 25.

29 ibid, p. 60.

30 ibid, p. 42.

31 In 'Front Garden Plan for Cottage and Villa', published in *The Australian Home Beautiful*, March 1929.

32 Writing in *The Australian Home Beautiful*, June 1933.

33 Interview with Glen Wilson, 31 March 1998.

34 Walling, *Gardens in Australia—Their Design and Care*, p. 11.

35 Wilson has described how Walling would make a Photostat, which made a negative and then a positive. Walling would provide Eric Hammond with the positive Photostat to work from. (Interview with Glen Wilson, 31 March 1998.)

36 ibid.

37 Walling papers, La Trobe MS 13048 3727/2.

38 The property was established in the 1850s by the Swan family, who built the homestead, and was bought by the Youngman family in 1888.

39 Walling, *Cottage and Garden in Australia*, p. 41.

40 A term she used often, including in *On the Trail of Australian Wildflowers*.

41 Also, Walling insisted on using black and white or sepia photographs, rather than the newly popular colour, which she regarded as 'dirty'. Glen Wilson remembers that Walling refused to put a colour film in her Rolleiflex camera. The publisher Victor Crittenden discovered the manuscript in the possession of Jean Galbraith, to whom Walling had sent it when it had earlier been refused by publishers. Crittenden obtained permission to publish it from Barbara Barnes.

42 Walling, *On the Trail of Australian Wildflowers*, p. 6.

43 Walling, *Cottage and Garden in Australia*, p. 60.

44 Walling, *On the Trail of Australian Wildflowers*, p. 2.

45 ibid. p. 5.

46 Walling, *Country Roads*, p. 20.

47 Walling, *On the Trail of Australian Wildflowers*, p. 27.

48 Walling, *Gardens in Australia—Their Design and Care*, p. 102.

49 Edna Walling to E. M. Osborne of Bundarbo, Coolac, dated 15 May 1957, La Trobe.

50 She acknowledged her own determination in 'An Adventure in Rural Development', published in *The Australian Handbook* in 1939, of the building of Sonning. 'In blissful ignorance I commenced to build myself a house,' she wrote.

51 As early as 1925, in *The Australian Home Beautiful*. Also, interview with Barbara Barnes, 7 September 1997.

52 Interview with Glen Wilson, 31 March 1998.

53 Edna Walling to Daphne Pearson, August 1969, Walling papers, La Trobe MS 13048 3727/2.

54 Barbara Barnes private papers.

Kath Carr

1 Interview with Kath Carr's brother, Alan Baldick, 10 May 2003.

2 Alison McKinnon's discussion of women's education in the early twentieth century, 'Nowhere to Plant the Sole of the Foot?' in Yates (ed.), *Feminism and Education*, pp. 22–38, provides fascinating insights into the attitudes of the day toward the choices required between education and marriage.

3 One client, Miriam Skene, remembered, 'Kath just walked in Edna Walling's footsteps. She slept, ate and drank Edna Walling. The first time I showed interest in Kath's work, she said, "You really need to get a set of Walling's garden books".' (Conversation with Skene, 20 April 2000.)

4 Interview with Ronnie Henderson, 15 April 2000.

5 Kath Carr to Susie Sutherland, 8 October 1968.

6 Alan Baldick certainly remembers his sister taking him, with 'two carloads' of friends, to visit Mawarra. (Interview with Baldick, 10 May 2003.)

7 Conversation with Susie Sutherland, 11 October 2002.

8 Conversations with Kath Carr between 1990 and 1994.

9 Walling papers, La Trobe, MS 13048 3727/2.

10 Letter in possession of Susie Sutherland. Walling had designed the Albury garden of Sutherland's parents, Mr and Mrs G. K. Finley.

11 Many of Carr's friends and clients, including Winifred (Bin) Ross (interview, 11 May 1998), remember that Walling wanted Carr to move to Buderim with her in the early 1970s, and to design gardens with her in the tropical Queensland town. In her archive in the SLV is a small note-book of spiritual quotations which Walling advises is to go to Carr upon her death. (This bequest was later crossed out.)

12 Interview with Jean Holt, 18 March 2003.

13 Interview with Ross Flanery, 16 April 2000.

14 Kath Carr to Susie Sutherland, 8 October 1968.
Susie adds, 'it was lovely listening to her tell me how she used to just trail around after Edna when she was starting off, not paid, but privileged to be able to be with Edna as Edna didn't suffer people easily.

They got on very well.' (Letter from Sutherland to author, May 1999.)

15 Carr had earlier designed a garden for Rhonda's parents. Rhonda Daly interviews: 1998, 1999.

16 Walling, *A Gardener's Log*, p. 3.

17 Conversation with Miriam Skene, 2 October 2001.

18 Interview with Judith Friend, 19 February 1999.

19 Interview with Jean Holt, 7 May 2003.

20 Ker Conway, p. 198.

21 Interview with Ross Flanery, 1 April 2000.

22 Interview with Susie Sutherland, 3 October 2002.

23 Interview with Rhonda Daly, 15 April 2000. Tape-recorded conversation between Kath Carr and Rhonda Daly, 1991.

24 Walling, *Cottage and Garden in Australia*, p. 1.

25 Interview with Kath Carr, 20 September 1994.

26 Notes contained in Rhonda Daly's garden book.

27 Interview with Bin Ross, 20 July 2001.

28 Interview with Ronnie Henderson, 15 April 2000.

29 Interview with Judith Friend, 19 February 1999.

30 Interview with Ross Flanery, 1 April 2000.

31 Ker Conway, p. 32.

32 ibid., p. 40.

33 Walling papers, La Trobe, MSS 10408. Letter to her friend the architect Mervyn Davis, dated 7 June 1965.

34 A 'ha-ha' is a ditch dug into the land, so that the view from the garden, or house, into the surrounding landscape can be enjoyed, uninterrupted by a fence. It allows stock to graze within the garden picture, but prevents them from intruding into the garden.
Carr may have seen similar brolgas at Mawarra, where they happily wade in the famous octagonal pool.

This bibliography is divided into sections as follows:

Primary Sources

Manuscript Collections
Private Papers
Books and Printed Materials
Theses
Lectures

Secondary Sources

Books
Pamphlets and Journal Articles

PRIMARY SOURCES

Manuscript Collections

Mitchell Library (ML)

Una Falkiner: Diaries 1901–1948, MS 5715, MSS 423/1–113; papers, MSS 4342, ML 1725/78; sketchbooks PIC ACC 5715.

Linnaean Society: MSS 2009/2-22.

Macarthur Family: MPA2906, MPA2907, MPA2908, MPA2931, MPA2898, MPA2899

Macleay Family: Fanny Macleay's letters to her brother William: A4300–A4302.

Winifred West: MSS 3367/1-5.

Royal Botanic Gardens, Sydney, Library

Letterbooks

Minutes of the Acclimatisation Society of Victoria

National Library (NL)

Dutton Archive: Series 43, Folder 5.

La Trobe Collection (La Trobe)

Edna Walling: MS 13048 3727/2

Battye Library (BL)

Georgiana Molloy: 3278A/2, MN 768 3278A/1, GM Diary ACC 4730A/17, A4732 1-2, WAA 139, WAA 479; Lindley to Mangles 1839 BL 479A/1-2; Letters: WAA501.

Cumbria Records Office (Carlisle) (CRO)

Georgiana Molloy: D/Ken/3 Bundle 28/2, D/Ken/3 Bundle 28/9

Private Papers

Beatrice Bligh: Papers in possession of Michael Bligh.

Kath Carr: Papers in possession of Alan Baldick.

Mary Collins: Papers part of the estate of Margaret Persse Hockey.

Una Falkiner: Papers in possession of Suzanne Falkiner.

Edna Walling: Papers in possession of Barbara Barnes, and of Peter Watts.

Books and Printed Materials

Bigge, J. T., *Report of the Commissioner of Inquiry (J. T. Bigge) into the State of the Colony of New South Wales,* London, 1822.

Bligh, Beatrice, *Down to Earth,* Angus & Robertson, Sydney, 1968.

——*Cherish the Earth,* Ure Smith, Sydney, 1973.

Historical Records of New South Wales, Lansdown Slattery & Company, Sydney, reprint 1978, selected volumes.

Macedon Ranges Cultural Heritage and Landscape Study

Meredith, Mrs Charles, *Notes and Sketches of New South Wales,* John Murray, London, 1844.

——*My Home in Tasmania,* volumes 1 & 2, John Murray, London, 1852.

——*Over the Straits: A Visit to Victoria,* John Murray, London, 1861.

Meredith, Louisa Anne, *Tasmanian Friends and Foes—Feathered, Furred, and Finned,* Marcus Ward & Co., London, 1881.

Repton, Humphry, *Observations on the Theory and Practice of Landscape Gardening,* facsimile, Phaidon, Oxford, 1980 (first published 1803).

Tench, Watkin, *Sydney's First Four Years: A Narrative of the Expedition to Botany Bay and A Complete Account,* Royal Australian Historical Society, 1979 (first published as a facsimile in 1961).

Walling, Edna, *Gardens in Australia—Their Design and Care,* Oxford University Press, Melbourne, 1946 (first edition published 1943).

——*Cottage and Garden in Australia,* Oxford University Press, Melbourne, 1947.

——*A Gardener's Log,* Oxford University Press, Melbourne, 1948.

——*On the Trail of Australian Wildflowers,* Mulini Press, Canberra, 1984.

——*The Australian Roadside,* Pioneer Design Studio, Victoria, 1985 (first edition published 1952).

——*Country Roads: The Australian Roadside,* Pioneer Design Studio, Melbourne, 1985.

West, Winifred, *Addresses and Talks,* Angus & Robertson, Sydney, 1973.

Western Australian Historical Society Journal, vol. I, part iv, *Journal and Proceedings.*

Theses

Holmes, Kathryn (Katie), published PhD thesis, *Spaces in Her Day: Australian Women's Diaries, 1919–1945,* University of Melbourne, 1995.

Lectures

Seddon, George, 'Gardens as Paradise'. Keynote address at 17th Annual National Conference of Australian Garden History Society, published in *AGHSJ*, vol. 8, no. 4, Jan/Feb 1997.

SECONDARY SOURCES

Books

Aitken, Richard & Looker, Michael (eds), *The Oxford Companion to Australian Gardens,* Oxford University Press, Melbourne, 2002.

Atkinson, Alan, *Camden: Farm and Village Life in Early New South Wales,* Oxford University Press, Melbourne, 1988.

Beadle, N. C. W., Evans O. D., & Carolin, R. C., *Flora of the Sydney Region,* Reed, Sydney, 1991.

Benson, Doug & Howell, Jocelyn, *Taken for Granted: The Bushland of Sydney and its Suburbs,* Kangaroo Press, Sydney, 1990.

Bickel, Lennard, *Australia's First Lady, The Story of Elizabeth Macarthur,* Allen & Unwin, Sydney, 1991.

Bisgrove, Richard, *The English Garden,* Viking, London, 1990.

——*The Gardens of Gertrude Jekyll,* Frances Lincoln, London, 1992.

Blainey, Geoffrey, *The Tyranny of Distance,* Macmillan, Melbourne, 1988 (first published 1966).

Boldrewood, Mrs Rolf, *The Flower Garden in Australia,* Mulini Press, Canberra, 1995.

Bonyhady, Tim, *The Colonial Earth,* Melbourne University Press, Melbourne, 2001.

Boswell, Annabella, *Further Recollections of My Early Days in Australia,* Mulini Press, Canberra, 1992.

Broadbent, James, *Elizabeth Farm, Parramatta: A History and Guide,* Historic Houses Trust, Sydney, 1995 (first published 1984).

——*Australian Colonial House, The Architecture and Society in New South Wales 1788–1842,* Hordern House, Sydney, 1997.

——& Hughes, Joy, *The Age of Macquarie,* Melbourne University Press, Melbourne, 1992.

Brown, Jane, *The Pursuit of Paradise,* HarperCollins Publishers, London, 1999.

Buckland, Jill, *Mort's Cottage Impressions of Sydney People and Their Times 1838–1988,* Kangaroo Press, Sydney, 1988.

Cannon, Michael, *The Long Last Summer: Australia's Upper Class Before the Great War,* Nelson, Melbourne, 1985.

Carson, Rachel, *Silent Spring,* Penguin Books, London, 2000 (first published 1962).

Cazneaux, Harold, *The Frensham Book,* Ure Smith, Sydney, 1959 (first published 1934).

Chambers, Douglas D. C., *The Planters of the English Landscape Garden: Botany, Trees, and the Georgics,* Yale University Press, London, 1993.

Chick, Neil, *The Archers of Van Diemens Land: A History of Pioneer Pastoral Families,* Pedigree Press, Tasmania, 1991.

Clark, C. M. H., *A History of Australia, Vol. III. The Beginning of an Australian Civilization, 1824–1851,* Melbourne University Press, Melbourne, 1992 (first published 1973).

Clark, Patricia, *Pioneer Writer. The Life of Louisa Atkinson: Novelist, Journalist, Naturalist,* Allen & Unwin, Sydney, 1990.

Clarke, P. & Spender, D., *Life Lines: Australian Women's Letters and Diaries 1788–1840,* Allen & Unwin, Sydney, 1996.

Clifford, Derek, *A History of Garden Design,* Frederick Praeger, New York, 1963.

Cresswell, Gail, *The Light of Leeuwin: The Augusta–Margaret River Shire History,* Scott Four, Perth, 1989.

Crittenden, Victor, *The Front Garden: The Story of the Cottage Garden in Australia,* Mulini Press, Canberra, 1979.

——*A Shrub in The Landscape of Fame,* Mulini Press, Canberra, 1992.

——*Yesterday's Gardens: A History and Bibliography of Australian Gardening Books,* Mulini Press, Canberra, 2001.

Crowley, F. K., *Australia's Western Third: A History of Western Australia from the First Settlements to Modern Times,* Macmillan, London, 1960.

Cuffley, Peter, *Cottage Gardens in Australia,* The Five Mile Press, Melbourne, 1983.

——*Traditional Gardens in Australia,* The Five Mile Press, Melbourne, 1991.

Cunningham, Peter, Surgeon RN, (David S. Macmillan ed.), *Two Years in New South Wales,* Angus & Robertson, Sydney, 1966 (first published 1827).

Curr, Edward, *An Account of the Colony of Van Diemen's Land Principally Designed for the Use of Emigrants,* George Cowie & Co., London 1824; 1967 facsimile, Platypus Publications.

Daniels, Stephen, *Humphry Repton: Landscape Gardening and the Geography of Georgian England,* Yale University Press, London, 1999.

Davidoff, Leonore, *Worlds Between: Historical Perspectives on Gender and Class,* Polity Press, Cambridge, 1995.

——& Hall, Catherine, *Family Fortunes: Men and Women of the English Middle Class 1750–1850,* Hutchinson, London, 1987.

Davison, Graeme, *The Rise and Fall of Marvellous Melbourne,* Melbourne University Press, Melbourne, 1978.

——, Hirst, John, & Macintyre, Stuart (eds), *The Oxford Companion to Australian History,* Oxford University Press, Melbourne, 2001 (first published 1998).

Day, David, *Claiming a Continent: A New History of Australia,* HarperCollins, Sydney, 2001 (first published 1996).

De Falbe, Jane, *My Dear Miss Macarthur: The Recollections of Emmeline Macarthur,* Kangaroo Press, Sydney, 1988.

De Vries-Evans, Susanna, *Pioneer Women, Pioneer Land: Yesterday's Tall Poppies,* Angus & Robertson, Sydney, 1987.

Dixon, Trisha & Churchill, Jenny, *In the Footsteps of Edna Walling,* Angus & Robertson, Sydney, 1988.

——*The Vision of Edna Walling,* Blooming Books, Melbourne, 1998.

Dutton, Geoffrey, *The Squatters,* Currey O'Neil Ross, Melbourne, 1985.

——*Out in the Open,* University of Queensland Press, Brisbane, 1994.

Dyster, Barrie, *Servant & Master: Building and Running the Grand Houses of Sydney, 1788–1850,* University of New South Wales, Sydney, 1989.

Earnshaw, Beverley, Hughes, Joy, & Davidson, Lindy, *Fanny to William: The Letters of Frances Leonora Macleay 1812–1836,* Historic Houses, Sydney, 1993.

Ellis, M. H., *Lachlan Macquarie,* Angus & Robertson, Sydney, 1973.

Falkiner, Suzanne, *Ethel. A Love Story,* Macmillan, Sydney, 1996.

——*Haddon Rig: The First Hundred Years,* Valadon Publishing, Sydney, 1996.

Flannery, Tim, *The Explorers,* Text Publishing, Melbourne, 1998.

——*The Birth of Sydney,* Text Publishing, Melbourne, 1999.

——(ed.), *Watkin Tench 1788,* Text Publishing, Melbourne, 1996.

——(ed.), *Life and Adventures 1776–1801 John Nicol,* Text Publishing, Melbourne, 1997.

Ford, Gordon, *The Natural Australian Garden,* Blooming Books, Melbourne, 1999.

Frazer Simons, Phyl, *Historic Tasmanian Gardens,* Mulini Press, Canberra, 1987.

Gelding, J., *Three Sydney Garden Nurseries in the 1860s,* Mulini Press, Canberra, 1983.

Griffiths, Nesta, *Some Northern Homes of N.S.W.,* Shepherd & Newman, Sydney, 1954.

——*Some Southern Homes of New South Wales,* Fine Arts Press, Sydney, 1976.

Griffiths, Tom, *Hunters and Collectors*, Cambridge University Press, Melbourne, 1996.

Grimshaw, Patricia and Strahan, Lynne, *The Half-Open Door*, Hale & Ironmonger, Sydney, 1982.

Hampton, Susan & Llewellyn, Kate (eds), *The Penguin Book of Australian Women Poets*, Penguin Books, Ringwood, 1986.

Hanson, Susan & Pratt, Geraldine, *Gender, Work and Space*, Routledge, London, 1995.

Harris, Mrs. T., *Woman—The Angel of the Home and the Saviour of the World*, 1890.

Hasluck, Alexandra, *Portrait with Background: A Life of Georgiana Molloy*, Oxford University Press, Melbourne, 1976.

Hassam, Andrew, *No Privacy for Writing: Shipboard Diaries 1852–1879*, Melbourne University Press, Melbourne, 1995.

——*Through Australian Eyes: Colonial Perceptions of Imperial Britain*, Melbourne University Press, Melbourne, 2000.

Henderson, John, *Observations of the Colonies of New South Wales and Van Diemen's Land*, Baptist Mission Press, Calcutta, 1832.

Heney, Helen, *Australia's Founding Mothers*, Thomas Nelson, Melbourne, 1978.

——*Dear Fanny*, ANU Press, Canberra, 1982.

Hewat, Tim, *Golden Fleeces: The Falkiners of Boonoke*, Bay Books, Sydney, 1980.

Holmes, Katie, *Spaces in Her Day: Australian Women's Diaries 1920s–1930s*, Allen & Unwin, Sydney, 1995.

Howe, G., *Australia's First Gardening Guide of 1806: Observations on Gardening*, Mulini Press, Canberra, facsimile, 1980.

Howitt, William, *Land, Labour & Gold, or Two Years in Victoria with Visits to Sydney and Van Diemen's Land*, Lowden Publishing Company, Kilmore, 1972 (first published 1855).

Hughes, Joy, *Journal & Letters of Elizabeth Macarthur 1789–1798*, Historic Houses, Sydney, 1984.

Hughes, Robert, *The Fatal Shore: A History of the Transportation of Convicts to Australia, 1787–1868*, Vintage, London, 2003 (first published 1986).

Inglis, Ken, *Australian Colonists*, Melbourne University Press, Melbourne, 1993.

Irvine, E. Marie, *Certain Worthy Women*, New Century Press, Sydney, 1939.

Irving, R. (ed.), *The History and Design of the Australian House*, Oxford University Press, Oxford, 1985.

Irwin, Frederick Chidley, *The State and Position of Western Australia: Commonly Called the Swan-River Settlement*, Simpkin, Marshall, London, 1835.

Isaacs, Jennifer, *Pioneer Women of The Bush and Outback*, Lansdowne Press, Sydney, 1998.

Jekyll, Gertrude, *Colour in the Flower Garden*, Mitchell Beazley, London, 1995 (first published 1908).

——& Weaver, Lawrence, *Gardens for Small Country Houses*, Antique Collectors Club, Suffolk, 1981 (first published 1912).

Jellicoe, G. & S., *The Landscape of Man: Shaping the Environment from Prehistory to the Modern Day*, Thames & Hudson, London, c.1975.

——,Goode, P.,& Lancaster, M., *The Oxford Companion to Gardens*, Oxford University Press, Oxford, 1991.

Johns, E., Sayers, A., Kornhauser, E. M. & Ellis, A., *New Worlds From Old: 19th Century Australian & American Landscapes*, National Gallery of Australia, Canberra, 1998.

Kennedy, Priscilla, *Portrait of Winifred West*, Fine Arts Press, Sydney, 1976.

Ker Conway, Jill, *The Road from Coorain*, Random House, Sydney, 1990.

Kerr Forsyth, Holly, *The Australian Country Woman's Garden*, Random House, Sydney, 1998.

——*The Garden Lover's Guide to Australia*, Random House, Sydney, 1998 (first published 1996).

——*Gardens in my Day*, New Holland, Sydney, 2000.

King, Hazel, *Elizabeth Macarthur and Her World*, Sydney University Press, Sydney, 1980.

Kingston, Beverley, *My Wife, My Daughter, and Poor Maryann*, Thomas Nelson, Sydney, 1975.

——*The Oxford History of Australia*, vol. 3: *Glad, Confident Morning 1860–1900*, Oxford University Press, Melbourne, 2001.

Knightley, Phillip, *Australia: A Biography of a Nation*, Jonathan Cape, London, 2000.

Kociumbas, J, *The Oxford History of Australia*, vol. 2: *Possessions*, Oxford University Press, Melbourne, 1995 (first published 1992).

Kyle, Noeline, *Her Natural Destiny: The Education of Women in New South Wales*, UNSW Press, Sydney, 1986.

Lansbury, Coral, *Arcady in Australia: The Evocation of Australia in Nineteenth Century English Literature*, Melbourne University Press, Melbourne, 1970.

Latreille, Anne, *The Natural Garden. Ellis Stones: His Life and Work*, Viking O'Neil, Melbourne, 1990.

Law-Smith, Joan, *A Gardener's Diary*, C S Graphic, Melbourne, 1976.

——*The Garden Within*, National Trust, Melbourne, 1991.

Lines, William J., *An All Consuming Passion: Origins, Modernity, and the Australian Life of Georgiana Molloy*, University of California Press, Berkeley, 1996.

——*Taming the Great South Land: A History of the Conquest of Nature in Australia*, University of Georgia Press, Athens, Georgia, 1999.

Loudon, J. C., *Encyclopaedia of Cottage, Farm and Villa Architecture and Furniture*, Longman, Rees, London, 1833.

——*The Villa Gardener: Comprising the Choice of A Suburban Villa Residence; The Laying out, Planting, and Culture of the Garden and Grounds; and the Management of the Villa Farm and more particularly for the use of Ladies*, 2nd edition, edited by Mrs Loudon, Wm S Orr & Co., London, 1850.

——*An Encyclopaedia of Gardening; comprising the Theory and Practice of Horticulture, Floriculture, Arboriculture, and Landscape Gardening;* (and) *A General History of Gardening in All Countries*, edited by Mrs Loudon, Longmans, Green and Co., London, 1865.

Loudon, (Jane) Mrs., *Loudon's Encyclopaedia of Plants*, Longmans, Green and Co., London, 1872.

——*The Ladies' Companion to the Flower Garden with Full Directions for the Culture of Ornamental Plants in Gardens and Shrubberies, and Hints on Garden Formation and Management*, Bradbury, Agnew & Co., London, 9th edition (first published 1843).

Lucas, Clive & Joyce, Ray, *Australian Country Houses, Homesteads, Farmsteads and Rural Retreats*, Lansdowne, Sydney, 1994.

Luffman, Charles Bogue, *The Principles of Gardening for Australia*, Book Lover's Diary, Melbourne, 1903.

Lycett Joseph, *Views in Australia or New South Wales and Van Diemen's Land Delineated*, J. Souter, London, 1825, facsimile edition.

McAfee, Robert, *Dawe's Meteorological Journal*, Australian Government Publishing Service, Canberra, 1981.

Macarthur, Maria, *Advice to a Young Lady in the Colonies*, Greenhouse, Melbourne, 1979.

Macarthur Onslow, Sibella, *Some Early Records of the Macarthurs of Camden*, Angus & Robertson, Sydney, 1914.

Mackaness, George (ed.), *Fourteen Journeys Over the Blue Mountains of New South Wales 1813–1841*, Horwitz-Grahame Publications, Sydney, 1965.

Mackerness, E. D. (ed.), *The Journals of George Sturt 1820–1927*, Cambridge University Press, London, 1967.

McWilliam-Tullberg, Rita, *Women at Cambridge*, Cambridge University Press, Cambridge, 1998 (first published 1975).

Maguire, Paul, *Australian Journey*, William Heinemann, London, 1943.

Massey, Doreen, *Space, Place and Gender*, Polity Press, Oxford, 1994.

Meinig, D. W. (ed.), *The Interpretation of Ordinary Landscapes*, Oxford University Press, Oxford, 1979.

Merchant, Carolyn, *Reinventing Eden: The Fate of Nature in Western Culture*, Routledge, New York, 2003.

Midgley, Clare (ed.), *Gender and Imperialism*, Manchester University Press, Manchester, 1998.

Molony, John, *Native Born: The First White Australians*, Melbourne University Press, Melbourne, 2000.

Morgan, Sharon, *Land Settlement in Early Tasmania: Creating an Antipodean England*, Cambridge University Press, Cambridge, 1992.

Morris, Colleen, et al., *Interwar Gardens: A Guide to the History, Conservation and Management of Gardens of 1915–1940*, The National Trust of Australia (NSW) Parks and Gardens Conservation Committee, 2003.

The New South Wales Pocket Almanack and Colonial Remembrancer, facsimile edition published by Victor Crittenden, Mulini Press, Canberra.

Nicolson, Nigel, *Portrait of a Marriage*, Weidenfeld & Nicolson, London, 1973.

Page, Russell, *Education of a Gardener*, Penguin Books, London, 1985.

Perrott, Monica, *A Tolerable Good Success: Economic Opportunities for Women in New South Wales 1788–1830*, Macquarie Colonial Press, Sydney, 1983.

Pike, Douglas, et al. (eds), *Australian Dictionary of Biography*, vols 1–15, (1788–1980), Melbourne University Press, Melbourne, 1966–2000.

Radford, R. & Hylton, J., *Australian Colonial Art 1800–1900*, Art Gallery of South Australia, Adelaide, 1991.

Rae-Ellis, Vivienne, *Louisa Anne Meredith: A Tigress in Exile*, St David's Park, Hobart, 1990.

Ratcliffe, Richard, *Australia's Master Gardener: Paul Sorensen and his Gardens*, Kangaroo Press, Sydney, 1990.

Ritchie, John, *Lachlan Macquarie: A Biography*, Melbourne University Press, Melbourne, 1986.

Robin, Libby, *Defending the Little Desert: The Rise of Ecological Consciousness in Australia*, Melbourne University Press, Melbourne, 1998.

Robinson, Portia, *The Women of Botany Bay*, Penguin Books, Melbourne, 1993.

Rowan, Ellis, *Flower Hunter*, Angus & Robertson, Sydney, 1995.

Russell, Charles, *Jimbour: Its History and Development*, Dalby Herald, Dalby, 1982.

Schaffer, Kay, *Women and the Bush: Forces of Desire in the Australian Cultural Tradition*, Cambridge University Press, Melbourne, 1988.

Searl and Sons, *Searl's Key to Australian Gardening*, Sydney, 1922.

Seddon, George, *Landprints: Reflections on Place and Landscape*, Cambridge University Press, Melbourne, 1997.

Serle, G., *The Golden Age: A History of the Colony of Victoria 1851–1861*, Melbourne University Press, Melbourne, 1977.

Shaw, A. G. L., *Convicts and the Colonies: A Study of Penal Transportation from Great Britain and Ireland to Australia and Other Parts of the British Empire*, Melbourne University Press, Melbourne, 1998 (first published 1966).

Shepherd, Jock & Jellicoe, Geoffrey, *Italian Gardens of the Renaissance*, Taranti, London, 1966.

Shepherd, Thomas, *Lectures on the Horticulture of NSW*, W. M. McGarvie, Sydney, 1836.

Smith, Bernard, *European Vision and the South Pacific*, Harper & Row, Sydney, 1984.

Snape, Diana, *Australian Native Gardens*, Lothian Books, Melbourne, 1992.

——*The Australian Garden: Designing with Australian Plants*, Bloomings Books, Melbourne, 2003.

Stearn, William T., *John Lindley, 1799–1865: Gardener-Botanist and Pioneer Orchidologist*, Antique Collectors' Club, Woodbridge, 1999.

Stones, Ellis, *Australian Garden Design*, Macmillan, Melbourne, 1971.

Stratford, Elaine (ed.), *Australian Cultural Geographies*, Oxford University Press, Melbourne, 1999.

Strong, Roy, *Country Life 1897–1997: The English Arcadia*, Boxtree, London, 1996.

Tankard, Judith, & Van Valkenburgh, Michael, *Gertrude Jekyll: A Vision of Garden and Wood*, John Murray, London, 1988.

Tankard, Judith, & Wood, Martin, *Gertrude Jekyll at Munstead Wood*, Sutton Publishing, Glouc., 1997.

Tanner, Howard, *Converting the Wilderness: The Art of Gardening in Colonial Australia*, Sydney, Langridge Press, 1979.

——*Towards an Australian Garden*, Valadon Publishing, Sydney, 1983.

——& Begg, Jane, *The Great Gardens of Australia*, Macmillan, Melbourne, 1976.

Taylor, Arthur, *Taylor Family, A Short Account of their Experiences in Tasmania*, self-published, Launceston, 1975.

Taylor, Vera, *Winton Merino Stud 1835–1985*, Neptune Press, Geelong, 1985.

Teo, Hsu-Ming & White, Richard, *Cultural History in Australia*, UNSW Press, Sydney, 2003.

Timms, Peter, *The Nature of Gardens*, Allen & Unwin, Sydney, 1999.

Tooley, Michael and Arnander, Primrose (eds), *Gertrude Jekyll: Essays on the Life of a Working Amateur*, Michaelmas Books, Durham, 1984.

Trollope, Anthony, *Australia*, Thomas Nelson, Sydney, 1966 (first published 1873).

Ward, Russell, *The Australian Legend*, Oxford University Press, Melbourne, 1978.

Watts, Peter, *Historic Gardens of Victoria*, Oxford University Press, Melbourne, 1983.

——*Edna Walling and Her Gardens*, Florilegium, Melbourne, 1991.

Wilson, Glen, *Landscaping with Australian Plants*, Nelson, Melbourne, 1975.

Windschuttle, Elizabeth, *Taste and Science: The Macleay Women*, Historic Houses Trust, Sydney, 1988.

Winzenreid, A. P., *Green Grows Your Garden: A Centenary History of Horticultural Education at Burnley*, Hyland House, Melbourne, 1991.

Wright, Judith, *Collected Poems 1942–1985*, Angus & Robertson, Sydney, 1994.

——*The Generations of Men*, ETT Imprint, Sydney, 1995 (first published 1959).

Young, Ann R. M., *Environmental Change in Australia Since 1788*, Oxford University Press, Melbourne, 1996.

Pamphlets and Journal Articles

Pamphlets

Fletcher, Brian, 'John Macarthur, A Man of Controversy', Elizabeth Farm Series, Historic Houses Trust, Sydney, 1984.

Hughes, Joy, 'John Macarthur and the Wool Industry', Elizabeth Farm Series, Historic Houses Trust, Sydney, 1984.

——'The Macarthurs: A Brief Family History', Elizabeth Farm Series, Historic Houses Trust, Sydney, 1984.

Kingston, Beverley, 'Elizabeth Macarthur', Elizabeth Farm Series, Historic Houses Trust, Sydney, 1984.

Sansom, Ian, 'The Conservation of Elizabeth Farm', Elizabeth Farm Series, Historic Houses Trust, Sydney, 1984.

Journal Articles

Cavanough, Jane, et al., 'Gardens of the Southern Highlands NSW 1828–1988', *Australian Garden Journal*, Bowral, 1988.

Fox, Paul, 'Over the Garden Fence', *Historic Environment*, vol. iv, no. 3, 1985, pp. 29–36.

——'The Simla of the South', *Proceedings of the 15th Annual Meeting of the Garden History Society*, October 1994, pp. 10–13.

Holmes, Katie, 'Fertile Ground: Women and Horticulture', *Australian Garden History*, vol. 10, no. 6, May/June 1999, pp. 6–9.

Hosking, Susan, '"I 'ad to 'ave me a Garden": A Perspective on Australian Women Gardeners,' *Meanjin*, vol. 47, no. 3, Spring 1988, pp. 439–43.

Jones, David, 'A Plea for Tradition: The Ideas of Walter Hervey Bagot and his Mediterranean Landscapes', in John Dixon Hunt (ed.), *Studies in the History of Gardens and Designed Landscapes*, vol. 21, no. 2, Taylor & Francis, 2001, pp. 93–101.

Kingston, Beverley, 'The Lady and the Australian Girl: Some Thoughts on Nationalism and Class', in N. Grieve and A. Burns (eds), *Australian Women: New Feminist Perspectives*, Oxford University Press, Melbourne, 1986, pp. 28–9.

Lake, Marilyn, 'The Politics of Respectability: Identifying the Masculinist Context', *Historical Studies*, vol. 22, 1986, pp. 116–23.

McKinnon, Alison, 'Nowhere to Plant the Sole of the Foot?: Women, University Education and Subjectivity in the Early Twentieth Century', in Lyn Yates (ed.), *Feminism and Education*, La Trobe University, Melbourne, 1993, pp. 22–38.

Martin, Susan, 'On Our Selection: Class, Gender and the Domestic Garden in Nineteenth-Century Australia', *Studies in the History of Gardens & Designed Landscapes*, vol. 21, no. 1, Spring 2001, pp. 27–32.

Seddon, George, 'The Australian Back Yard', *Australian Studies*, no. 7, November 1993, London, pp. 23–35.

——'Gardens as Paradise,' keynote address to the 17th Annual National Conference of Australian Garden History Society, published in *AGHSJ*, vol. 8, no. 4, Jan/Feb 1997, pp. 8–12.

——'The Landscapes of Australia', *Studies in the History of Gardens & Designed Landscapes*, vol. 21, no. 1, Spring 2001, pp. 1–10.

Shepherd, Jane, 'Women at Work: Melbourne's 20th Century Landscape Designers', *National Trust News*, July 1990.

Skene, Judy, 'Gardens of Their Own: Exploring the Garden as Feminine Space', *Limina*, vol. 2, 1996, pp. 18–27.

Walling, Edna, 'An Adventure in Rural Development', *The Australian Handbook*, The Australia Hotel, 1939.

Wilken, Rowan, 'Horticulture for Women', *Journal of Australian Garden History Society*, March 1998, vol. 9, no. 5, pp. 6–8.

Plant Index

General Index

THE MIEGUNYAH PRESS

This book was designed by Mary Callahan
The text was typeset by J & M Typesetting and Mary Callahan
The text was set in 10.5 point Minion with 5 points of leading
The text is printed on 130 gsm matt art

This book was edited by Clare Coney